Organizational Behavior
Critical Incidents and Analysis

Organizational Behavior
Critical Incidents and Analysis

John V. Murray
Thomas J. Von der Embse
Wright State University

Charles E. Merrill Publishing Company
A Bell & Howell Company
Columbus, Ohio

Published by

Charles E. Merrill Publishing Company
A Bell & Howell Company
Columbus, Ohio 43216

International Standard Book Number: 0-675-08963-8

Library of Congress Catalog Card Number: 72-95928

1 2 3 4 5 6 7 8—78 77 76 75 74 73

Printed in the United States of America

To Allecia and Jean

ACKNOWLEDGMENTS

The authors wish to acknowledge their indebtedness to graduate students at Wright State University who prepared most of the incidents in this book. We are also indebted to the many graduate students who provided meaningful discussion of the analyses which appear in Part II of the book.

We are further indebted to Arthur C. MacKinney, Dean of Graduate Division, Wright State University, who assisted the authors in teaching the Organization Behavior course where the incidents were tested.

We thank the many authors and publishers who granted us permission to quote copyrighted material. The material quoted and its source is indicated in the analyses of the various incidents in Part II of the book.

Finally, we wish to express our appreciation to Christine Jones, Rebecca Kraft, Mary Schock, and Shirley Armstrong for their assistance in preparing the manuscript.

We acknowledge the many and varied contributions from others, but the authors assume full responsibility for the contents of the book.

PREFACE

Most incidents texts contain problem situations which the student is asked to study, analyze and solve. In this decision-making process, it is expected that the student will develop analytical and decision skills which are transferable to real-world situations. The incident approach, as the theory goes, will thereby help to sharpen, condition and prepare the student's capacity for managerial decision making.

Given a highly capable instructor and the proper set of conditions, it might be possible to develop decision-making skills through the incident method. But, as will be demonstrated in Part I, there are several difficulties involved in using incidents for problem-solving purposes. Basically, the issue is a philosophical one. Too often, the incident is viewed as a small case. The diagnosis and treatment of the situation, consequently, tends to parallel that of the case study method.

This text offers alternatives to the traditional incident approach. In it, the incident is used not as a tool for problem solving, but (1) as an instrument for facilitating the application of abstract concepts and theories in organizational behavior, and (2) for identifying the behavioral aspects of critical situations and determining what additional knowledge would be needed to make a decision were the situation encountered in real life. At the present time, there is no text—at least none in organization behavior—which treats the incident quite this way.

Designed to allow maximum flexibility, the text can be used for executive development and training programs, or at either graduate or undergraduate levels. It is especially appropriate as a companion to an organizational behavior, organization theory or human relations text. Or, it can be used effectively with a readings text and/or current articles from periodicals. The incident approach suggested here provides an excellent springboard for class and seminar discussions, whether among undergraduates, graduate students, or practicing managers. The flexibility offered also extends to the course level. For example, where students have had prior course work in organization behavior, readings can be assigned in greater depth and breadth, thereby advancing the level of application and analysis consistent with the background of the class.

The text is organized into three parts. Part I explains the use of the incident as a pedagogical tool and demonstrates how the incident approach can assist in bridging theory and application. Part II contains thirty incidents which are organized into topical areas. Each incident in Part II is followed by two sample analyses, written by the authors of the text. We have attempted, in these analyses, to implement the approach to incident study which is outlined in Part I, and have included appropriate, up-to-date documentation for the concepts applied in the analysis. Part III provides thirty incidents which are neither classified by topical area nor accompanied by analyses. Further explanation of Parts II and III is given in the section that follows. All incidents in the book are real-life situations; only the names have been changed for the protection of those involved.

As a class project in a management development program, a graduate course or an undergraduate course, the instructor might ask the students to develop critical incidents from their own experience and present analyses of these incidents. Selected incidents can then be distributed to other class members for their analysis. In this way, a variety of ideas is encouraged, and the author of the incident receives a bonus of free consultation.

All of the incidents in Part II and many in Part III have been developed and tested through the approach suggested above. Credit is given the author of the incident at the beginning of each section. Not only has this approach enhanced the student's contribution to the organization field, but the method of instruction has elicited favorable response from the students. It holds their interest and stimulates them to study and understand behavioral concepts in greater depth than is possible through lecture and discussion alone. As stated by Champion and Bridges, incident study increases student interest and results in an accelerated incentive to read assigned material. In addition, there is high retention of subject matter. The approach in this text should result in an even greater understanding and retention than that precipitated by the traditional incident method.

John V. Murray
Thomas J. Von der Embse

CONTENTS

PART I

THE CRITICAL INCIDENT APPROACH

INTRODUCTION   3

The Critical Incident Approach as a Pedagogical Technique   3

Critical Incidents in Bridging Theory and Application   6

PART II

INCIDENTS WITH ANALYSES

PERCEPTION   13

MOTIVATION   34

COMMUNICATION   60

STATUS AND ROLE   84

GROUP BEHAVIOR AND CONFLICT   109

AUTHORITY   137

POWER   158

LEADERSHIP   183

CHANGE   207

ORGANIZATIONAL CLIMATE   230

PART III

INCIDENTS WITHOUT ANALYSES

Thirty Uncategorized Incidents with No Topical Head-ings or Labels

INDEX TO PART III INCIDENTS   257

PART I

The Critical Incident Approach

INTRODUCTION

THE CRITICAL INCIDENT APPROACH AS A PEDAGOGICAL TECHNIQUE

The Critical Incident Method is a variation of case study, which most of us have at some time experienced. The Critical Incident is the summary of something that actually happened or that realistically could happen. It normally provides a minimum of data so that the analyst must determine information that is needed before proceeding with his/her analysis. The incident itself is short in length, generally not more than one typewritten page.

In comparing the Case Method with the Critical Incident Method, a major difference lies with the presentation of the data. The typical case tends to be relatively complete with background material, several episodes, and a lengthy buildup to a problem. A critical incident, on the other hand, tends to be a portrayal of a single action and leaves out much of the background and long-term information. Identification of the significant issue in the incident together with identification of additional information needed is therefore the key to successful analysis.

The student is challenged in the Critical Incident process to ascertain additional needed information in order to complement the small amount of data provided. In this respect the student is required to identify this additional information together with his reasons or justification for needing it. In providing his justification he must refer to what he considers as applicable concepts, research findings and theories that would dictate the need for this additional information.

The incident is more appropriate than the case method when used as a vehicle to assist the student in understanding a body of knowledge on the current developments, concepts, research findings and theories in organizational behavior. The Case Method, with its comparatively vast amount of background data, often results in time-consuming periods in the classroom where students debate various and sometimes trivial matters that may be reported in the case. With reference to the levels of perception, Svenson suggests that the case method rarely attains the degree of discovery associated with seeking and applying new knowledge. He maintains that the case method "is cluttered with non-pertinent details which impede under-standing. Furthermore, too many old problems with pat answers obstruct creativity." In this sense, the case might pose as a "barrier between the student and business reality."[1]

The case method, at its inception, was a refreshing alternative to the traditional principles approach, but there is some point at which the solutions tend to proliferate, although new twists and games are often intro-duced into cases to give them unique character.[2] On the other hand, proponents of the case method cite this approach as a vehicle for learning and for developing analytical skills. They contend that, from long experi-ence with case study, it is a useful vehicle for developing breadth, judgment, and experience as well as for integrating knowledge and understanding.[3]

It is not our purpose to construct a "straw-man" of the case method, but rather to distinguish the case and incident approaches in relation to their respective purposes. Indeed, we have utilized both methods advantageously and can attest to the strengths of the case approach in seminar-type courses where integration is of major importance and where the input of abstract and fundamental knowledge is not an overriding consideration.

It is also true of the Case Method that often students try to express feelings about the cases that can impede discussion of the underlying con-cepts. The instructor may find it difficult to intervene, especially when students become engrossed in the case to the point of heated interchange over actions, solutions and interpretations. The Incident Method, in con-trast, does not provide the background information that the student can get involved with, and therefore, he/she is forced to relate to the incident those concepts and research findings that have been read and studied prior to the class meeting. The result is that students apply in a particular situation what is otherwise abstract material. Where the Incident Method has been used for this purpose, it has shown to be a successful motivating technique to teach and communicate concepts and theories and place them in a more meaningful context.

The incident also affords the student the opportunity of developing and sharpening analytical skills by relating abstract ideas to specific managerial situations. It provides the student with the opportunity to understand the viewpoints and motives of others, gain insight into the job that must be done, and most importantly, develop skills in defining and isolating those concepts, research findings and theories that may be applicable to particular situations along with those which probably are not applicable.

The ability to relate specific material to specific situations is not gained through the accumulation and memorization of a body of facts. Through the Critical Incident technique the student learns to cope with many prob-lems or potential problems which are unique, each of which must be ana-lyzed and evaluated in its setting. Thus, the student is less apt to derive distorted views of some of the theories. First, he rapidly learns that there is no one all-inclusive theory that applies to all situations. By being exposed to various theories and by being forced to relate them to various unique situations he becomes flexible enough in his thinking to select those theories or combinations of theories that are most likely applicable. Secondly, he learns that a theory is not necessarily completely wrong just because it does not apply in a given situation. The student is exposed to so many possible and varied circumstances that he/she soon understands that practically all the theories contain some elements of applicability and cannot be rejected just because they are not completely relevant.

The use of the Critical Incident, then, can be summarized in two ways. First, the student must identify the additional information that is needed and justify his reasons thereof. The justifications must be based on theory and research in the field of organizational behavior. The second purpose of the Critical Incident is that the student must identify the concepts, research findings and theories that may be applicable to a particular situation and explain why they must be applicable. At the same time he should offer reasons why other similar concepts are not applicable.

The 30 incidents in Part II of this book provide situations in the area of perception, role, motivation, leadership, power and authority, communication and other related organizational behavior subjects. The incidents are categorized and classified by topics which appear to be the most significant issue within the incident. Additionally, each incident contains two analyses, by the authors, which relate concepts and research findings to the particular incident. These analyses provide the student with a variety of different views relative to the issues involved. The analyses should be construed as only samples of various interpretations and are not necessarily all-inclusive or "ideal" approaches. They vary from heavily-documented, encyclopedic discussions to more intuitive oriented analyses. We have attempted to vary the mechanics in order to demonstrate how the approach can be flexibly applied.

In the classroom exercise, students might first study the incident, then evaluate the accompanying sample analyses. Their evaluation based on additional readings assigned by the instructor provides an opportunity for the student to critically evaluate the analyses that have been presented. The instructor and student have considerable flexibility in the use of these incidents by being able to relate both classical and recently-developed concepts and research findings to the incidents.

In Part III of the text the incidents are not classified in terms of any particular problem area, nor are they accompanied by analyses. This format is more characteristic of how the student would encounter a situation in a real-world setting. The manager is seldom provided clues to specific areas applicable to the problem. He must make this determination through his own analysis and insight—whether through trial-and-error or out of systematic exploration developed through education and past experience.[4] Therefore, to provide a valuable learning experience, it is helpful to begin with the incidents in Part II for an initial exposure, then proceed to the unlabeled incidents in Part III for exercise in searching out relevant concepts and approaches to solution. The next section offers further examples and suggestions for using the Critical Incident in applying behavioral ideas and theories.

CRITICAL INCIDENTS IN BRIDGING THEORY AND APPLICATION

It is important to reiterate that an incident is only a partial representation of a situation. It is analogous to an insert on a road map which highlights a point of interest, leaving it to the navigator to relate it into the perspective of the geographical environment. However, in the incident technique, environmental information and context are rarely adequate; thus, the student has primarily two options in approaching the incident: (1) to assume the necessary background and proceed toward a solution, or (2) to view the incident as a demonstration or example of certain abstract, fundamental concepts, with little concern as to the outcome of the situation. As previously suggested, the first alternative tends to lead to superficial analyses and solutions, often culminating in the disparaging conclusion that insufficient information prevents any further analysis.

The second option, however, incorporates the incident in its more proper role—as a vehicle for applying theories and concepts, fostering a more cogent analysis by providing a point of reference for understanding the theory or concept.

SOME BEHAVIORAL EXAMPLES

Consider for instance, the theory of cognitive dissonance. Examples abound in the marketing literature, but in a specialized context, usually the marketing research and advertising rubric. Yet, its application in a management context has been somewhat limited, not because of a dearth of literature on the subject, but due more to the relative absence of documented situations which demonstrate the theory.

Theory: Cognitive Dissonance. Leon Festinger is generally credited with the development of the theory of cognitive dissonance. He explains it in terms of perceptual consistencies and inconsistencies. Thus, "cognitive" refers to the process of perceptual awareness, and "dissonance" to the inconsistency of that awareness with one's feelings, attitudes and opinions. The theory states, in effect, that when dissonance exists, the individual will try to reduce it and achieve consonance, or consistency. In addition, when dissonance exists, an individual will attempt to avoid those circumstances which would heighten the dissonance and the accompanying psychological discomfort.[5]

While it is not the purpose here to analyze the theory, it is instructive to note that it contains a number of powerful implications for management. For one, restoration of consonance is roughly equivalent to need satisfaction. An individual experiencing dissonance seeks to eliminate it through various means which range from complete subconscious submergence to direct confrontation. The following incident will demonstrate:

For ten years, Joe Dykes had been supervising one of the most productive departments in the plant. Over that period he received considerable recognition from his superiors, both as "supervisor of the year" and in the form of other non-monetary rewards. However, this past year has been another matter. Out of ten departments in the plant his productivity index at mid-year is second lowest.

In two hours, Joe will meet with his immediate superior, the plant manager, for his semi-annual performance review. Not wanting to give excuses for his performance, Joe thought about confessing that he was simply losing confidence and interest in his unit. Too, he thought, many things had happened this year. Some of the productive "old hands" retired, new procedures had become confusing to the men, and then there was the new man—Bob Ryan —who just a couple of days ago asked Joe when there will be a supervisory job open in the plant, because that's what he (Bob) eventually wants to become.

Further reflecting on what to tell his superior, Joe knew that if he were completely honest about it, he'd tell the superior that he is no longer able to cope with the rapid changes, that Bob is intelligent and shows leadership capability and should probably be promoted as supervisor.

He further thought to himself, as he glanced toward the wall at his "supervisor of the year" plaque, "No, Bob's too young and inexperienced. Hell, I can handle the job. Now that we're over the hump on changes, we'll rally and come out on top at the end of the year. That's what I'll tell the boss." And with that, he marched confidently toward the office of the assistant plant manager.

In examining this situation, one is no doubt tempted to want to solve the problem and/or to role-play the impending performance review. While there may be merit in role-playing the situation, the proper use of the incident technique in the context of this book suggests that a more fruitful approach would involve seeking answers to questions such as "What additional information would be needed in order to solve the problems observed?" and "What behavioral concepts are involved and how are they demonstrated in the incident?"

The theory of cognitive dissonance was demonstrated deductively in the above incident. Joe Dykes was characterized as a person experiencing a conflict of awareness and feelings. The dissonance in this instance was reduced by accepting and internalizing another perception that supported certain feelings conditioned by past need-satisfying behavior; i.e., recognition. One could argue that his rationalization was unsound, but support for the position would require considerable information not provided in the illustration.

The application of concepts might also be approached inductively. Thus, in the above incident, one could infer not only cognitive dissonance but other behavioral concepts such as motivation, performance evaluation, leadership style and communication.

The approach, deductive or inductive, depends upon the purpose or objective. If the objective of the exercise is to demonstrate a single concept or theory, a deductive approach should suffice. If, on the other hand, the purpose is to ferret out as much behavioral "meat" as possible, an inductive approach would be more appropriate. In practice, the two analytical approaches can be readily combined, as above, where the initial objective was that of exemplifying cognitive dissonance, but subsequent analysis uncovered other behavioral insights.

If the learning objective involves developing skill in recognizing behavioral implications in a situation, it is better to approach the incident inductively. To achieve this objective, the incident should be untitled and prior analysis by other "experts" should not be made available. The incidents in Part III of this text encourage the type of exercise which will help to broaden one's perceptual skills. The absence of topical headings encourages a decidedly "real world" experience in that managers do not encounter actual situations with labels attached. In this setting, various concepts might emerge, many of which had not been previously applied in a situational context. The following example will illustrate.

> The West wing of Metropolitan Hospital houses the psychiatric ward. The first floor of this wing is for women patients and the second floor for men. Judy Anderson is a shift supervisor of nurses on the second floor. She reports directly to the ward head nurse, Paula MacIntyre.
>
> Besides ministering to the medical needs of patients, the nurses are very conscious of the loneliness many of the patients feel—related both to their psychological conditions and to the physical surroundings. Thus, the nurses

will sometimes play cards with the patients, watch TV or just talk with them. Judy usually encourages this whenever possible, especially in the evening when the schedule is not as tight. Paula is personally opposed to the practice, but does not openly object since she is aware that the physicians tend to favor it.

Lately, Room 214 had become a center of activity. In it are two young men who are there primarily for tests. Neither has severely disabling physical or psychological symptoms, unlike many of the other patients. One evening a group of young nurses congregated in Room 214, talking, laughing, and—as Judy aptly put it after the incident—flirting with these patients.

Judy didn't consider herself a prude, but when she witnessed what was happening, she felt something had to be done immediately. So she summoned all of the nurses on the floor to the nurses' room and told them that it was time to put a stop to close fraternization with the patients, and, except where medical treatment was required, no more than one nurse at a time would be permitted in a patient's room. Further, any socializing would be done in a very brief fashion in order to avoid involvements which might reflect unfavorably on the hospital and nurse's staff.

After this brief pronouncement, there was general silence and the nurses dispersed to tend to their respective duties. The next day Judy told Paula what had happened and Paula agreed completely with Judy's handling of the situation. Paula even suggested that the nurses involved be placed on report for possible disciplinary measures.

In reviewing this incident, it is obvious that a number of behavioral areas can be discussed. But a disciplined approach requires that an initial question be answered: What additional information is needed in order to intelligently and realistically attempt to seek solutions and decisions? There is little known about the background of the individuals and of the group. The situation did not occur in a vacuum; similar incidents must have taken place before. How were they handled? What is the official hospital policy? What led to the nurses' congregating in Room 214? Perhaps it was their attraction to the young men—but *maybe* something else. The questions could continue ad infinitum, but that is of course not the purpose here.

It is, however, possible to comment on and inductively show how behavioral concepts are involved. Communication is an example. Judy's was primarily a one-way approach and in a radial configuration or network. This practice should not be summarily condemned, for it is known to be appropriate in some instances. But it is not unexpected that the nurses were left in silence, since it is obvious that feedback was not invited by Judy's action.

Leadership style is another concept observed in the incident. Judy was obviously eclectic—normally consultive but in this instance quite directive

—which, again, can be highly appropriate. Paula exhibited a directive style, from the brief description of Judy's encounter with her. Still another area —and a controversial one—is the individual-to-group vs. individual-to-individual manner of handling situations such as this which involve corrective action. Judy called a meeting of all the nurses on the floor while the incident involved only part of the group. But, then, she wanted to establish a policy which obviously would affect everyone. Nevertheless, principles of disciplinary action enter the picture; i.e., objectivity, uniformity, immediacy, flexibility and proportionality of infractions and penalties. Judy's response was uniform and immediate, but other characteristics of effective disciplinary action are not apparent.

It should be possible to glean a number of other concepts from this incident. Approached inductively, this kind of "brainstorming" should be encouraged if the objective of the exercise is the development of breadth, awareness, understanding and appreciation of the dynamic nature of behavioral theory and concepts in organization. It is the authors' position that incident analysis, as presented in this text, is highly appropriate to that objective, and that the objective itself involves skills essential for vigorous, effective decision-making in behavioral situations.

Relationship to Problem-Solving. As we have indicated, the approach in this text is not focused on the solution of problems identified in the incidents. Nevertheless, the logic of the approach suggests that it can and should lead to problem-solving. Further, the processes underscored in the text are essential to intelligently and scientifically handling the incidents. From a managerial perspective, the incident technique incorporates several phases which require different postures and skills. For our purposes, we will refer to these phases as synonymous with problem-solving.

1. Size up the situation.
2. Get relevant information.
3. Analyze the data and the situation.
4. Develop alternative solutions.
5. Experiment and test alternative solutions.
6. Decide on the best solution.
7. Implement.

In the context of these problem-solving phases, the approach suggested in these pages emphasizes primarily the first three, along with occasional reference to the last four. There is, of course, good reason for this. Without the relevant information, there is little realistic basis for moving toward solution. It is always possible to make assumptions, however, but the labyrnth of assumptions required in some incidents would tax the limits of credibility. Rather, we have chosen to devote the pedogogical effort toward augmenting the reader's analytical base, out of which realistic and conceptually-sound decisions will likely follow.

FOOTNOTES

[1]Arthur L. Svenson, *Management Experience: The Short Case* (Englewood Cliffs, N.J.: Prentice-Hall, Inc., 1968), p. 3.

[2]*Ibid.,* pp. 5-6.

[3]George A. Smith, Jr., C. Roland Christensen, and Norman A. Berg, *Policy Formulation and Administration* (Homewood, Ill.: Richard D. Irwin, Inc., 1968), pp. ix-xiii.

[4]Livingston, in a recent and somewhat controversial article, identifies problem recognition as a vital managerial skill not developed in formal education for managers. See J. Sterling Livingston, "The Myth of the Well-Educated Manager," *Harvard Business Review* (January-February, 1971), pp. 79-89.

[5]Leon Festinger, *A Theory of Cognitive Dissonance* (Stanford, Calif.: Stanford University Press, 1957), pp. 1-30.

PART II

Incidents with
Analyses

PERCEPTION

Incident	*Page*
A POSSIBLE RESIGNATION	14
Richard S. Scranton	
Analysis 1	15
Analysis 2	17
GRIEVING CASEWORKERS	21
James R. Hoke	
Analysis 1	22
Analysis 2	23
THE COMPUTER PRINTOUT	27
R. N. Ritner	
Analysis 1	27
Analysis 2	29

A POSSIBLE RESIGNATION

The senior partners of the law firm of Schmidt and Snodgrass decided to automate the preparation of routine legal documents. Mr. Knock, a junior member of the firm, who also acted as office manager, was assigned the task of accomplishing this. Originally, Miss Lohman, a woman with three years of prelaw training, was selected to implement the program. She had quickly proven too technically incompetent and socially incompatible to do the job.

Somewhat in desperation, Mr. Knock then chose Mrs. Jones, one of the younger and more capable secretaries, as her replacement. The system implementation was then successful to the satisfaction and surprise of all concerned. Mrs. Jones, through special schooling and diligent effort, had learned the intricacies of the relatively complex system and managed to convert many of the standard documents into forms such that they could be readily produced automatically.

At the end of the year, which was review time for all office personnel, Mrs. Jones was given a minimum raise. Mrs. Jones was of the opinion that her dual efforts, as secretary and system operator, were worthy of a greater reward and stated this to Mr. Knock. His explanation was that due to her past raises, resulting from her excellence as a secretary, she was already approaching the pay standard of the secretaries of long tenure and that a more substantial increase would create dissension and dissatisfaction among these women. Mrs. Jones responded by refusing the small raise, claiming that it was an insult.

While it was not stated in so many words, Mr. Knock read this as a precursor to her resignation. Knowing that this would set the automation program back at least another six months, an event certain to dismay the senior partners, and being of the opinion that a greater raise would cause disharmony in the office, he was faced with a dilemma. What should he do to insure the continued success of the automation program and at the same time to maintain a reasonable level of harmony in the office force?

ANALYSIS 1: *A Possible Resignation*

An analysis of this incident shows initially that perception is playing an important part in the relationship that has developed between Mr. Knock and Mrs. Jones. Mrs. Jones has developed a frame of reference based on her outstanding performance while implementing and operating the relatively complex automated documents system as well as performing as a secretary. Mr. Knock continues to view her as a secretary, as shown by his evaluation of her and comparing her pay with that of the other secretaries in the office. If the perceptions of the two principals were closer, or more coincidental, much of the problem would have been eased from the beginning. Leavitt[1] points out that because people see things differently, the same set of facts may be viewed differently by various people. He further states that managers must develop an awareness of these differences through the mechanism of feedback.

Elements of motivational friction, as described by Scott,[2] are evident between Mrs. Jones and Mr. Knock. Mrs. Jones is experiencing a large measure of frustration since the formal system of authority in the organization is placing a barrier between her and the satisfaction for which she is striving. Although she is showing dissatisfaction with her salary increase, the expression of economic aspects of the raise is symbolic, and the true needs she is attempting to satisfy are probably those of esteem and self-actualization. Mr. Knock, on the other hand, is facing conflict—a conflict because he is confronted with the need for choice between goals—keeping the group satisfied, and keeping Mrs. Jones satisfied. This approaches the avoidance-avoidance conflict which Scott describes as a dilemma between two threats.[3]

Mrs. Jones is also engulfed in a role conflict. On one hand, she is regarded in the role of a secretary with rewards based on that role. On the other hand, she has received special schooling, has met the challenge of establishing an automated records system and is now performing as a system operator as well as secretary. Scott does an excellent job of showing the importance of this type of conflict when he states "An individual in an organization is required to play a number of roles. Traditionally, good management practice tries to ensure that role conflict does not occur in formal job requirements because of the consequent inefficiencies and employee dissatisfactions. As far as possible, well-managed organizations spell out the functions required of employees and arrange that these functions are not incompatible."[4]

Mrs. Jones has not been given the benefit of practice or the consideration of human needs. Maslow identifies five sets of goals as human needs: physiological, safety, love, esteem, and self-actualization. He regards man as a "perpetually wanting animal" and regards the average member of our society as only partially satisfied in what he wants. Maslow's hierarchical approach places increasing percentage values of nonsatisfaction as one progresses up the ladder of needs. Maslow further states that any thwarting of these basic goals or danger to the conditions on which they rest would be considered a psychological threat.[5] What Mrs. Jones is seeking under this concept is esteem. She desires a high evaluation of her competency and mastery of establishing the automated system, and performing as a secretary in addition. Mrs. Jones is perceiving a need for recognition of her performance and worth in her own eyes as well as in the eyes of others in the office. She is also perceiving the need for self-actualization which in her case is recognition as a systems operator. These two needs are particularly important in Mrs. Jones's case, since they occupy the top two positions in Maslow's hierarchical array. As Scott points out, the literature of industrial humanism, which is traceable to Maslow and supported by Argyris, has emphasized that the organization should be designed to increase the opportunities for its participants to achieve self-actualization.[6]

Additional analysis of this incident reveals a communication breakdown between Mr. Knock and Mrs. Jones. An interpersonal communication relationship between the two appears somewhat weak since Mr. Knock was communicating with Mrs. Jones as performing in one role, and she was communicating while viewing herself in a far more expanded role. This easily could have led to a lack of acceptance of communications on her part. In this respect, Escher states, "Since unconscious selection (of information) is closely allied to our psychological needs and desires, it may be said quite aptly that we hear what we want to hear and reject what we don't want to hear."[7]

CONCLUSION

It can be concluded that Mrs. Jones has been frustrated and hindered while seeking some of her goals and in not receiving satisfaction of certain basic needs. Two separate and diverse viewpoints of her duties, position, and worth in the organization have developed; one by Mr. Knock and the other by herself. Part of the problem could have been avoided had communications between the two been more effective.

It is possible for Mr. Knock to be relieved of his dilemma. Mrs. Jones should continue in her expanded role to insure continued success of the automation program. Since she is carrying extraordinary responsibilities, she should be recognized. With increased responsibility she should be given a commensurate increase in authority to cover all of the operations for which she is charged. Most important, however, she should be given the status of her higher level responsibilities. This can be done by giving her a title or job description of a higher level than that of secretary. Physical symbols of status could also be provided her. Her physical location could be removed from those normally occupied by the secretaries. Mr. Knock must communicate with her on the extent of her duties in the expanded role. He could explain to her that once reclassified, she will receive another evaluation based on her new position and her salary would be weighed accordingly.

ADDITIONAL INFORMATION NEEDED

What is the size of the office force and organization of the group? Was there a recognizable informal group leader? What was the extent of social interaction within the group towards Mrs. Jones?

To what extent were interpersonal communications carried on between Mr. Knock and Mrs. Jones when she was preparing for her new duties? What was the nature and degree of rapport between the two?

What was Miss Lohman's reaction to her removal from the automated systems job? Was she, or is she still resentful and must she be considered in resolving the dilemma?

How many people received raises in addition to Mrs. Jones and what was the extent of such raises relative to hers?

What is the extent of the workload now and in the future for the automated documents system? Will it support a full-time employee?

With additional information, consideration could be given to the alternatives available to Mr. Knock. He might want to create a position for Mrs. Jones in which she would be a full-time program operator or supervisor of the activity. This would give her the role, status, esteem and self-actualization she seeks. She could be evaluated for salary purposes upon establishing the new position.

ANALYSIS 2: *A Possible Resignation*

In order to make a more accurate analysis of the incident, it would be helpful to have certain additional information. Rarely, of course, would a decision maker have complete information about a situation, but the following should realistically be obtainable. For example, what were the amounts of merit increases, if any, of other employees? What type of orientation had Mrs. Jones received? In other words, what expectations were developed which she might later perceive as commitments by the organization? Since

Knock was assigned the task of overseeing the automation program, what were his own sentiments concerning this change and his role in implementing it? In Knock's interpretation, what did he assume to be the needs and attitudes of employees?

It would also assist in problem solution to know more about the informal organization. Was it cohesive? Positive in sentiments toward the automation program? Were its work norms consistent with formal standards? These questions regarding the group are crucial, since any solution to the compensation problem must consider the reaction of the group. There was already evidence that the other workers were not sympathetic toward high merit increases. Nor had they fully accepted Mrs. Jones as a member of the group.

In analyzing the situation it is evident that Mr. Knock was involved in a frustrating avoidance-avoidance type of conflict. An obvious dilemma existed between two threats. He perceived the necessity of giving Mrs. Jones a substantial raise in order to keep her on the job to insure continuing progress of the automation program while at the same time, he realized that other employees would be dissatisfied if she (Mrs. Jones) received more money than they did. What Knock actually did, as a result, borders on manipulation. In order to assuage other workers, he compromised on Mrs. Jones' reward. But what he probably had not realized was that Mrs. Jones would react critically. Studies have shown, for example, that exploitive behavior tends to increase when a continuing relationship with the "opponent" is not expected.[8] In other words, Knock was not anticipating the possible future consequences, but rather protecting his immediate position.

PERCEPTION

Perception, or the question of "what we see," has a definite bearing on this situation.[9] What one person sees as fact might be viewed by another as fantasy or as nonexistent. Consequently, it should be no great surprise to find that situational conditions take on different meanings among the parties involved.

Mrs. Jones has certain needs which require satisfaction and, in turn, the organization has needs in the form of services which must be performed. There is, in other words, an opportunity for a reciprocal relationship between person and organization.[10] But in this incident the relationship has been disturbed by a perception of inadequate compensation. Theoretically, Mrs. Jones would be experiencing cognitive dissonance, in that her cognitions of effort and reward are incompatible. One would also expect a similar dissonance in Knock's perception, but it might not surface here because there are many ways that he can justify any perceived exploitation.[11] For example, Knock rationalized the group's reaction, e.g., by stating that it would not be fair to the secretaries with greater seniority. For this reason, it will be difficult to reduce the dissonance experienced by Mrs. Jones regarding her compensation. Knock has, in effect, a "logic-tight" argument from the standpoint of expressing solicitude over the effects of Mrs. Jones's compensation on other workers. He may, of course, be feigning this concern, but that would not alter the strength of the rationalization.

One of the values in sizing up a situation such as this in a behavioral science framework is that of generating predictions. Mrs. Jones will respond, for example, in a manner which will restore cognitive consonance.[12] But what are her options? For one, she can reduce her effort to a level more compatible with her perception of her compensation. Thus, her reward might have served as productive of a kind of Pygmalion in reverse.[13] Indeed, there is evidence that workers will tend to contribute according to their perception of justice/injustice in their rewards. Higher than expected reward, for example, tends to be followed by greater effort, and lower than expected reward by less effort.[14]

As time progressed and the project was successfully implemented, Mrs. Jones no longer perceived herself as a mere secretary but as a systems analyst who was quite distinct from others in the secretarial group. On the other hand, Knock, who was rather surprised but satisfied at the successful outcome of the project, still did not perceive Mrs. Jones as being a systems analyst, distinct from the others in the group. Knock failed to exercise what Koontz and Bradspies call "feed-forward control."[15] In other words, Knock did not anticipate, nor did he prepare for, the changing perceptions of role and status that often occur under circumstances such as those in the incidents. Feed-forward (contrasted with feedback) control relies heavily on forecasting and prediction at the input stage.[16] While the authors refer to it in more general management terms, its relevancy here to a behavioral situation is quite apparent.

OTHER SALIENT ISSUES

Throughout the situation, Mrs. Jones has experienced role conflict. She is being asked to perform the role of systems analyst rather than that of a secretary. But, with respect to rewards and status, she is expected to be satisfied with the latter. Therefore, the conflict is compounded in the sense that the secretarial and systems analyst expectations are in competition, and the reward system is incongruent with the higher of the expectations.

There is another way to approach the above enigma; i.e., in terms of Mrs. Jones's self-perceptions. She developed, through performing highly-skilled tasks, a favorable self-perception which would be more consistent with the

systems analyst role. At the same time, her perception of Knock's supportiveness also changed. A study by Thompson relates appropriately in this
context. Thompson found that employees with favorable self-perceptions
reported lower levels of satisfaction and did not perceive their supervisors
as supportive, in contrast with employees having lower self-perceptions.[17]
It would not be taking excessive liberty to interpret this as meaning that an
individual in Mrs. Jones's situation, given an (assumed) upward shift in her
self-perceptions, would also require more supportive leader behavior from
her supervisor in order to attain and maintain a desired level of satisfaction.
The mere fact that she is highly dissatisfied with her salary increase is
indicative of the self-perception phenomenon in operation.

While our purpose in these analyses is not to solve the problems but
rather to suggest an approach which will lead to solution, it obviously
behooves Knock to somehow differentiate Mrs. Jones from others in the
secretarial group. Her role, status, and compensation must be consistent
with her level of responsibility, which is greater than that of others in the
work group. By creating a new position for her, it might become possible
to also circumvent the salary problem. In other words, the seniority factor
would not be so relevant in determining salary in relation to the other
secretaries.

GRIEVING CASEWORKERS

Late one afternoon Mr. Jones, one of five city commissioners and head of the committee on Health, Education and Welfare, received a petition of grievances bearing some 200 signatures of social workers connected with one of the county social agencies. The petition urged Mr. Jones along with the other members of his committee to take some action to alleviate the poor working conditions which prohibited these workers from doing the professional job they felt was necessary. Among those things cited were such matters as high individual case loads, ever-increasing case enrollment with no apparent effort by the director of the agency to hire new caseworkers or introduce new methods of handling the multiplying paperwork. The petition went on to include other problems such as poor physical working conditions, incompetency of supervisory staff, and low wages. Lastly, the petition threatened that if immediate action was not taken to correct these problems, the caseworkers would be forced to refuse to take any additional cases, which would result in a period of extreme distress at a critical time in the city's economy.

Having had no problems with this particular agency previously, Mr. Jones was somewhat alarmed at the sudden appearance of numerous problems. He immediately phoned Mr. Phillips, assistant to the director of the agency, with whom Mr. Jones was acquainted and had previously worked, in an effort to gain a better picture of the situation. He knew Mr. Phillips was in charge of employee relations at the agency and would probably be able to better explain what was happening. However, Mr. Phillips was off work for medical reasons and would not be returning for several weeks. Then Mr. Jones placed a call to Mr. Frank, director of the agency, and bluntly asked him what the petition was all about. Mr. Frank said he had received no petition from his staff and was sure that Jones need not worry, since there was no problem he (Frank) couldn't handle. Mr. Jones called in one of his assistants to look into the matter and get back with him in a day or so with more information.

ANALYSIS 1: *Grieving Caseworkers*

The petition sent by the caseworkers to Mr. Jones, the city commissioner, was a highly significant communication. The fact that nearly 200 social workers signed it has import. Even though we do not know the total number of workers in the agency, 200 would appear to be a significant number who are unified in their perception of conditions in the department. We have a group of workers with a common perceived need. As Scott states, ". . . a human need exists to solve problems . . . and to achieve a balance in human relationships,"[18] hence an informal group has formed. We may speculate that the caseworkers believed that a consensus was necessary to provide support for one another and lend emphasis to their appeal.

The concept of perceived role looms large as an implicit factor in the caseworkers' petition. They indicated that because of the identified poor working conditions, they were unable to do the "professional job" they felt was necessary. Role, according to Scott, is ". . . a collection of activities peculiar to a position or function in society at large, . . . (or) a formal organization . . ."[19] The petitioners are indicating that they perceive their position as one in which they render a professional service to those with whom they deal. Their threatened capability for continuing to perform this service at the desired professional level is the reason they give for the requested agency changes.

We might categorize the caseworkers as experiencing a variation of Kahn's "person-role conflict."[20] They perceive their position as requiring the rendering of professional services, but the developing environmental conditions are denying them the capability of performing at the desired level. Kahn states: "Any person who is confronted with a situation of role conflict . . . must respond to it in some fashion."[21] The response of the caseworkers as a group was to write and send their petition; and to be certain that it would generate an urgency to correct the identified conditions they included a threat: refusal to handle any new cases if their requests were not met.

A significant topic of the petition pertains to the agency director and supervisors. The caseworkers suggest that, despite what they consider serious problems in mounting caseloads and attendant paperwork, the director is not taking effective action. They label their supervisory staff as incompetent. It would appear that they have lost confidence in their formally designated superiors. The caseworkers probably perceive their supervisors as nonprofessionals who are not supporting their professional role.[22]

Mr. Frank, the director of the welfare agency, assured Mr. Jones that he had received no petition and that if a problem existed he (Frank) could handle it. We should examine two aspects of the incident:

1. The concept of role again as we look at Mr. Frank.
2. What is implied about communication within the agency.

It is possible that Mr. Frank was not aware of the conditions. There may be factors in the agency that are causing communication problems. From among "barriers" that Stieglitz discusses that may cause communication breakdowns, the following may pertain here: (1) the top man; (2) organization structure; and (3) poor supervision.[23] Mr. Frank's policies and personality might be directly responsible for his not knowing about the undesirable conditions. His philosophy and practice of management may be such as to create an organization where policies and climate discourage the communication of problems and needs from the caseworker level. The organization structure might be a factor. Perhaps the supervisors, because of incompetence and constraints of their perceived role, are acting as barriers to communications. There are no facts given in the incident to support analysis on any of these possibilities.

What are the alternatives for dealing with this problem? A possibility is that Mr. Frank is correct in saying that if a problem exists he can handle it. It would appear naive, however, to believe that Mr. Frank has not been aware of these identified conditions, even though he did not know of the petition. If he were aware of the conditions and took no effective action or if he were not aware because of various communications barriers in the agency, Mr. Frank exhibits deficiencies in his management of the agency.

It would seem necessary for Mr. Jones and his committee to follow up on this situation and provide whatever assistance is necessary to adequately resolve it. Whatever the resolution of this immediate problem, Mr. Frank should be questioned regarding management of the agency. It should be determined why these conditions were not identified as problems earlier, either to be effectively solved within the agency or brought to the attention of the parent controlling committee of the commission. Based upon the results of the investigation of Mr. Frank's effectiveness as a manager, certain actions might be taken. Perhaps Mr. Frank needs to be replaced. At the least, it would appear that the implementation of new management practices and the regular, more complete reporting of agency problems by the director to the committee would be called for.

ANALYSIS 2: *Grieving Caseworkers*

This incident will be analyzed in three parts: a discussion of various items of missing information and why they are important to the analysis; a consideration of several aspects of the incident in light of organizational behavior concepts; and a discussion of the action taken by the commissioner.

There are at least five elements of missing information, the availability of which is highly necessary for a thorough analysis. Probably the most obvious omission is that which relates to the signatories of the petition. While seemingly a large figure, what percentage of social work employees of the particular agency does 200 represent? Also, the backgrounds of the signatories are important; it would make quite a difference if 170 were fresh out of college and relatively inexperienced, or if the same number were employees with over 20 years' experience, for example. Do they all work with, say, juvenile delinquents or do they represent welfare workers and other groups? These items of information about the petition-signers would be required for any insights into the behavioral system, and for any conclusions regarding possible actions.

Second, the analyst would certainly desire more information about the Health, Education and Welfare committee. What power does it have, both to influence the activities of the social workers and to alleviate these conditions, if they do in fact exist? Is this a city committee dealing with a county agency in an advisory capacity, or is it just coincidental that a city commissioner chairs a county committee? These data seem quite relevant for the analysis.

Third, the analyst would like to know how the petition was received. Did it come up through established channels? Does this committee function as an appeal agency? Or, if the committee does not ordinarily act on grievances such as these, was the existing appeal system tried previously by the petitioners in this matter? If not, why? Also, was the petition carried by hand? If so, perhaps the courier is the informal leader of the group, or can identify the leader, with whom the issues may be discussed at a subsequent time. Answers to these questions would be useful in sizing up this situation.

Fourth, it would be desirable to have some type of objective data about the past performance of this agency. The fact that the committee has had no previous problems with the agency does not indicate that things have always been going well. If its function is juvenile delinquent counseling, for example, how does the counselees' rate of recidivism compare with other counties, and what have recent trends been in the area of the agency's efforts? The answer to this would help to determine what relation, if any, exists between morale and productivity of the staff. It would appear that morale is low. How well are the people doing under this condition? The answer might indicate more about the nature of the personnel involved.

Finally, it would be helpful to learn more about the employee relations conditions in the past which have led to this seemingly drastic step. Have the workers complained to the powers within the agency previously? Is this just another, albeit louder, incident in a series of defensive reactions which has been blown out of proportion by the staff? In such an instance, it would be difficult to remove the dissatisfactions which appear to be voiced here. Or this could be a precipitatory event, suggesting an accumulation of past grievances. Understanding these phenomena would aid in developing the "big picture" along with an historical perspective.

This incident is an excellent example of one that is very difficult to identify topically. Perception, however, is one of the dominant issues; thus, it will be first examined from that perspective.

PERCEPTION

The question has already been raised as to whether the grievances are representative of the actual occurrences at the time, or are an accumulation of past dissatisfactions. It is important to realize that quite frequently perceptions made at a single point in time have been forming through cumulative experience. Nor are the complaints always representative of the real problems. Petitions might itemize tangible grievances and leave more important intangible matters unexpressed because of employee perceptions of management's lack of understanding of less tangible problems.

In this respect, concepts of motivation relate very closely to the perception problem. Assuming that perception is determined partly by the state of motivation[24] one could examine several interesting aspects of the incident. By far the most apparent is that virtually all of the Herzberg hygiene factors were mentioned in the incident.[25] But, following Herzberg, one could not expect an improvement in performance upon modifying the conditions which are creating dissatisfaction. Elimination of these factors cannot produce positive motivation, according to motivation-hygiene theory. Rather, their removal will reduce dissatisfaction. This aspect of the two-factor theory has, of course, been disputed, along with the identification of satisfiers and dissatisfiers themselves.[26]

Then, too, there is the question of the extent to which value systems affect the determination of motivation and hygiene factors. Grigaliunas and Herzberg have raised the question whether self-report statements in the motivation-hygiene studies relate to the respondents' value systems or to actual work incidents.[27] In other words, in the context of this incident it could be questioned whether the caseworkers would perceive these factors as dissatisfiers. It could be that, individually or taken together, they constitute real motivational barriers, even though the caseworkers report them as matters related to hygiene.

Therefore, a first requirement would be for the administrators involved to obtain an accurate reading on the perceptions of the caseworkers and of the underlying causes of these perceptions.

OTHER IMPORTANT ISSUES

It appears that Frank occupies a position of headship, as opposed to leadership, in the agency. His authority hasn't been legitimized in the minds of the staff, and, according to Barnard's consent theory of authority,[28] Frank probably possesses none. An informal leader has undoubtedly arisen with the consent of the staff, who for them holds legitimate authority.

Many of the problems of the agency may well be the result of communication filtering processes which have apparently been occurring. It may well be that Phillips has filtered any dissatisfaction from reaching Frank. It may also be that Frank had previously distorted the dissatisfaction which reached him. Or, it may also be that Frank had previously filtered the dissatisfaction from his superiors and the committee.

Another indicator of poor communication is the fact that Jones appears to be avoiding a proper communication channel by first trying to reach the assistant director regarding the petition. There is more here than a question of short-circuiting the channel of communication. It is also a matter of keeping the top man informed regarding the situation. By approaching Frank, it might stimulate him to find out what is happening in the organization.

THE COMPUTER PRINTOUT

In early February, 1969, Colonel "Rock" Jones informed his division by word of mouth that Headquarters, United States Air Force, had published directions concerning a computerized information retrieval and storage system which was to be created in each unit. This system was to contain management information on all projects evolved. When the system was finally completed, the Army, Navy, and Department of Defense could receive information from the other organizations.

Colonel Jones selected a civil service employee, Mr. Floor, to design and implement the information system within the organization. Mr. Floor was known for being the first to accept a new project and the last to finish it. Due to a manpower shortage, Colonel Jones had no choice but to assign the project to Mr. Floor and hope that he would complete it on time.

Virtually every member of the unit was opposed to the computer retrieval system and made comments such as: "It will always be two months out of date. We work in a fast-moving field." "Management is admitting they can't do their job and they need an electronic brain to do it for them." "It is just plain silly. We already have weekly and monthly management reports which report the same information."

Mr. Floor, after securing specific information on each project, created the computer program to process and store it. He gave the printout to Colonel Jones in late November (it was due at Headquarters in early December) for final review. Much to the surprise of Colonel Jones, about 80 percent of the information appeared to be incorrect. It was quite obvious that either false information had been provided or the information was purposely changed when entered into the computer. Time was running out.

ANALYSIS 1: *The Computer Printout*

There are several initial questions which relate to the type of information needed to solve the problem(s) with the computer system. For example, did the project managers provide incorrect data in order to sabotage the system?

Why were project managers not given a more active role in designing and implementing the system? Did Floor alter any of the information given him, either for purposes of protecting the interests of others or for his personal ego-satisfaction? It would be helpful, too, to know more about the nature of the projects. Were they critical to the extent that information error was an extremely serious matter? Finally, how did Col. Jones interpret the directives from Headquarters? Insofar as he disseminated the information by word-of-mouth, it is highly possible that the intent of the original message was garbled. It could be, too, that this was perceived by Jones as an opportunity to impress the Pentagon "brass" and, therefore, he ordered the change regardless of the urgency of the original directive.

PERCEPTION

There was obviously a difference in the way Colonel Jones and the project managers perceived the situation. The latter saw it as another "make work" project; the former, as an important change. This is an example of a situation in which communication has an important effect on perceptions. First, there was the word-of-mouth medium of communication. While this medium is not always associated with low-priority messages, it does give rise to variations in the understanding and interpretation of their meaning and wording. In that sense, word-of-mouth is not only less reliable than written communication—it leads to ambiguity and lack of direction as well. One would expect, for example, that a group of project managers would prefer having the directions presented to them in detail. In this regard, House, et.al., found that higher level occupational groups tend to respond more favorably to initiating structure than do lower-status occupational groups. The reason could relate to another finding of that study which suggests that initiating structure does not adversely affect one's satisfaction with freedom.[29] Thus, by not adequately structuring his communication, Jones is creating ambiguity among the project directors.

OTHER IMPORTANT ISSUES

The incident as reported does not indicate whether the projects are of a scientific nature. If we assume for the moment that they are, one could raise strong criticisms of Jones's approach. The cognitive-level difficulties posed by Jones were mentioned above. Regarding *cognitive* behavior, his approach can also be described as highly inappropriate. Scientific performance, for example, depends largely upon sharing information and decisions. Smith found that, especially where practical objectives are involved, scientific productivity relates positively to multiple consultation and shared decision-making.[30] Jones obviously did not consult with the project directors; i.e., those who would be most directly affected by the system change. Moreover Jones placed Floor, who was held in low esteem, in charge of a project which interfaces with highly-sensitive areas.

Floor's position as an integrator would be a difficult one for even a highly competent individual.[31] It requires considerable interaction and consultation, which apparently Floor has not been involved in to this point.

Perhaps one of the major factors for consideration was the resistance to change on the part of the project managers. In this incident, it might be more aptly described, in Longenecker's terminology, as "resistance to authority."[32] The reason for viewing it in this way is basically that the way the system was introduced and the approach taken by Floor in installing it are largely responsible for the apparent failures. The project managers would understandably resent this intrusion by an individual of Floor's stature. Nor are they inclined to give tacit assent to Jones's directives. Returning to an earlier point regarding communication, the introduction of the change by Jones lacked the official "ring" that a more affirmative pronouncement would possess. Moreover, the lack of prior information and participation constitutes an open invitation for the opposition to join ranks and torpedo the effort.

ANALYSIS 2: *The Computer Printout*

It is assumed that the only communication between Colonel Jones and members of his division concerning this project was his verbal statement in February, 1969. It is also assumed that the only direct involvement of Jones in the project was his final review of it.

Communication and perception appear to be major behavioral problems in this incident. Jones should have followed up his verbal message with a written communication of some sort. This could have lessened the possibility of misinterpretation and distortion of facts.

The members of Jones's division apparently perceived the project as inconsistent with the purpose of the organization, and incompatible with their personal interests. Their perception may have been false, but what is perceived is most important to the individual, regardless of its truth or falsity.[33]

Possibly in Jones's case, and certainly in Floor's case, we have reason to question the effectiveness of the communicator. There is no evidence that a problem-solving approach was pursued in communicating the necessity for the project.[34] Feedback was lacking; feedback would have made possible an exchange of ideas which might have generated greater acceptance of the project. Frequent communication and periodic checks of the project by Jones would also have revealed the false information earlier.

The attitude of the division members toward the project and toward Floor, whose reputation they were undoubtedly aware of, might have been responsible for the incorrect data. Filtering of the communication by members of the division to Floor could have occurred.[35]

Authority might also have been a problem area. It is possible that there was a status-ego threat existing between the civil service employee and the military personnel. Floor's reputation would lead us to believe that he might lack functional status. This might have undermined the legitimacy of his authority, as perceived by the people he dealt with.

It is possible that the false information was the result of a pathological role defense by members of the division. It is at least certain that we have resistance to change. Individual comments tend to support this conclusion.

In summary, this incident is the result of poor communication, inadequate informal authority, pathological role defenses, and, intermingled with each of these, faulty perception.

ALTERNATIVES

1. Jones could issue verbal and written instructions to the members of his division, instructing them to correct the mistakes and assist Floor in developing an accurate program by the deadline date. It could be made perfectly clear that this was to be an all-out, no excuses acceptable, effort. This alternative may accomplish the task on time, but would probably cause other problems. Floor's inefficiency would be blamed for the problems, and Jones would be blamed for assigning him to the project. This would take place regardless of who actually caused the problem. Morale would be low and future efficiency within the division might be hampered.

2. Jones could ask for an extension of time for the project. This would certainly not improve his image at the United States Air Force Headquarters. If additional time was granted, he could issue an order similar to the above, but without such a tight time schedule. The results of this approach would be similar to those mentioned under alternative 1.

3. Jones could call a meeting with Floor and the formal leaders of the division present. He could pursue a problem-solving approach and hope the results would permit the successful completion of the program by the target date. He could also, on a less formal basis, attempt to explain the program, how it would benefit the division, what was yet to be done, etc., to the informal leaders. He could elicit their suggestions as to how the job could

be completed on time. Past circumstances might prevent him from effectively doing this on a personal basis, but he could work through his formal leaders toward this end. To a large extent the past experience of the group and their relationship with Jones will determine the success of this alternative. The normal reaction to this approach would probably be suspicion of manipulation coupled with an "I knew the project would flop" attitude. Developing trust would require time. If this approach had been attempted at the outset of the project, the incident under discussion might not have occurred.

CONCLUSION

If time were not so critical, alternative three would be the best choice. However, using a combination of alternatives one and three may be necessary to complete the project on time. The instructions suggested in alternative one must exist to point out the importance of both the project and the deadline. While issuing the verbal instructions, Jones could address members of the division, shoulder the responsibility for the current situation, explain the potential benefits of the project, indirectly appeal to esprit-de-corps, and request assistance in solving the problem. If he can eliminate the impulse to be defensive concerning past actions, remove the need to place blame on an individual or group, and generate a spirit of cooperation, the problem might be solved.

ADDITIONAL INFORMATION DESIRED

It would be helpful to have additional facts concerning Jones. Background information concerning his education, leadership style, and personality profile may help explain why he allowed the problem to develop in the first place. How he was perceived by the personnel in his division would be beneficial. Exactly what did he say when transmitting the directive from Headquarters?

It would be helpful to know how Floor earned his reputation. Was he inefficient, overly thorough, or a victim of circumstances? What was Floor's attitude toward the project?

Who changed the information and why? Was this an act of sabotage or a misguided effort to anticipate conditions as they would exist at the target date? If this was the case, did Floor change the information? Or, if he didn't, why wasn't the false information obvious to Floor? Why wasn't information periodically checked for validity?

FOOTNOTES

[1]Harold J. Leavitt, *Managerial Psychology* 2nd ed. (Chicago and London: The University of Chicago Press, 1964), pp. 28–40.

[2]William G. Scott, *Organization Theory: A Behavioral Analysis for Management* (Homewood, Ill.: Richard D. Irwin, Inc., 1967), p. 78.

[3]*Ibid.,* p. 79.

[4]*Ibid.,* p. 197.

[5]A. H. Maslow, "A Theory of Human Motivation: The Basic Needs," in D. R. Hampton, C. E. Summer, and R. A. Webber, *Organizational Behavior and the Practice of Management* (Glenview, Ill.: Scott, Foresman and Company, 1968), pp. 39–40.

[6]Scott, *Organization Theory,* p. 78.

[7]Albert J. Escher, "But I Thought . . .," *Supervision,* July, 1959, p. 24.

[8]See D. Marlowe, K. J. Gergen, and A. N. Doob, "Opponent's Personality, Expectation of Social Interaction, and Interpersonal Bargaining," *Journal of Personality and Social Psychology* 3 (1966): 206–13; also, Kenneth J. Gergen, *The Psychology of Behavior Exchange* (Reading, Mass. Addison-Wesley Publishing Company, 1969), pp. 59–63.

[9]Joseph A. Litterer, *The Analysis of Organization* (New York: John Wiley and Sons, Inc., 1965), p. 41.

[10]Alvin Gouldner, "The Norm of Reciprocity: A Preliminary Statement," *American Sociological Review* 25, no. 2 (April, 1960): 161–78.

[11]Ellen Berscheid and Elaine Hatfield Walster, *Interpersonal Attraction* (Reading, Mass.: Addison-Wesley Publishing Company, 1969), pp. 14–28.

[12]Co-author Von der Embse has suggested, in a perverse vein, that the theory should be termed "cognitive consonance" rather than "cognitive dissonance," because the behavioral dynamics appear to center more on the mechanisms of reducing dissonance.

[13]J. Sterling Livingston, "Pygmalion in Management," *Harvard Business Review,* July-August, 1969, pp. 81–89.

[14]See J. Stacy Adams, "Toward An Understanding of Inequity," *Journal of Abnormal and Social Psychology* 67 (1963): 422–24.

[15]Harold Koontz and Robert W. Bradspies, "Managing Through Feedforward Control," *Business Horizons,* June, 1972, pp. 25–36.

[16]*Ibid.,* pp. 27–28.

[17]Duane E. Thompson, "Favorable Self-Perceptions, Perceived Supervisory Style and Job Satisfaction," *Journal of Applied Psychology* 55, no. 4 (1971): 349–52.

[18]Scott, *Organization Theory,* p. 83.

[19]*Ibid.,* p. 192.

[20]Robert L. Kahn, "Role Conflict and Ambiguity in Organizations," in S. G. Huneryager and I. L. Heckman, *Human Relations in Management* (Cincinnati: South-Western Publishing Co. 1967), p. 645.

[21]*Ibid.,* p. 647.

[22]For a comprehensive analysis of professionals in organizations, see Fremont E. Kast and James E. Rosenzwieg, *Organization and Management: A Systems Approach* (New York: McGraw-Hill Book Company, 1970), Chap. 17.

[23]Harold Stieglitz, "Barriers to Communication," *Management Record,* 20, no. 1 (January 1958): 2–5.

[24]This assumption appears to be widely accepted in both texts and articles in the field.

[25]See Frederick Herzberg, *Work and the Nature of Man* (Cleveland: World Publishing Co., 1966).

[26]See Raymond L. Hilgert, "Satisfaction and Dissatisfaction in a Plant Setting," *Personnel Administration,* July-August, 1971, pp. 21–27.

[27]Benedict A. Grigaliunas and Frederick Herzberg, "Relevancy in the Test of Motivator—Hygiene Theory," *Journal of Applied Psychology* 55, no. 1 (1971): 73–79.

[28]Chester I. Barnard, *The Functions of the Executive* (Cambridge: Harvard University Press, 1938).

[29]Robert J. House, Allan C. Filley, and Damodar N. Gujarita, "Leadership Style, Hierarchical Influence, and the Satisfaction of Subordinate Role Expectations: A Test of Likert's Influence Proposition," *Journal of Applied Psychology* 55, no. 5 (1971): 422–32; especially, 430–31.

[30]Clagett G. Smith, "Consultation and Decision Processes in a Research Laboratory," *Administrative Science Quarterly* 15 (1970): 203–15.

[31]For a more extensive discussion of this role, see R. C. Ziller, B. J. Stark, and H. O. Pruden, "Marginality and Integrative Management Positions," *Academy of Management Journal,* December, 1969, pp. 487–95; also, Paul R. Lawrence and Jay Lorsch, "New Management Job: The Integrator," *Harvard Business Review,* November-December, 1967, pp. 142–51.

[32]Justin G. Longenecker, *Principles of Management and Organizational Behavior* (Columbus, Charles E. Merrill Publishing Co., 1964), p. 354.

[33]Walter Nord, *Concepts and Controversy in Organizational Behavior* (Pacific Palisades, Calif.: Goodyear Publishing Co., 1972), p. 19.

[34]Jack R. Gibb, "Communication and Productivity," in S. G. Huneryager and I. L. Heckman, *Human Relations in Management* (Cincinnati: South-Western Publishing Co., 1967), pp. 520–29.

[35]William G. Scott and Terence R. Mitchell, *Organization Theory: A Structural and Behavioral Analysis,* Revised Edition (Homewood, Ill.: Richard D. Irwin, Inc. and The Dorsey Press, 1972), pp. 159–61.

MOTIVATION

Incident	*Page*
TO WORK ON SATURDAY	35
Joel S. Eichenholf	
Analysis 1	36
Analysis 2	38
THE CROSSWORD PUZZLE	42
William K. Maxwell	
Analysis 1	43
Analysis 2	45
JOB PERFORMANCE	49
Robert J. Bunyard	
Analysis 1	50
Analysis 2	54

TO WORK ON SATURDAY

Mr. Ward is a manager of a computer software group. He personally wrote large portions of a time-sharing executive now being used throughout the engineering division of the corporation he works for. He is in the process of phasing out of the participative end of the project and is turning the maintenance and tuning of the executive over to Mr. Holt. To enable the system to run faster some additional hardware was purchased. The system needed some major changes to take advantage of the new hardware. Since Mr. Ward is phasing off the project he could not do it. Mr. Holt had a work load far above the level that would allow him to take on this extra task and complete it within a reasonable length of time. For that reason Mr. Jones, one of the group's best programmers, was asked to take on this six-month project.

For a few months all went well. Mr. Holt spent most of his time keeping the present system functional while Mr. Ward supervised Mr. Jones's reworking of the executive to handle the new hardware. The conflict did not arise until the new code was ready to be tested. At that time the computer was being used for the time-sharing system during the entire working day. Mr. Ward and Mr. Holt always worked overtime when it was necessary to do work on the executive. All three men are salaried professionals and are not paid extra for overtime efforts. Mr. Jones's testing required the use of the computer system for long stretches of time which were only available at night or over the weekend. Mr. Jones refused to work on weekends without overtime pay. He agreed to work for an hour after five if he could arrive an hour late. This slowed the testing down considerably and angered Mr. Ward.

Mr. Ward wanted the new code used as soon as possible. He assumed that Mr. Jones was aware from the start that this overtime would be necessary. After all Mr. Jones could readily observe that Mr. Ward worked at least fifty hours each week and that when truly necessary Mr. Holt worked overtime without question. Mr. Jones felt that he should have been informed at the inception of the project that this extra time would be necessary so that an equitable agreement could have been reached in advance.

Mr. Ward went into a slow burn about the situation and Mr. Jones held firm. The project is now more than a month late and is still being delayed.

ANALYSIS 1: *To Work on Saturday*

This incident, as with many others, involves more problem areas than would be justified under a single topic, such as motivation. Mr. Ward's managerial capabilities are obviously facing a severe test. It is often too easy to overlook a fact of organizational life: the managerial job involves far more than simply motivating others in pursuit of a set of objectives. Nevertheless, motivation is a useful starting point—and from there, we can let the analysis flow into other significant issues.

MOTIVATION

The incident mentions the fact that Mr. Ward usually works at least fifty hours per week (all three men are considered professionals and are not paid extra for overtime). Obviously, someone who works on this basis should be motivated at the higher end of Maslow's scale. Mr. Jones, on the other hand, wants to work only forty hours per week. This behavior could imply that he is working primarily for money. Research has shown that higher-level personnel in organizations are motivated at a higher level on Maslow's scale than lower ranking people.[1]

While it seems reasonable that Jones should not be as highly motivated as Ward; it seems that he is high enough in the organization to be more intrinsically motivated than appears from the facts. After all, Jones is a senior programmer. While the exact nature of his work is not revealed, he is probably involved with relatively long-range projects; at least it appears he would rather work with long-term projects since the natural time span for technical work is generally long compared to other work in an organization.[2] Since this project to which he has been assigned is a relatively short one, his refusal to work overtime may be symptomatic of his dissatisfaction with the temporal nature of the work.

There are ways Mr. Ward can attempt to motivate Mr. Jones. Probably the best in this case would be to ease the control Ward is placing on Jones by supervising him. Since Jones is a senior analyst, it seems reasonable to assume that he is capable of modifying the executive without too much help from Ward. This loosening of control would in no way dilute the requirement that the job be done in six months.[3] Another form of motivation is increasing responsibility. If it is possible to give Jones responsibility and authority in this matter it would be wise to do so.

GROUP AND INTERGROUP BEHAVIOR

There is ample reason to believe that the programmers are rather close socially. There are many reasons why people belong to informal groups: they get a feeling of security, belonging, sympathetic ear for troubles, aid on the job.[4] It is easy to see that if Jones starts to work all of this overtime he will do so alone and thus lose many of the benefits that he derives from the group. Therefore, he will probably want to reduce his overtime to a bare minimum.

There is also reason to believe that Jones's performance during regular working hours isn't up to expectations. Even though during working hours he spends most of his time physically with the group, the nature of the work he is doing can isolate him from the social interactions occurring within the group. Since his job is now so specialized, he will tend not to take part in the usual consultations that transpire, and he will have little reason to discuss his work with his fellow group members. Thus, he will not receive the social satisfactions that accrue to group members.

Mr. Ward probably holds membership in a different managerial group than Mr. Jones. Ward identifies more as a manager and probably associates with other managers. Since Ward did write some of the time-sharing executive and he is Jones's supervisor, and since Jones is a senior programmer (and probably a better programmer than Ward), there is a real problem in defining (in Jones's mind) who is the higher status person. When this type of situation occurs, communication between people and (or) groups tends to be severely limited.[5] Since Jones is not communicating either, it is easy to see why he seems bitter about this whole job—his attitude clearly isn't favorable toward overtime.

There is still another area for possible trouble in the relationship between Jones and Ward. If Jones feels as though he is being taken advantage of he may be engaged in a deliberate work slowdown in order to set this relationship into what he perceives as a more stable and equitable footing.[6]

LEADERSHIP AND LEADERSHIP STYLE

Naturally the relationship between a superior and his subordinate is a very important one. We would expect too that if there was something wrong with this relationship, performance would suffer. We have a good clue that the leadership style of Ward isn't appropriate when we find that Ward didn't make it clear that the job would require a good deal of overtime. There is yet another symptom of poor communication and that is the fact of Ward's refusal to talk to Jones about the problem. Since the most effective way to improve communication between subordinates and superiors is face-to-face interchange,[7] there isn't a good chance of immediate improvement.

All supervisors have power relative to their subordinates. The base of this power is of extreme importance in managing employees, especially technically oriented ones. The least desirable type of power, as far as motivation is concerned, is coercion (use of punishments and threats); and the most desirable kind is expertise (power based on superior knowledge).[8] It seems unlikely that Ward would have more skill at programming than a senior programmer, so we know that his power base isn't really ideal—although it probably isn't purely coercive either.

ANALYSIS 2: *To Work on Saturday*

The three major behavioral concepts or combinations of them which are applicable to this incident are in the areas of Communication, Leadership and Motivation. Also, functionally interdependent are the concepts of Role Conflict, Perception and Authority.

COMMUNICATION

Certainly there were communication breakdowns in this incident at the outset of the assignment as well as during the administering of the program. What were the probable causes or reasons? Scott and Mitchell[9] would probably say there was distortion because both parties perceived different requirements for the job. Possibly, also, because of lack of communication with others, the actual job requirements, namely the necessity for odd hour testing of the code, was unknown until too late to avoid the conflict. Possibly this job requirement was filtered or distorted during the communications between Mr. Jones and Mr. Ward. One requirement of an effective organization, and one that possibly applies to this incident, is a clear understanding of organization purpose and goals; this is especially important when employing participative management and job enlargement. Possibly Mr. Ward did not communicate these needs and the specific need for the code in the larger context. Mr. Ward should have communicated these job requirements rather than assume that Mr. Jones had knowledge of them. As discussed by Scott and Mitchell[10] communication could possibly have avoided this lack of "role effectiveness" between Mr. Jones's individual needs and his selection for the task assignment.

LEADERSHIP STYLE

First, did Mr. Ward use participative management in selecting Mr. Jones? Did Mr. Jones have some say on the assignment? According to Tannenbaum and Schmidt, an effective leader must be aware of the forces in the manager, the situation and the subordinates.[11] Mr. Ward must not have been aware of Mr. Jones's personal motivation. It is quite possible that work was not the central interest in Jones's life.[12]

According to MacGregor[13] the effective leader will integrate the goals of the individual and the goals of the organization. This was not done nor was the need for doing it perceived by Mr. Ward. However, we must also question if Mr. Ward can motivate Mr. Jones. Is Mr. Jones's behavior indicative of his personality or emergent from Mr. Ward's leadership and group interactions?[14]

MOTIVATION

Mr. Jones's dysfunctional attitude would appear to stem from his personality or demotivation. We mentioned under communication some of the possibilities due to inadequate communication of organizational goals and needs. Secondly, we discussed some possible demotivating reasons due to the leadership style of Mr. Ward. Now we will look at possible individual and group demotivators.

First, possibly the intrinsic job satisfaction and interest is not prevalent due to the job itself. Additionally, Mr. Jones, for one of many reasons, may not be interested in this task.

Secondly, Mr. Jones may feel no need for a "norm of reciprocal rights and duties." Possibly he has nothing to reciprocate, no outstanding "duty" to the others of the group or division, and hence feels no requirement to perform "extra" duties to accomplish the task.[15]

ROLE CONFLICT

Mr. Jones is undoubtedly experiencing role conflict. Kahn's[16] role conflict is seen here as inter-role conflict between the job requirement and Mr.

Jones's personal desires. These role conflicts probably could have been detected and avoided by early awareness through communication.

PERCEPTION

The job task was certainly perceived differently by the two people. Adequate communication and feedback and role empathy would have helped resolve the different perceptions.[17]

POWER AND AUTHORITY

Here we see Mr. Ward's positional authority challenged. According to Goldhammer and Shils[18] power is legitimate only if recognized by the subordinate while, on the other hand, legitimate power is the maximum potential ability to control.[19]

ADDITIONAL INFORMATION

To completely analyze the incident and provide some guidelines for corrective action, the following additional information would be needed.

Organization. What was the structure of the organization? Did Mr. Ward have other programmers in his group to choose from, or access to others in the division? Was Mr. Ward a new supervisor? Did he usually do coding himself? How many individuals worked for Mr. Ward? What leeway did Mr. Ward have in supervising his workers? Could he determine their hours, pay, overtime, control their job, and hire and fire as required?

Formal and Informal Pressure. What were the formal and informal pressures and forces involved in the situation? Was Mr. Ward pressured by time, scalar authority, limited by unions, individual needs, needs of the division, and so on?

Leadership. What was the leadership style of Mr. Ward? Was there conflict of some sort? Was Mr. Jones's behavior emergent and/or basic? Did Mr. Ward have adequate authority, or were his leadership abilities limited by organizational constraints? Why was this problem with Jones not anticipated? Surely Ward was not aware of the individual situation with Mr. Jones not willing to work overtime at the time he appointed him to the project. Why not? Was this an unknown force in Mr. Jones or brought on by Mr. Ward? In any case, Mr. Ward lacked knowledge about one of his individuals.

Communication. Obviously there was a communication breakdown somewhere, but where and when? Possibly at the time of the project assignments, Mr. Ward and Mr. Jones had different perceptions of the job requirements. Was there any two-way communication with feedback?

Individual Personalities. Certainly some of the emergent behavior is personality determined; however, we do not have adequate information to analyze this background factor in the emergent behavior of those involved.

SUMMARY

The incident would appear to result from Mr. Jones's not agreeing to working "extra" hours to accomplish a required task and so to assure timely completion. The behavior could be fundamental to Mr. Jones or emergent from the group or leadership for several reasons; however, it would appear that this conflict could have been avoided by proper role congruency in the selection of Mr. Jones for the specific job, proper communication with feedback, early recognition of all job requirements by all parties, and better motivation and teamwork through reciprocity and group forces.

THE CROSSWORD PUZZLE

As the officer in charge of reorganizing the equipment management branch of a military medical research laboratory, Lieutenant Horngren requested that a noncommissioned officer be assigned to assist him in the task. The personnel office obliged by assigning Sergeant G. R. Kovak, an inventory management specialist, to the equipment management branch. Sergeant Kovak had been assigned to a nearby laboratory, and even before his arrival, rumors were circulating that Sergeant Kovak was a "problem." Lieutenant Horngren had enough problems and he was determined to cure the rumored laziness of Sergeant Kovak.

Upon Sergeant Kovak's arrival to the equipment management office, he was instructed by Lieutenant Horngren to begin a long-needed physical inventory of all of the equipment in the laboratory. Sergeant Kovak suggested that the inventory be delayed until the quarterly computer listing of the equipment was available as a cross reference to the actual physical count. This method, he explained, would save time and result in a more accurate inventory. Lieutenant Horngren became visibly angry and told Sergeant Kovak that his delay tactics would not work and he should get busy on the inventory immediately. The inventory progressed at a slow rate at first but was quickly completed after the computer listings were finally made available.

Sergeant Kovak's lack of initiative in the next few weeks convinced Lieutenant Horngren that the rumors he had heard were true. Lieutenant Horngren and Mr. Jim Aldren, a civilian subordinate, worked together to formulate new policies and programs while Sergeant Kovak was given only routine clerical tasks. He was soon very efficient at these and they were not enough to keep him busy. As a result, he spent his idle time working crossword puzzles. People began to kid Sergeant Kovak about his inactivity and he became progressively more withdrawn. Sergeant Kovak complained to his friends in the barracks, "I thought that this new assignment would be a real opportunity but it's just like any other assignment. I didn't join the Air Force to be a flunky."

Lieutenant Horngren's duties required him to be out of the office a good portion of the time, so he was not aware of Sergeant Kovak's clerical efficiency. However, he did hear several office jokes about Sergeant Kovak's crossword puzzles. These reports prompted the Lieutenant to tell Jim Aldren, "Jim, I had hoped to use Sergeant Kovak to help plan and implement some new materiel programs, but he just doesn't seem to have the desire to help. He's going to have to get motivated, or I will have to replace him."

ANALYSIS 1: *The Cross Word Puzzle*

This incident centers around the relationship between Lieutenant Horngren and Sergeant Kovak. Kovak was assigned to assist Lieutenant Horngren in the reorganization of the equipment management branch of a medical research laboratory.

Kovak had a prior reputation of being lazy. Before Kovak was officially assigned, Horngren had made up his mind to cure Kovak of his problem.

MOTIVATION

Kovak appears to be a fairly competent and intelligent person. From his talks with his friends, we might conclude that his level of need satisfaction is quite high. He also appears to be technically knowledgeable when he suggested to Horngren to wait on the inventory until the quarterly computer listing came out.

As soon as he was assigned to Horngren, however, he was given only simplistic tasks to perform which he mastered quickly. As he became more proficient at these tasks, he grew more withdrawn and bitter. This behavior seems logical from his point of view, since people are usually satisfied to the degree that they are able to use their skills and abilities in their work.[20] Clearly, Horngren has Kovak operating below his level of skills.

Aside from job content, there appears to be yet another reason why Kovak is not motivated. Horngren has determined that to motivate Kovak it is necessary to give him orders. We can conclude, however, that this only works when the person giving the orders is prepared to let the receiver influence him and when there is a consistency between the speaker's actions and words.[21] It is quite apparent that Horngren fails on both of these counts thus adding to the frustration that Kovak is experiencing.

A fundamental consideration in motivating others is that the manager must develop an environment in which sincerity, integrity, trust, and mutual respect are the rule. This means that the manager must get to know his workers and enable them to know him.[22] This environment will allow the manager to know the capabilities of his workers and thus match each worker with the job that worker is capable of doing.[23] In the incident Horngren does not know Kovak's capabilities and Horngren and Kovak do not know each other. This leads to a situation in which the worker is not motivated.

According to Myers the factors which motivate are "achievement, recognition, responsibility, growth, advancement, and other matters associated with the self-actualization of the individual on the job."[24] These factors can be applied in the incident, because possibly Kovak is looking for a position in which he can achieve and grow. The position which Kovak holds does not allow him any meaningful achievement. This failure to achieve is a dissatisfier.[25]

LEADERSHIP STYLE

According to Myers, "Motivation is strongly related to the style of the immediate boss: 'developmental' supervisors stimulate motivation; 'reductive' supervisors inhibit motivation."[26] Developmental supervision can be described as Theory Y Supervision, and reductive supervision can be described as Theory X supervision.[27] In the incident, Horngren appears to believe that "people do not like to work and avoid it when they can, they must be coerced, controlled, directed and threatened, and people prefer direction and dislike responsibility."[28] This describes the assumptions of Theory X. Horngren appears to follow the management style of a Theory X manager. Perhaps based upon the conclusion stated above—that reductive supervisors inhibit motivation—we can conclude that the management style of Horngren is an important part of the motivation process.

Horngren appears to be an autocratic manager, who uses his rank and the threat of punishment to get things done. Some research reveals that this basis for authority is the least desirable that can be used to handle employees.[29] This leadership style has been shown to generate resentment and slowdowns among subordinates.

One of the principal activities of a supervisor is that of evaluating his subordinates. To do this successfully he needs to take time to minimize mistakes, be objective and avoid the use of descriptive phrases that tend to type the person being evaluated.[30] A quick examination of how Horngren obtained his impression that Kovak was "lazy" suggests that Horngren has been hasty in evaluating his subordinate.

ADDITIONAL INFORMATION DESIRED

It would be helpful to know more about Kovak's and Horngren's personalities and attitudes. We have made some assumptions based on indicators in the incident that may not be true. For example, we have assumed that Kovak really wants a challenging job. If this assumption is correct, job enrichment would surely help motivate him.[31] This enrichment would take the form of actually letting Kovak in on the planning, which is what Horngren originally stated. Having subordinates participate in the planning has been found to be an effective motivator available to managers.[32]

We have also assumed that Horngren is an autocratic manager, and there is some evidence in the incident to indicate that this assumption is correct. However, we would want to know more about Horngren. We would also want to know the organizational climate prevailing in the medical research laboratory. It is quite possible that because of the attitudes of top management, Horngren has little opportunity to change his leadership pattern without encountering some difficulty with his superiors.

ANALYSIS 2: *The Crossword Puzzle*

On the surface, this incident would appear to lend itself to a fairly straightforward analysis; however, there are several complicating factors. One is the set of assumptions upon which Lieutenant Horngren apparently based his actions toward Sergeant Kovak. Another is the puzzling behavior of Lieutenant Horngren who, while appearing to perceive the job as one of high importance, behaved in reality as if it were simply a clerical assignment with literally no responsibility. There are several areas and viewpoints which can be utilized in analyzing this situation. On balance, though, one of the main issues appears to be motivation. This, along with other areas involved, constitutes the framework of analysis.

MOTIVATION

There are numerous motivational concepts which apply to this incident. For example, Sergeant Kovak appears to have many of the basic needs fulfilled by membership in the military, a situation which would seem to suggest an emphasis on the higher order needs; that is, provided one subscribes to the Maslow hierarchy of needs and its implications.[33] M. Scott Myers summarizes the process as follows: "As people satisfy their lower order needs, they need to move up to their higher order needs."[34] In this regard, one would expect that Lieutenant Horngren had not concerned himself with satisfying higher level needs and, consequently, was failing to unlock the motivation level appropriate to Sergeant Kovak's situation. This explanation would indeed follow the clear-cut textbook model. However, reality is much more complex. For one, the Maslow Theory and its conceptual first cousins, the Herzberg Motivation-Hygiene Theory and McGregor's X and Y Theory, are not without their detractors.[35] Thus, while one may be quick to criticize Lieutenant Horngren for not recognizing what appeared to be obvious shortcomings in his perception of the situation, it is also equally possible that Sergeant Kovak's rumored laziness was an accurate description of his attitude.

Another way of putting it is that perhaps life in the military, with the apparent vacillation between security orientation on the one hand and crises on the other might engender a kind of fixation at the security level. Moreover, the retirement system in the military, with its opportunity for exiting at a relatively early age, might discourage a central work orientation in the individual. The central life interest concept of Robert Dubin could perhaps apply in this situation.[36] Assuming for the moment that this observation is correct, this would not necessarily mean that it is impossible to motivate people. There is, after all, evidence that Sergeant Kovak was capable of producing very good work. There is further evidence that Kovak was looking for the kind of opportunity that would give access to what may be a dormant need for self-esteem or perhaps self-realization.

This leads us back to the motivation-hygiene concept and the possibility, in this incident, of job enrichment for Sergeant Kovak.[37] Were Lieutenant Horngren to apply the concept of job enrichment, he would first of all need to structure the job in such a way that Sergeant Kovak or any other incumbent, for that matter, would have real decision-making authority, at least insofar as control of his work is concerned. This, of course, would not imply an abdication of authority on the part of Lieutenant Horngren, but rather the delegation of decision-making authority with accountability for results. This suggests a supportive and developmental role for the supervisor in satisfying this basic and higher-order psychological need. The employee-centered approach suggested by Likert and others[38] would be central to this role.

One of the standout qualities of a good leader is that he or she must extend the leader-follower relationship beyond the formally prescribed structural behavior. The Etzioni model suggests this and most leadership research confirms this observation.[39] Lieutenant Horngren obviously used the authority of his position in traditional, vertical fashion. Horngren formally was authorized to delegate what he so chose. Horngren's own accountability was, most likely, to simply get the job done. The experience of one of the authors of the text relates to this situation. The author, while an enlisted man in service, was in charge of a radio section when a new ROTC-trained lieutenant was assigned as communications platoon leader. Although the new lieutenant could have taken control very directively by spelling out exactly how he wanted the section to perform, he chose a highly consultative route, working with the section leader to determine what objectives and plans presently existed and what problems the section faced. For the first two months, he successfully delegated almost complete decision-making authority to the section leader to determine the resources needed, to make assignments and to schedule the day-to-day equipment maintenance activities.* Had the lieutenant taken the more autocratic route, compliance would have resulted, but at the risk of inviting a certain amount of mischief in the form of malicious obedience, or as Gouldner puts it, "bureaucratic sabotage."[40]

AUTHORITY AND POWER

One is tempted to regress toward the traditional assumptions regarding military leadership, i.e., submergence of power in the formal status system centered around rank. There is evidence that Horngren's orientation is in this direction. He apparently is willing to work on a co-equal basis with a civilian subordinate, Jim Aldren, in developing new policies. Yet, he perceived Sergeant Kovak according to his status as an enlisted man—a distinction which is clearly emphasized in the training of both officers and enlisted men. No doubt status differences are necessary and even desirable, but when they interfere with the accomplishment of work—a distinct possibility in this incident—the formal status system obviously becomes dysfunctional. Energies which should be channeled toward mutual task objectives tend to be misdirected toward maintenance of the authority structure. More importantly, this situation results in loss of trust, an essential attribute in any productive authority relationship. Taken together, those areas considered thus far—motivation, leadership, and authority—suggest a Theory "X" attitudinal orientation on the part of Lieutenant Horngren, but with some differentiation and vacillation due partly to the nature of the task.[41]

---

*The author recalls this experience as undoubtedly the most productive and rewarding in his brief military career.

OTHER RELEVANT ISSUES AND QUESTIONS

There are a number of communication barriers involved, foremost of which is lack of empathy on the part of Lieutenant Horngren. Some authorities, such as Rogers and McMurry, have cited empathy as the manager's most important communicative skill.[42] Horngren obviously did not attempt to view the situation from Kovak's frame of reference. Nor did Horngren have an accurate conception of what the task entailed. Once the work was underway, he relied on grapevine reports in evaluating Kovak's productivity. While the grapevine is an accurate channel of communication for nonthreatening information, for value-laden messages such as performance, accuracy decreases considerably.[43] Horngren did occasionally observe first hand, but the preconception of Kovak's "lack of initiative" had already been formed, in which case selective perception could easily support the conclusion the lieutenant formed prior to the actual observation.

Finally, there is the issue of what should be further known about the situation in order to solve the problems involved and, especially, why this information is necessary. For example, background facts are needed in order to accurately size up the incident. How did Sergeant Kovak, for example, perform in his previous assignments? What was the basis of the rumors circulating about Kovak? Similarly, what was Lieutenant Horngren's previous record and training? What were the specific pressures involved in getting the task completed? In order to more accurately estimate the motivation factors, what specific inducements and climate were present in the situation? Possible promotion? Award? Rank? Reassignment? Did the incident itself occur stateside or overseas?

In summary, this incident represents the type of managerial action commonly found in the situation and environment involved. In the interest of completing a task, what is often overlooked is that "one becomes a participating member (of an organization) through a process of exaltation which may be as difficult as the process of becoming Americanized is difficult for some immigrants."[44]

JOB PERFORMANCE

Carl Marrell, 35 years old, began working at the ABC Steel Corporation in the Metallurgical Department as a Zinc Checker twelve years ago. After spending three years at this zone six job, Carl progressed to a zone eight job as Processing Control Observer. After he had spent two years as Processing Control Observer, Carl advanced to a zone ten job as Melting Control Observer. He has been working at this job during the past seven years.

Carl was able to move upward in the Metallurgical Department much faster than average, by bypassing several job positions. Carl possesses above average intelligence and potential. He had a good scholastic and athletic record in high school, and also completed two years of college. Of the eight observers in the melting area, Carl is the youngest in age and lowest in seniority.

The highest hourly pay zone in the Metallurgical Department is twelve. Metallurgical Technician would be the next possible advancement following the line of progression for observers in the melting area.

Each lab is under the responsibility of a metallurgist. For example, the Zincgrip, Processing, Hot Rolling, and Melting Laboratories each have one or more assigned metallurgists. Each metallurgist is given supervisory type responsibilities but is not given the title of supervisor. Each metallurgist is responsible for observer performance, training, conducting safety meetings and observations, weekly and monthly quality reports, and some projects in his area. Each metallurgist reports to a supervisor.

Observers are responsible for making routine quality checks. Each job has a written job description outlining the procedure to follow. Typical observer jobs include checking weight of nonmetallic coatings, temperature charts, hardness results, surface defects, etc.

Carl apparently did a good job during his first several years of employment. This is evidenced by his rapid progress in the department. During the past five years, Carl's job performance has been considered poor by supervisors and lab metallurgists.

Some of the complaints heard most often are: (1) frequent errors on heat logs, (2) lack of detail as to heat history on the log, (3) lack of interest in the job, (4) frequent loss of safety equipment, (5) tardiness and absenteeism, (6) and sleeping on the job. ABC policy states that sleeping on the job is cause for discharge.

During the past five years, although allegedly performing in a manner that constituted grounds for disciplinary action, Carl was not disciplined until September, 1970. Because of economic conditions, production cutbacks were made. As a result, Carl was demoted to his former job as Processing Control Observer. Carl had not worked this job regularly for about seven years. During the first week on the job, Carl was caught falsifying hardness readings. ABC must certify steel strip hardness on many government orders and orders whose end use must conform to military specifications. Deliberately falsifying records is a serious offense and, as a result, Carl was laid off for five days.

In late 1970, as business conditions improved, Carl again returned to his regular job as Melting Control Observer. Carl was advised that his past job performance would no longer be tolerated. When his previous type performances continued, Carl was called in by the supervisor in May, 1971. Carl was again disciplined by being laid off for seven days and advised that he was subject to discharge if his performance did not come up to that of the other observers.

In his spare time, Carl contracts to build houses. Most of the work is subcontracted out by Carl. He has been engaged in building for about five or six years. During early 1970, Carl also bought a restaurant in partnership with another person.

ANALYSIS 1: *Job Performance*

There are several unanswered but vital questions related to this incident. Before proceeding to analyze the known areas, it would be helpful to spell out what especially should be explicated in order to enable one to size up the situation more fully. These question areas can be summarized in terms of Carl's career goals, his need for "moonlighting," the company's delay in disciplinary action, Carl's status in the informal group, his perception of himself as a person and the reasons for his outside involvements.

CAREER GOALS

Marrell was relatively young, 23, when he began working at ABC. He had worked in the Metallurgical Department for twelve years. Did he perceive his activities outside ABC as more important than his job in the Metallurgical Department? Carl may have been "serving his time" until his outside activities became profitable enough to allow him to devote more effort to them. If this were true, it could account for his inadequate job performance.

NEED FOR MOONLIGHTING

Does Marrell have to work at ABC to attain a satisfactory standard of living? Perhaps his restaurant business and his building ventures are profitable. Whether his businesses are profitable or not, he could have a negative attitude toward working at ABC due to his psychological investment in outside activities.

DISCIPLINE

Why did ABC delay disciplinary action on Carl until September, 1970? For the previous five years, Carl's performance had been unsatisfactory; yet, ABC did not discipline him until September of 1970. Were Carl's superiors attempting to delay an unpleasant confrontation, or were they simply unsure of their position and authority in the organization?

INFORMAL GROUP STATUS

What was Carl's status in the informal group? Apparently, he had bypassed several job positions. He was also the youngest observer by age and seniority. Was he uncomfortable in his relationships with other employees? Did his values and interests conflict with those of other employees?

CARL'S SELF-PERCEPTIONS

What was Carl's perception of himself as a person? Did he feel that he was superior to the people in the Metallurgical Department? Or did he feel that his talents were not being fully utilized by performing relatively routine jobs in this department? Was his comparative youth a dissonant factor in others' perceptions of his capability and performance?

REASONS FOR OUTSIDE INVOLVEMENTS

Why did Marrell enter the building contracting business? Was it a hedge against possible loss of job security at ABC or out of genuine interest in the work? Or, as indicated earlier, because of perceived financial need? The same questions could be asked in relation to the restaurant venture.

MOTIVATION

A basic problem is that Carl Marrell is no longer motivated to accept organization goals. He is satisfying his higher-level needs with his off-job activities. He is probably experiencing little job satisfaction at ABC; he is therefore, no longer motivated to perform his job satisfactorily.

The point is made consistently in the literature that normal adults are not really motivated by physiological, safety and love needs.[45] Thus, the needs for esteem and self-actualization are the only truly motivating forces. It follows that organizations must recognize this factor in designing work and promotion systems.

One could question whether Carl Marrell's position at ABC was commensurate with his abilities and if it was consistent to his desires for self-actualization. Carl may perceive the company as a barrier to meaningful achievement. He could be experiencing an avoidance-avoidance conflict whereby he is confronted with the decision to continue performing his dull, routine, and unfulfilling job at ABC or leave his job to devote more time to his building and the restaurant. He may avoid quitting due to the fear of economic insecurity; however, he still retains some vestige of independence although performing poorly on the job. There is considerable evidence to suggest job dissatisfaction. For instance, some frequent complaints about Carl were lack of interest in the job, frequent tardiness and absenteeism, sleeping on the job, and falsifying records.

All of these symptoms suggest that Carl would quit for his own and the company's welfare. Little wonder he is sleeping on the job, not to mention the potential effects on his family life. Nevertheless, building construction is highly seasonal and the restaurant business in most communities is quite competitive. Therefore, his trade-offs are such that quitting the job at ABC would upset this very delicate balance.

The central life-interest thesis enters importantly in this respect.[46] In essence, this concept suggests that for some individuals, work is the main focus of their lives; for others, it is not. Related to Dubin's view of work behavior, in contrast with that of Argyris and others, there are many workers who prefer to invest only a small portion of their mental, physical and psychological selves at the workplace and—this is the rub of the controversy—not because management has failed to enrich the jobs, but because of personal choices concerning the locus of their energy output.[47] Carl's behavior pattern, however, departs from the central life-interest concept in that while not apparently involved in his work at ABC, he has immersed himself in the type of entrepreneurial activities which are ordinarily rather demanding of an individual's time and effort. A "pure" central life-interest application would be exibited in a situation where a person channels his/her talents primarily toward nonwork activities such as hobbies, recreation, avocations or other nonremunerative endeavors.

Therefore, to uncover Carl's motivation fabric, management will need to determine his basic life interests. It would be foolish at this point to assume that Carl's goals are identical with those of ABC's. Moreover, in Carl's and other workers' minds, perhaps ABC's are either misunderstood or not satisfactorily articulated. In this regard, applying concepts such as work planning[48] and MBO[49] might help to tap the wellspring of motivation that obviously impels Carl to derive satisfaction from his moonlighting activities. Determination of these underlying motivation factors would help to answer some of the questions raised at the outset and also lead to solving this and other similar problems in the organization.

AUTHORITY AND POWER

One way an organization attains its goals is through the judicious use of authority and power. Carl's perception of his superior's authority, especially that of the metallurgist, enters here in an important way. Perhaps herein lies the reason for the delay in disciplining action. The consent theory of authority is appealing here, but in a limited way, because acceptance of authority relates directly to the motivation problems discussed above.[50] In other words, given little interest on Carl's part to internalize the standards and values of the organization, it is doubtful that acceptance or nonacceptance of authority would be a major issue here. He has apparently decided, perhaps unconsciously, to disregard the decrees and entreaties of those in authority.

A clarification of the metallurgist's authority might help to alter Carl's perception of the locus of authority. It would lead to more definitive action in disciplinary cases. Moreover, it could change the informal group relationships as far as the group-supervisor interface is concerned. The technical-supervisory mix of the metallurgist's position is ambiguous, at best. If the metallurgists are given little support for their supervisory decisions, they will be accorded little respect by workers.[51] At least Carl would develop expectations about the reaction of the metallurgist to his performance, regardless of whether it would lead to positive motivation or acceptance of their authority. Over a period of time, it is possible that the power and influence of the metallurgist would substantially increase, given a more definitive role in making decisions. This would also increase their willingness to make decisions on the human problems that confront them, of which Carl's situation is probably only a sample.

ANALYSIS 2: *Job Performance*

From the incident one can readily discern that we have an employee who has changed from a motivated employee into one exhibiting dysfunctional behavior. Carl, an ambitious, intelligent man, is in a job which really demands very little—the pace is routine, and the instructions are specific. Initially, Carl moved up quickly, probably because the jobs he held were easy for him and the organization recognized his abilities. Now, however, this upward movement has slowed and, in Carl's mind, will not continue. His academic background would indicate that he probably had high expectations of advancement.

PERCEPTION

In his first five years at ABC, Carl was advanced twice. He has held his last job for seven years. Leavitt suggests that a significant determinant of a person's behavior is the manner in which he perceives the world and the people in it.[52] Applying this concept to the incident, we can conclude that Carl has changed his perception concerning his work.

Based on his rapid advancement in his first years of employment with ABC, Carl could easily have assumed that his future was almost unlimited. After holding his latest job for two or three years, Carl again expected to be advanced. As revealed by Kuhn, Slocum and Case, satisfaction is a function of both magnitude and frequency of rewards as well as expectations.[53] When Carl was not recognized for his efforts, he probably began to exhibit signs of dysfunctional behavior.

MOTIVATION

Dubin, in discussing the concepts of an individual's motivation states, "If the social setting is one not central to his life interests, then he will participate in it as required (as is true in work) without expecting or needing these rewards to continue his performance . . . He finds the rewards that sustain his personal integrity in other institutional settings central to his life."[54] Carl apparently looked elsewhere such as building houses and operating a restaurant to satisfy his high order needs. This type of behavioral pattern was also found in the research findings reported by Kuhn, Slocum and Case.[55]

Why then did Carl turn to outside interests eventually to fullfill his higher order needs? As stated earlier, his failure to continue to advance was particularly important. The new self-employed positions offered more status and new challenges. As is true of many jobs, the average employee spends his first year or two learning all of the duties involved and then proceeds to routinely do them the rest of his life. For an above average employee such as Carl, the recognition and challenges were important motivational factors.

THE LEADERSHIP APPROACH

The formal organizational structure at ABC corresponds somewhat with the concept of dual leadership as expressed by Etzioni.[56] The functional duties in each job are under the responsibility of a metallurgist. Each metallurgist reports to a supervisor. The supervisor is responsible for the administration of personnel policies and procedures.

The statement that Carl, although allegedly performing in a below average manner for the previous five years, was not disciplined until September, 1970, indicates that the leadership style employed was one of abdication. The discipline that was finally adopted could not be considered progressive discipline as advocated by Odiorne.[57] Additionally, the action, being infrequent, probably did not encompass any significant degree of communication between Carl and his supervisors.[58]

It is interesting to note that the methods of punishment by the organization apparently have had no effect. Supposedly, the organization has authority and could exercise it over Carl, but power does not exist because the sanctions have not influenced Carl's behavior.[59] According to Odiorne, discipline must be voluntarily accepted; otherwise, it is not legitimate.[60]

ADDITIONAL INFORMATION DESIRED

First, what is the degree of dissatisfaction among other workers at the ABC Company, as evidenced by absenteeism, poor performance, turnover and the like? The results of a study of the ABC Company such as the type reported by Herrick[61] would provide some insight as to the degree of satisfaction or dissatisfaction among the employees of the company.

Second, what was Carl's status in the work group—a regular, an isolate, or a deviate?

Third, more information on the philosophy of top management would be helpful. We have some indication of loose supervision, but at the same time, there is an indication that participative management is limited, if not nonexistent.

CONCLUSION

The present ABC management approach of applying sporadic and fluctuating disciplinary penalties to "cure" Carl's dysfunctional behavior has relatively little hope of succeeding. A better approach would be a series of counseling sessions between Carl and his supervisor, and possibly participative management that would heighten Carl's self-esteem.[62] However, Carl should understand that if he is to continue in the employ of ABC, his outside activities must not interfere with his job performance in the future.

Personally, from the data given in this incident, it is believed that Carl will leave ABC in the relatively near future unless positive action is taken by the company to keep him.

FOOTNOTES

[1]L.L. Cummings and A.M. Elsalmi, "The Impact of Role Diversity, Job Level, and Organization Size on Management Satisfaction," *Administrative Science Quarterly,* March, 1970, pp. 1–10.

[2]J.W. Lorsch and P.R. Lawrence, "Organizing for Product Innovation," in Gene W. Dalton, Paul R. Lawrence, and Jay W. Lorsch, *Organizational Structure and Design* (Homewood, Ill.: Richard D. Irwin Inc. and The Dorsey Press, 1970), pp. 280–96.

[3]M. G. Eavens, "Herzberg's Two-Factor Theory of Motivation: Some Problems and a Suggested Test, " *Personnel Journal,* January, 1970, p. 33.

[4]William F. Dowling, Jr. and Leonard R. Sayles, *How Managers Motivate: The Imperatives of Supervision* (New York: McGraw-Hill Book Company, 1971), pp. 78–82.

[5]J. E. Kelly, *Organizational Behavior* (Georgetown, Ontario: Irwin-Dorsey Ltd., 1969), pp. 225–27.

[6]Alvin Gouldner, "The Role of the Norm of Reciprocity in Social Stabilization," In P. R. Lawrence and J. A. Seiler, et. al., *Organizational Behavior and Administration* (Homewood, Ill.: Richard D. Irwin, Inc, and The Dorsey Press, 1965), pp. 565–68.

[7]S. D. Hoslett, "Barriers to Effective Communication," in Max D. Richards and William A. Nielander, *Readings in Management* (Cincinnati: South-Western Publishing Co., 1969), p. 149.

[8]J. W. Slocum, Jr., "Supervisory Influence on the Professional Employee," *Personnel Journal,* June, 1970, pp. 484–88.

[9]William G. Scott and Terence R. Mitchell, *Organization Theory: A Structural and Behavioral Analysis,* Revised Edition (Homewood, Ill.: Richard D. Irwin, Inc., and The Dorsey Press, 1972), pp. 158–59.

[10]*Ibid.,* pp. 209–10.

[11]Robert Tannenbaum and Warren H. Schmidt, "How to Choose a Leadership Pattern," *Harvard Business Review,* March-April, 1958, pp. 95–101.

[12]Robert A. Dubin, "Person and Organization," in William T. Greenwood, *Management and Organizational Behavior Theories* (Cincinnati: South-Western Publishing Co., 1965), pp. 486–89.

[13]Douglas MacGregor, *The Human Side of Enterprise* (New York: McGraw-Hill Book Company, Inc.), chap. 4.

[14]Arthur N. Turner, "A Conceptual Scheme for Describing Work Group Behavior," in Paul E. Lawrence and John A. Seiler et al. *Organizational Behavior and Administration* (Homewood, Ill.: Richard D. Irwin, Inc., and The Dorsey Press, 1965), pp. 154–64.

[15]Paul R. Lawrence and John A. Seiler et al. *Organizational Behavior and Administration* (Homewood, Ill.: Richard D. Irwin, Inc., and The Dorsey Press, 1965), p. 566.

[16]Robert L. Kahn, "Role Conflict and Ambiguity in Organizations," *The Personnel Administrator,* March-April, 1964, pp. 8–13.

[17]Scott and Mitchell, *Structural and Behavioral Analysis,* p. 208.

[18]Herbert Goldhammer and E. A. Shils, "Types of Power and Status," in D. R. Hampton, C. E. Summer and R. A. Webber, *Organizational Behavior and the Practice of Management* (Glenview, Ill.: Scott, Foresman and Company, 1968), p. 480.

[19]Scott and Mitchell, *Structural and Behavioral Analysis,* p. 214.

[20]John W. Slocum and Michael J. Misshauk, "Job Satisfaction and Productivity," *Personnel Administration,* March-April, 1970, pp. 53–58.

[21]Joseph G. Happel, "To Motivate—Communicate," *Personnel Journal,* December, 1969, pp. 984–87.

[22]Frank M. Sterner, "Motivate—Don't Manipulate," *Personnel Journal,* August, 1969, p. 626.

[23]M. Scott Myers, "Who Are Your Motivated Workers?" *Harvard Business Review,* January-February, 1964, pp. 73–88.

[24]*Ibid.,* p. 73.

[25]*Ibid.*

[26]M. Scott Myers, "Conditions for Manager Motivation," *Harvard Business Review,* January-February, 1966, p. 58.

[27]*Ibid.,* p. 59.

[28]Sterner, "Motivate," p. 625.

[29]Slocum, "Supervisory Influence," pp. 484–88.

[30]William H. Newman, Charles E. Summer, E. Kirby Warren, *The Process of Management,* Second Edition (Englewood Cliffs, N.J.: Prentice-Hall, Inc., 1967), pp. 271–76.

[31]Curt Tausky, H. Roy Kaplin and Bhopinder S. Bolaria, "Job Enrichment," *Personnel Journal,* October, 1969, pp. 791–98.

[32]Robert C. Miljus, "Effective Leadership and the Motivation of Human Resources," *Personnel Journal,* January, 1970, pp. 36–40.

[33]A. H. Maslow, "A Theory of Human Motivation," in William P. Sexton, *Organization Theories* (Columbus, Ohio: Charles E. Merrill Publishing Co., 1970), pp. 143–66.

[34]M. Scott Myers, "The Human Factor in Management Systems," Journal of Systems Management, November, 1970, p. 10.

[35]James A. Lee, "Behavioral Theory and Reality," *Harvard Business Review,* March-April, 1971, pp. 20–28, 157-59.

[36]Dubin, "Person," pp. 486–89.

[37]William J. Paul, Jr., Keith B. Robinson, and Frederick Herzberg, "Job Enrichment Pays Off," *Harvard Business Review,* March-April, 1969, pp. 61–78.

[38]Renses Likert, *The Human Organization* (New York: McGraw-Hill Book Company, 1967).

[39]Amitai Etzioni, "Dual Leadership in Complex Organizations," in Donald E. Porter, Philip B. Applewhite and Michael J. Misshauk, *Studies in Organizational Behavior and Management,* 2d ed. (Scranton, Pa.: Intext Educational Publishers, 1971), pp. 323–39.

[40]Alvin W. Gouldner, "About the Functions of Bureaucratic Rules," in Joseph A. Litterer, *Organizations: Structure and Behavior* (New York: John Wiley & Sons, Inc., 1963), p. 394.

[41]See Fred E. Fiedler, "Engineer the Job to Fit the Manager," *Harvard Business Review* September-October, 1965, pp. 115–22, and George F. Lombard, "Relativism in Organizations," *Harvard Business Review,* March-April, 1971, pp. 55–65.

[42]Robert N. McMurry, "Empathy: Management's Greatest Need," in S. G. Huneryager and I. L. Heckmann, *Human Relations in Management* (Cincinnati: South-Western Publishing Company, 1967), pp. 722–38.

[43]Keith Davis, *Human Behavior at Work* (New York: McGraw-Hill Book Company, 1972), pp. 261–70.

[44]Walter S. Neff, "Understanding Difficulties in Work Adaptation," *Management of Personnel Quarterly,* University of Michigan Bureau of Business Research (Spring, 1971), p. 10.

[45]See Frederick R. Herzberg, *Work and the Nature of Man* (New York: World Publishing Company, 1966); also G. Halpern, "Relative Contributions of Motivator and Hygiene Factors to Overall Job Satisfaction," *Journal of Applied Psychology* (1966), pp. 198–200; Charles L. Hulin and Patricia A. Smith, "An Empirical Investigation of Two Implications of the Two-Factor Theory of Job Satisfaction," *Journal of Applied Psychology* 51, no. 5 (1967), pp. 396–402.

[46]See Robert Dubin, "Industrial Workers' World: A Study of the 'Central Life Interest' of Industrial Workers," *Social Problems* 3 (January, 1956): 131; and John G. Maurer, "Work as a 'Central Life Interest' of Industrial Supervisors," *Academy of Management Journal,* September, 1968, pp. 329–39.

[47]Edwin B. Flippo, *Management: A Behavioral Approach* (Boston: Allyn and Bacon, Inc., 1970), p. 113.

[48]See Stanley C. Duffendack, *Effective Management Through Work Planning* (Schenectady, N. Y.: Maqua Company, 1970).

[49]George S. Odiorne, *Management by Objectives* (New York: Pitman Publishing Corp., 1965).

[50]Robert Bierstedt, "The Problem of Authority," in John H. Turner, Allen C. Filley, and Robert J. House, *Studies in Managerial Process and Organizational Behavior* (Glenview, Ill.: Scott, Foresman and Company, 1972), p. 69.

[51]Martin Patchen, "Supervisory Methods and Group Performance Norms," *Administrative Science Quarterly,* December, 1962, pp. 275–93.

[52]Harold J. Leavitt, *Managerial Psychology,* 2d. ed. (Chicago and London: The University of Chicago Press, 1964), p. 35.

[53]D. G. Kuhn, J. W. Slocum and R. B. Case, "Does Job Performance Affect Employee Satisfaction?" *Personnel Journal,* June, 1971, pp. 455–60.

[54]Dubin, "Person," p. 488.

[55]Kuhn, Slocum and Case, "Job Performance," pp. 455-460.

[56]Amitai Etzioni, "Dual Leadership in Complex Organizations," *American Sociological Review,* October, 1965, pp. 688–98.

[57] George S. Odiorne, "Discipline by Objectives," *Management of Personnel Quarterly,* Summer, 1971, pp. 13–20.

[58]M. Sorcher, "Motivation, Participation and Myth," *Personnel Administration,* September-October, 1971, pp. 20–24.

[59]Herbert Goldhammer and Edward Shils, "Types of Power and Status," in Hampton, Summer and Webber, *Organizational Behavior,* p. 480.

[60]Odiorne, "Discipline," pp. 13–20.

[61]Neal Q. Herrick, "Who's Unhappy at Work and Why," *Manpower,* January, 1972, pp. 2–7.

[62]Sorcher, "Motivation," pp. 20–24.

COMMUNICATION

Incident	*Page*
THE ADAMS SCHOOL	61
Raymond D. Mager	
Analysis 1	61
Analysis 2	64
THE UNWANTED GIFT	67
Alexander J. Laslo	
Analysis 1	68
Analysis 2	71
THE DEADLINE	75
James Quinn	
Analysis 1	76
Analysis 2	79

THE ADAMS SCHOOL

Mr. Jack W. Robbins is the principal of both the Adams and Green Elementary Schools and is directly responsible for the work of 26 teachers, 10 teacher's aides, 8 administrative and custodial personnel, and 700 students. Being principal of both schools is both a trying and time consuming position; it also means that at times Mr. Robbins may be absent from one school for a period ranging from a few hours to a few days. Miss Thelma Smith (age 29) of Adams and Mrs. Frieda Jones (age 43) of Green are both teachers in the system. They also hold the title of Assistant Principal and are responsible for their respective schools during Mr. Robbins's absence.

On several different occasions the teachers of Adams School had requested that a meeting be set up between themselves and Mr. Robbins to make various changes in the school curricula and to re-establish various school procedures that had become lax or unclear over the past year. At each instance the teachers were rebuffed by Mr. Robbins because of a lack of time, prior commitments or his being needed at the other school.

Finally, the teachers called an informal meeting at which criticisms were levied at Mr. Robbins because of his apparent lack of interest over a potentially explosive situation. In a discussion that followed, Miss Smith became very emotional. She felt completely helpless. She had previously tried to express the teachers' feeling to Mr. Robbins, but was unsuccessful. Miss Smith also felt that the other teachers blamed her for the lack of communication that existed and questioned whether she was really doing her job. Green School was also experiencing similar types of problems, but apparently was able to handle them more successfully.

ANALYSIS 1: *The Adams School*

The salient issues that appear relevant to this incident are in the areas of communication and organization. Prior to analyzing these two areas, it is necessary to assume that neither Miss Smith nor Mrs. Jones were provided any training nor delegated authority as administrators prior to being assigned as Assistant Principals. This assumption is based on the fact stated in the incident that they hold the title of assistant principal and are responsible for their respective schools only during the absence of Mr. Robbins.

COMMUNICATION

The teachers at both Adams and Green Elementary Schools obviously recognize that they are not accomplishing their goals. It would also appear that they perceive their roles to be somewhat ambiguous. This is evident from the statement in the incident,

> On several occasions the teachers of Adams School have attempted to make various changes in the school curricula and to re-establish various school procedures which are unclear, but on each occasion the teachers were rebuffed by Mr. Robbins because of his lack of time or prior commitments.

It appears that Mr. Robbins practices, at the least, one-way communication. Probably even more important, it would appear that he does not understand the need for communication. Prior to assuring effective communication in an organizational setting, the parties to the situation must perceive a need for it. The ambiguity and lack of clarity in the communication situation as perceived by the group causes tension within the organization.[1] A situation of this type can be resolved through the establishment of an adequate communication system which provides for feedback and hence control. The communication system must fit the organization. Any system developed must be evaluated constantly by both the principal and the teachers. This evaluation apparently is not taking place or, at least, is not being performed by Mr. Robbins. As implied by Strenski, management will often set up a communication plan without considering the need for feedback nor will it consider the need for evaluating the system.[2]

ORGANIZATION

Closely related to communication is the organization structure and arrangement that Mr. Robbins has adopted. He obviously has not delegated authority to his assistant principals. They, therefore, cannot effectively use the problem-solving approach as advocated by Gibb,[3] but must rely upon the persuasion approach. According to Weiss, the supervisor must determine exactly what can be delegated and determine those who are capable of performing what is delegated. Additionally, the organization and the job must be prepared for the delegation.[4]

SOLUTIONS

One solution, as advocated by Gelfand, would encompass the establishment of a program for communicating through supervisors.[5] Briefly, this program, as it applies to this incident, would encompass the assistant principals talking to each group of teachers for at least fifteen minutes each week and taking a few minutes whenever necessary to talk to each group about topics that interest them followed by a meaningful question and answer session. As stated by Gelfand, this is a deceptively simple program but has proven successful. This program, however, would not be successful in the Adams School incident without first taking actions, as previously mentioned, to delegate to the assistant principals the necessary authority for them to use a problem-solving approach.

ADDITIONAL INFORMATION DESIRED

It would be helpful to know the differences, other than age as given in the incident, between Miss Smith and Mrs. Jones and their relationships with Mr. Robbins. It is obvious that Mrs. Jones is more successful than Miss Smith. Even though neither one has formal authority, it appears that Mrs. Jones has been conferred authority by the teachers in the Green Elementary School, whereas the teachers in the Adams School have not conferred authority upon Miss Smith. It is possible that Mrs. Jones enjoys a better reputation with Mr. Robbins. If this is true, it is possible that the teachers perceive Mrs. Jones as having upward influence whereas on the other hand it is quite obvious that Miss Smith is not perceived by the teachers as having upward influence with Mr. Robbins. This lack of perceived upward influence could have a detrimental impact on Miss Smith's ability to perform as an assistant principal.[6]

It would also be beneficial to know the background, experiences and attitudes of Mr. Robbins. We would also want to know more about his leadership style and his responsibilities. For example, is it true that he lacks time to communicate with his teachers? Does he have other responsibilities that preclude him from doing so? If this were true, then we may have a mechanical barrier to communications of the type expressed by Stieglitz.[7]

ANALYSIS 2: *The Adams School*

An initial size-up of the situation would suggest that the problems lie at the assistant principal level rather than with Robbins, the Principal. The incident appears to demonstrate the importance of selection and training of administrative assistants in organizations. However, there are other issues which require investigation in order to more fully analyze the incident. One obvious problem area is that of communication—specifically, the misunderstandings and distortions that have developed in the administration of the Adams School.

COMMUNICATION

Jack Robbins is apparently in the role situation of a "boundary agent," with all of the attendant interactional and communication problems. The boundary agent, referred to elsewhere in this text (The Nitrous Oxide Incident) must interact with various groups and satisfy different constituencies.[8] The accompanying stress can be potentially dysfunctional, especially because of the difficulty of balancing one's effort among the interests involved.

The reason for viewing Robbins as a boundary person is that the principal's role generally involves considerable ambience—interacting with groups and factions outside the school. This probably explains Robbins's frequent absences, notwithstanding the fact that he is principal of two schools. It does not, however, exonerate him from his responsibility to attend to the important problems of the schools. Nor does his difficult role mitigate the communication problems which exist in the Adams School.

One reason for the communication problem can apparently be traced to Thelma Smith. She has failed to effectively relate the teachers' problems to Mr. Robbins. In Robbins's absence, it would appear to be her responsibility to accurately assess and administer the requests of the teachers. Whether upward filtering has occurred is not certain, but it is possible that Thelma Smith, for reasons of not wanting to appear incompetent before her superior, would distort the unpleasant messages that confront her. One cannot overlook, also, the potential physical barrier to communication that exists due to Robbins's dual principalships. Robbins's absence does not contribute to spontaneous, interpersonal communication. Argyris, for example, reports that a large percentage of employees feel appreciative when managers visit them in person.[9] Whether this observation applies in this situation is not certain, but the principle should remain; namely, the individual problems cannot be adequately handled through impersonal channels and that recognition as individuals can be cathartic in itself. There is a reflection here on another facet of the situation—that of the quality of leadership demonstrated by both Robbins and Smith.

LEADERSHIP AND RELATED ISSUES

It is questionable whether Robbins has adequately delegated to Thelma Smith the necessary authority for handling the teachers' problems. Delegation, though, is basically an act of trust. Robbins might not have the necessary confidence in Miss Smith to assign to her any serious responsibilities. Robbins might also fear the loss of his own authority through delegation. There is adequate belief, though, that delegation does not weaken authority of the delegator, but rather establishes a social bond between delegator and delegatee. Especially where autonomy is absent, the "social delegation" process becomes more important.[10] There is evidence, though, that Robbins was rather selective in delegating authority, having apparently permitted Mrs. Jones to deal with a similar situation at the Green school.

Perhaps what Robbins's actions demonstrate is the necessity to exercise discretion in utilizing participative management. As Fitzgerald points out, the opportunity costs need to be adequately weighed in considering whether or not to exercise participative decision making.[11] In this instance, Robbins might have perceived Thelma Smith as incapable of handling complex responsibilities. The question invariably would arise, though, regarding why Miss Smith would not be replaced if she is, in fact, unqualified. Theoretically, of course, it might be possible to transfer or fire her, but the reality of modern organizational life gives compelling evidence that this is very difficult to do, especially in bureaucracies such as municipal school systems (assuming this to be a large school system).

What Robbins might need to do instead, assuming that removing her is not feasible, would be to develop her administrative capabilities. Of the skills often alluded to in the literature—conceptual, human and technical[12] —Miss Smith would appear to need the first two in large measure. In the human skill area, effective interpersonal relationships are extremely important to her role. In this regard, the tenets of organization development (OD) systems could apply. As Eddy suggests, OD emphasizes interpersonal and membership capabilities, often in conjunction with a social system perspective on organization.[13] He indicates, too, that the goal of OD programs is change.[14] While Miss Smith apparently needs interpersonal skill development, it is questionable whether the goal—change—is sufficient. Change for the sake of change is comparable to profit for the sake of profit, an anachronism whose burial is long past, partly due to the efforts of human relationists and organization behavioralists.

For very practical reasons, the Adams School needs capable administratorship from both Jack Robbins and Thelma Smith. Any training and development effort in this instance must have as its ultimate goal the improvement of the quality of education through teamwork and administrative action. There are indications that OD, laboratory training and similar process-teamwork-relationships oriented programs are not entirely capable of delivering what is sometimes purported, partly because they are not adequately issue-oriented or because they subordinate the task to the process.[15] Then, too, a more modest effort, stressing management (as distinct from organization) development, might be more appropriate inasmuch as the skills needed in this situation include also the conceptual areas—internal and external planning, organizing, abstracting, and modeling relationships. Whatever avenue for development is selected, it is essential that Robbins sort out the personal and organizational objectives to be achieved and to look beyond relationships, per se, toward improving the education of students. Viewed in that perspective, curriculum changes might or might not be necessary, but at least he and Miss Smith will need to work with the teachers toward arriving at an appropriate decision.

ADDITIONAL INFORMATION NEEDED

In order to more completely analyze the situation, it would be helpful to know more about the reasons for Robbins's dual assignment. Also, what is his background in the administrative area? How was Thelma Smith selected for the position and did Robbins have a voice in the selection? What was the background of the teachers' complaints? What proportion of teachers are represented in the complaints? Do other schools in the system share in the same type of administrative arrangement? Finally, is it possible for Robbins to arrange his schedule whereby attention to critical problems can be given, perhaps through regular faculty/administrative meetings?

THE UNWANTED GIFT

Transol Corporation is a national distributor of industrial chemicals with regional sales offices in twelve major manufacturing centers. Each office is staffed by a regional sales director, his assistant, ten to fourteen salesmen, and a secretary. It is a policy of Transol to transfer salesmen among regions more frequently than similar firms because in the opinion of Transol, "a rolling stone gathers no moss." As a result, salesmen expect to be transferred every three years on the average.

The New Orleans regional sales office is one of the larger offices with fourteen salesmen assigned. In the past five years, the New Orleans office has consistently been among the top five sales offices in volume of sales per salesman. Recently, the sales director of fifteen years retired and was replaced by George M. Carver, from outside the company.

During the first week of his tenure, Carver asked his assistant, White, to take a voluntary collection from the staff and select a reasonably priced, suitable going-away gift for a departing salesman. Shortly thereafter, White approached members of the staff and said Carver had decided that the office should present the departing salesman with an engraved pewter beer mug as a remembrance gift. Everyone contacted by White contributed, including the office secretary. A month later, Carver asked White to take a similar collection for another departing salesman. White approached the staff in the same manner as previously; however, one of the salesmen refused to contribute. In response, White doubled his contribution and concealed the incident from Carver. Several months later Carver again asked White to take a collection, but now three of the salesmen and the secretary refused to contribute. In addition, the departing salesman told White, "For my part, you can tell Carver that I don't even want the mug!"

This time White explained to Carver what happened, and at the next sales meeting Carver emphasized a relationship between "esprit de corps" and sales volume.

ANALYSIS 1: *The Unwanted Gift*

This incident contains many factors, both stated and implied, which have behavioral implications. Some of the areas are easy to isolate whereas others seem vague; but, with additional information, they too could be analyzed.

PERCEPTION AND PERSONALITY

Differences in perception of the same situation by different people is the rule rather than the exception. People perceive what they think will satisfy their needs. To ignore these differences in perception is to ignore a major determinant of behavior.[16] Mr. Carver perceives that the employees would like a remembrance of their time spent at the New Orleans office. He fails to recognize that their perspective is different from his even after they rebel against his idea, as witnessed by his emphasis at the sales meeting of the relationship between esprit de corps and sales volume. The sales volume per salesman has been consistently high compared to other regions in the past, and Mr. Carver is tampering with a seemingly well established regional office. His policies of the future, if carried out in the same manner, could lead to a decline of the esprit de corps that he seeks to perpetuate.

Mr. White's perception of Carver's request was that he himself should select the gift. This unilateral selection of the gift could be questioned as being ineffective. White could have used a participative approach in deciding on the gift; this could possibly have promoted "a sense of partnership in and responsibility for the affairs of the organization"[17] even if only in a small and inconspicuous way.

SMALL GROUP

The conflict appears to be between the group (subordinates) and Carver (the boss). Furthermore, the gift itself is probably no more than a precipitating factor of the conflict; the group's reasons behind the conflict as related to the group's goals are the real issues. The specific nature of the gift, that is, an engraved pewter beer mug, is only the battleground of an ongoing conflict. The personnel are strongly reacting to whatever the gift represents to them, and this reaction is increasing in strength. Assuming the New Orleans regional sales office previously lacked intrapersonal cohesiveness, a consensus or common orientation is now emerging which will solidify its personnel into an effective informal group and reinforce its polarity in the conflict with time.

Little more can be said about the group in terms of relevant group behavioral theory based upon the information given in the incident. Since group behavior is basic to our analysis of the incident, the group being the largest unknown of the three principals, the following questions need to be addressed in a search for additional information.

    a. Is the office composed of one or several groups, and who are their informal leaders?

    b. What are the group's attitudes and goals?

    c. What rumors and informal conversation pertaining to Carver's desire to establish a remembrance gift, and to his personality and leadership style, have evolved among members of a group and between groups?

STATUS AND ROLE CONCEPTS

Mr. Carver perceives that he possesses status because of his position as the regional sales director. This scalar status, which features the right to command others,[18] is not as prevalent in the "flat" organizational structure, but it is evidenced in this incident. Carver believes he has the right to ask for voluntary contributions in order to fulfill a goal which is evidently his and his alone. He feels that his role is one of creating and promoting esprit de corps, which could be defined as Scott's particularistic dimension of the role concept.[19] Carver evidently lacks the ability to "put himself in the other guy's shoes," which is known as empathy.

White exhibits role conflict when he doubles his contribution to the second collection because one salesman refused to contribute. He sees his role as being a successful "fund raiser" and does not want to look incompetent in the eyes of his supervisors. Kahn[20] would define this as inter-sender conflict, because White is pressured from the top by his supervisor's request and from the bottom by the salesman's refusal to donate.

COMMUNICATION CONCEPTS AND COMMUNICATION BREAKDOWNS

Mr. Carver asked Mr. White to take up the voluntary collection for the gift but did not ask for feedback from the employees. This one-way flow of communication is not conducive to a humanistic organization. At the sales meeting, Carver could have used effective two-way communication to solve the problem rather than to lecture the subordinates on sales volume and the necessity for esprit de corps. By using the persuasion approach rather than the problem solving approach,[21] Carver has undoubtedly impeded the very purpose he is trying to promote.

Mr. White, on the other hand, uses the process of filtering, as defined by Scott,[22] when he doubles his contribution in order to cover up for the salesman who refused to donate on the second collection. This is a barrier to communication in that it manipulates facts in order to make them more favorable for the sender and more acceptable to the receiver.

The group is not accepting Carver's message as communicated by White, resulting in ineffective communication because conduct is not following the intended meaning of the message. There is a breakdown in effective communication between Carver and the group, and the breakdown stems from nonacceptance of Carver's communication. At issue, and the basis for acceptance as seen by Scott are the "needs, motives, experience, and education of the receiver, plus the environment in which he finds himself."[23] It is easy to see that perception is closely related to acceptance, since an individual's view of reality defines his needs, motives, experience, and environment.[24] Scott states, "If these definitions (of reality) can be changed to conform with the manager's . . . view of reality, then higher levels of communication acceptance are reasonably assured."[25]

In a different plant it can be said that the goals of a group are based upon a consensus of needs as determined by the composite and similar views of reality among members of the group. Therefore, a positive approach to changing the group's definition of reality is the attainment of group goals congruent with the organization's goals.

POWER, AUTHORITY AND LEADERSHIP

Mr. Carver probably believes his value system is the same as that of his employees and therefore believes that the employees desire a departing remembrance; this is not a reciprocated value as evidenced by the reaction of the employees. At first, they could have felt obligated on behalf of their superior[26] since he had been there for only a short time, but Carver's use of his power privilege did not gain the good will of his sales force.[27]

Leadership by Mr. Carver in this incident is indeed lacking. Various authors define leadership in terms of the process involved, the individual involved, the act involved, etc., but Bavelas' view seems most applicable to this incident. He states that "the person who can assist or facilitate the group most in reaching a satisfactory state is most likely to be regarded as the leader."[28] If Mr. Carver had taken the time to analyze the goals and needs of the individuals and the goals of the organization and attempted to relate them, he might have come closer to reaching a state of accord in this situation. It is significant to note that he decided on the policy of a gift to departing salesmen after being in his position for only one week; this would not seem sufficient time for him to understand the organizational climate and the employees' needs and desires. If Mr. Carver truly desires to modify his sales organization, he first must determine how the organization has operated in the past. He should attempt to understand the organizational climate, get to know his employees better, and develop a better sense of timing.

Mr. White displays a lack of effective leadership techniques when he doubles his contribution rather than seeking the cause of the problem on the second attempt at collecting; this would have been the proper time to bring the problem out in the open rather than waiting until it had grown into larger proportions. White should have seen this and solved the problem immediately.

CONCLUSION

Suggestions have been implied in each area discussed. It can be said that Mr. Carver is indeed somewhat hasty in pushing his viewpoint and value judgments on the organization. The decision to present a gift to departing employees should be determined by the employees. A knowledgeable perception of the situation and the underlying factors would aid in assessing the appropriate action that Mr. Carver should now take.

ANALYSIS 2: *The Unwanted Gift*

There are several issues in this incident that should be addressed in the analysis. They include group behavior, leadership, perception and communication, among others. Primarily, though, the central issue appears to involve communication and this analysis, therefore, will focus in that area.

ADDITIONAL INFORMATION NEEDED

In order to more definitively analyze the situation, it would be helpful to have certain information not already given. For instance, how is Carver approaching the position managerially? Presumably, his gift idea is but a small and perhaps unrepresentative sample of his behavior as a manager. If the New Orleans sales office was one of the high-producing salesmen, why did Carver decide to implement the gift idea? In other words, it is questionable whether such a form of recognition would be needed, since high performance tends to produce its own satisfactions to which token gifts such as pewter mugs will add very little.[29] Also, what policies have other sales offices followed in regard to gifts? Perhaps Carver was establishing a prece-

dent which salesmen in other offices will come to expect. Finally, why did
Carver ask for contributions to defray expenses? It is one thing to collect
for unexpected tragedies or for weddings, birthdays, etc., but quite another
to ask employees to contribute for matters which are a result of company
policies. Surely, one would expect that Carver's budget would allow the
purchase of pewter mugs, if he feels so strongly about giving the salesmen
something tangible in recognition of their service while in that region. It
appears rather gauche to ask employees to contribute for gifts that constitute a form of company recognition.

COMMUNICATION

Aside from the question of Carver's method of funding his going-away gifts,
there is a question of what is communicated in the process itself. Returning
to a point made earlier regarding the motivational value of this form of
recognition, one could cite the Porter and Fowler studies in support of the
previous remarks. In short, there is a positive correlation between degree
of need satisfaction and job performance. Satisfaction of higher order needs
associates with performance among top, middle and lower-level managers.[30] Follow-up studies of the Porter-Fowler model have also confirmed
the basic performance-satisfaction relationship.[31] These findings relate, of
course, to the motivational aspects of the gift policy, but also in a large way
to the communication question involved. It is axiomatic that communication and motivation are inextricably related. This incident clearly demonstrates this relationship. The gift-giving is intended to communicate
appreciation; i.e., serve as a form of recognition for service to the regional
organization. Yet, the gifts accrue to everyone who transfers out, whether
a high or low performer. In other words, there is no real merit attached to
the gift.[32] Little wonder the salesmen are cynical about the mugs—they
only signify a transfer from one office to another, which could be a pleasant,
unpleasant or indifferent experience, depending upon how it is perceived.
For example, to the salesmen, the gift could be construed as what Schaub
calls a "managerial facade;" i.e., an hypocrisy between thought and action.[33] Perhaps to the salesmen, management is using the gift-giving in
order to disguise weaknesses in the transfer policy. Similar to retiring a
long-service employee and giving that employee a gold watch in recognition, the pewter mug might smack of insincerity and only serve to remind
the employee of the organizational inflexibility that forced the transfer in
the first place. Therefore, the communication involved is fraught with various other unintended, but very real, messages concerning the employee's
worth.

OTHER SALIENT ISSUES

One could raise serious questions with the transfer policy itself to which Carver is apparently committed at this point. Perhaps Transol's view that "a rolling stone gathers no moss" is a valid one, but neither do rolling stones build stable foundations. True, the salesmen expect to be transferred after about three years, but the effects on families and on the company could be more expensive than the effects of more permanent assignments. For example, salesmen develop client-vendor relationships which can be highly valuable to the organization. Families develop social and community involvements which are a part of individual need structures. If these are not satisfied off-the-job, it might be that salesmen will seek out social satisfactions within the organization at the expense of higher level satisfactions.

Then, too, the transient family would tend to have less identity with the community, a factor which indirectly could affect the company's status as a good citizen. Perhaps this aspect is not so important in a city of the size of New Orleans, but in other locations, it could be a factor. Another effect of transiency is even more important; i.e., in relation to customer service. The modern salesman does much more than just sell. The salesman represents the company as its interface with the customer. Particularly in industrial sales, one would expect identification with customers to be highly important. A study by one of the authors indicates its value in the retail firm where customers are not known by name and the interchange is relatively brief.[34] In industrial selling, confidence in a supplier relies heavily upon the salesman's ability to understand and interpret customer needs and the Transol Company may be trading off customer loyalty for salesman mobility.

Another study suggests that organizational indentification, service orientation, satisfaction of higher-order needs, and length of service associate together.[35] While the study was conducted in a setting involving U.S. Forest Service personnel, it is possible that the findings could apply to salesmen and others. At least it makes motivational sense to expect that salesmen would derive ego and/or self-fulfillment level satisfactions from having served client needs and that the service commitment would produce organizational identification—assuming the organization's service objective to be compatible with the salesmen's service efforts.

Rather than develop incentive schemes which can very well boomerang as in this incident, perhaps what Carver needs to do is to work toward modifying the organization's transfer policy. Along the way, it is imperative that, as a new manager, he develop trust among the salesmen. Little is known of his approach to supervising, quota-selling and appraisal. Yet, this incident could very well affect all of these vital managerial areas. The approach suggested by Golembiewski and Carrigan based on their laboratory experiences with salesmen and sales managers is one way of establishing trust through improved interpersonal relationships.[36] Perhaps the laboratory approach is not appropriate in the present situation, though, considering the current level of effectiveness of the salesmen—as well as Carver's relative newness in the company. Nevertheless, as Carver's style and attitudes become more familiar, there will be some point at which training and development needs can be determined and one of the alternatives, among others, would be a relatively unstructured, laboratory-type experience.

THE DEADLINE

Marvin Ellerbrock, Project Leader for the Hartsmoth Co., had fourteen computer programmers reporting to him. These programmers were working on the development of three major information systems, and each of his programmers was assigned to one of three teams. Each team was responsible for one of the information systems. Mr. Ellerbrock decided that he could better control the development of the projects, and free more time for his administrative responsibilities, by assigning team leaders to each project area. The team leaders, he decided, would be called "lead programmers." Before announcing his decision to all of his programmers, Mr. Ellerbrock decided to discuss it privately with each of his three prospective lead programmers. He wanted to be sure that they understood the project and were willing to accept this new responsibility.

Mr. Ellerbrock called Tom Hall into his office and told him that he would like him to be the lead programmer on projects related to the Billing and Pricing Systems. Mr. Ellerbrock carefully explained to Tom that this position carried the authority to direct the project-related activities of the people assigned to the project area. These people were John DeVance, Robert Swift, Jack Bell and Susan Proy. Mr. Ellerbrock clearly explained what was meant by project-related activities vs. areas of administrative authority, which he would retain. Tom Hall accepted the new position, and as he was leaving the office, asked Mr. Ellerbrock to announce and explain the new position to the other programmers. Mr. Ellerbrock assured Tom that he would on the next day. The following week Mr. Ellerbrock began his annual vacation.

One morning while Mr. Ellerbrock was still on vacation, Tom Hall asked Bob Swift to prepare the computer operator procedure for a system test which had to be run that night. Later that day, Tom asked Bob if the test procedure was ready; Bob replied that it was not.

Tom asked, "Why not, didn't you have enough time?"

"No," Bob replied, "I had enough time, but where I worked

before, that task was the responsibility of the project's systems analyst."

Tom was getting upset. "Fortunately or unfortunately, it is a programming responsibility here; I've explained that to you earlier. I'm the lead programmer on this project; now why didn't you do as I asked?"

"You're the lead programmer?" Bob seemed surprised. "To my knowledge, we don't have a lead programmer on this project."

Tom pondered what his next step should be. He knew that the test procedure had to be done within three hours, and Bob was the only one who had the knowledge to prepare it.

ANALYSIS 1: *The Deadline*

The incident involves several important behavioral areas, among which are group behavior, perception, leadership and authority. It is the intention here, though, to focus particularly on the communication problems involved, since these appear to be of overriding importance.

Ostensibly, Ellerbrock was accustomed to directing project-related activities and did not prepare formal assignments for each team member. Whether or not Ellerbrock advised most of the programmers of the new arrangement is a matter for conjecture; however, indications are that Tom's group was not informed. In this regard, Ellerbrock certainly should have defined individual responsibilities and the objectives or mission of each team prior to his departure. In other words, the delineation of project-related activities versus areas of administrative authority was insufficient.

John R. Maher and Darrell T. Piersol explored this area of communication based on experiments showing reactions to induced frustration. The variables they measured include the perception of clarity regarding individual job objectives, overall objectives of mission, rating of job, cohesiveness of groups and overall satisfaction. Of major significance to the individual with supervisory responsibility is the finding that perceived clarity of an individual's location or department mission and personal work objectives has a major impact on such key factors as satisfaction with job, company and work associates.[37] The major implication of this finding is that there is a need for a complete understanding of communication media as well as communication skills in order for an administrator to be successful. In talking about "management by objectives" the authors also point out that direct involvement by employees in establishing objectives has often led to greater clarity of expectations as well as increased mutual cooperation toward attaining stated goals. In this incident Ellerbrock clearly explained those project-related activities Tom had authority over, but he did not mention anything about expected results or objectives. Perhaps part of the reason Tom was upset was because he was unclear as to exactly how he should be directing the team. It is not known how much time had elapsed prior to the confrontation, but it appears fairly obvious that if Bob had initially been informed of his responsibility for the test procedure as well as of Tom's new role, the task would have been accomplished on time.

LEADERSHIP

Another important area in this incident is that of leadership, particularly in relation to Ellerbrock and Hall. Ellerbrock appears to have attempted to adapt his leadership approach to the "lead programmer" situation. He distinguished project authority and administrative authority, apparently acknowledging the differences between them.[38] Although it is not clear what Ellerbrock meant by administrative authority, it is assumed that he was referring to decisions which would involve the permanent assignments of the programmer; i.e., promotion, transfer, salary, and evaluation. The lead programmer positions were also temporary; i.e., for the duration of the project.

It appears that at least Ellerbrock is capable of making a decision, but he apparently does not follow through as thoroughly as he might. His "style" is not clear from the incident, but it apparently is not exactly consultative. The question of leadership style is complicated by the fact of Ellerbrock's going on vacation. Notwithstanding that factor, it would appear that Ellerbrock is deficient in human relations skill, as evidenced in not informing the other programmers of the change in project management. According to a study by Misshauk, engineers rate human skills highest in importance among administrative skills for supervisors. Moreover, the greater the difference between actual and perceived supervisory skill, the less satisfied is the employee with the supervisor.[39] While the employees here are programmers rather than engineers, there is a potential application of the above study in that the technical content of the work and the education backgrounds are quite similar. Related to the vacation matter, this could have been an opportunity for Ellerbrock to develop human capabilities through delegation. But he omitted the participative facet which is so important in projects such as this. Perhaps it was a mere oversight on his part, but Ellerbrock left a void in the ongoing direction of the project by not informing team members of the new function of lead programmers. Perhaps the project teams might have worked effectively in a leaderless condition.[40] It is not known, however, whether the interaction would be functional or dysfunctional. Presumably, interaction is to be valued in itself, and in this incident one could predict the type of interaction which attempts to structure an ambiguous situation—such as the development of norms and procedures which provide direction in the absence of the leader.

GROUP BEHAVIOR

The above analysis leads to a question of group behavior. The programmer group fits very appropriately the definition of a small group.[41] It is under ten in size, interacts face-to-face, and evidently has a common task objective.

It is not known how long the team members worked together and it would be difficult to describe the interpersonal relationships, based upon the given information. However, in view of Tom's confrontation with Bob, there is an indication of uncooperativeness or lack of cohesiveness. As a result, it may be useful to examine some of the research regarding group cohesiveness.

Adams and Slocum attempted to test various hypotheses regarding the effects of group cohesiveness. They viewed a highly cohesive group as one in which the members saw themselves as part of the group, preferred membership in the group, perceived their group to be better than others with respect to the way the men get along together as well as the way they help each other, and their tendency to stick together. They also defined satisfaction as the extent to which the environmental factors meet or exceed the employees' expectations. The study indicated that group cohesiveness is a significant force affecting satisfactions of unskilled groups, but not necessarily in the case of skilled workers, contrary to prior research cited.[42] Members of more highly skilled and cohesive groups were found to be significantly less satisfied than their unskilled counterparts. The suggested interpretation is that the prestige factor inherent in the higher-skilled jobs brought more direct satisfaction, perhaps making social satisfactions less important.[43]

Our programmers in this incident are obviously skilled workers, but there is often a required interaction factor in this type of work in contrast to, for instance, a lathe operator. In other words, the study findings cited above might not apply uniformly to this type of work. Regardless there does appear to be an individualized work system here, in the sense that each programmer has a specific assignment and must use technical skills in an atmosphere unpenetrated by distractive social intercourse. In that respect, interaction might be dysfunctional and impair satisfaction of ego and fulfillment needs.

ADDITIONAL INFORMATION NEEDED

It would be helpful to know more about Bob Swift's background. This may give a clearer understanding as to why he left his previous employer and why he alluded to the fact that certain people have specific responsibilities. Also, how much time had elapsed from the day that Tom received his new assignment until the confrontation with Bob? This could yield some insight as to whether or not Tom was a poor organizer or a poor planner. What type of instructions did Ellerbrock give the team members during the normal course of business? Were the members able to demonstrate initiative or were they accustomed to being told what to do? Why did Tom not check with the programmers to determine whether Ellerbrock had informed them of the new supervisory positions and the assignments of people who would fill them? One would expect that, having worked with an individual for some time, one could predict whether that person would follow through on his assurances. Regardless, it is advisable to make certain employees know about the change and this would also provide an opportunity for project leaders such as Tom Hall to orient the programmers concerning expectations, instructions, and responsibilities.

ANALYSIS 2: *The Deadline*

The major issues in this incident are in the areas of communication. The communication issues are also intertwined with the secondary issues of span of control, authority and unity of command.

COMMUNICATION

Three actual communication breakdowns may be cited. The first breakdown occurred when Marvin Ellerbrock failed to discuss with the other programmers the assignment of the lead programmers. This failure led directly to the incident in which Bob Swift showed that he was unaware of Tom Hall's position. Cooperation is more likely when people are told of changes and the reasons for them in advance.[44] Bob Swift showed some resistance when being confronted so abruptly with a change in who was giving him orders. A second communication breakdown occurred due to Tom Hall's failure to check back with Ellerbrock later to make sure that he had spoken with the other programmers. Hall should have sought this feedback to assure that proper communication had taken place. A third communication breakdown is the failure of Hall to have held some kind of meeting with the other programmers to make certain that they were aware of and understood the reasons for the assignment of lead programmers.

SPAN OF CONTROL

It is not possible to state for certain why the lack of effective communication was so apparent. However, it appears that the concept of span of control could provide a partial explanation for the problem. With fourteen programmers reporting to Mr. Ellerbrock, it is likely that this organization has been troubled in the past by poor communication. For example, Ellerbrock may have been too busy previously to make it clear to Bob Swift that it was his duty to prepare test procedures. Ellerbrock's busy schedule also may have been the reason why he did not discuss the assignment of lead programmers with the other programmers. Scott lists "failure to delegate" or "no time" as barriers to communication.[45] A person who carries too much of a work load and who fails to delegate stifles good communication. Although Ellerbrock did delegate some of his responsibilities to the lead programmers, conditions of poor communication and vagueness of individual duties may have existed due to his former excessive duties.

AUTHORITY

Mr. Ellerbrock told Tom Hall that, as lead programmer, he carried the authority to direct project-related activities. However, there was no clarity of responsibilities in the relationship between Hall and Swift. If Swift had understood the new responsibilities placed on Hall, cooperation would have been more likely. Obedience cannot be expected to be automatic without understanding. Swift's failure to respond to Hall's request to prepare the test procedures was due to his annoyance at being confronted with the changed relationship without having been given any prior information or reason.

Authority is usually acknowledged more readily by people when they have been given the opportunity to participate in the management processes.[46] It was particularly difficult for Swift to acknowledge Hall's authority because Swift had been completely left out of Ellerbrock's decision-making process.

UNITY OF COMMAND

Bob Swift recognizes Ellerbrock as his boss, and expects his orders to come from him. Ellerbrock, however, has changed this arrangement by appointing lead programmers for each project. However, it appears that there will be some confusion within each project with respect to who will be giving orders, Ellerbrock or the lead programmer. A written description of job responsibilities should be provided to all the programmers to prevent people from being confronted with incompatible orders. Similarly, each programmer should understand to whom he is accountable for proper execution of his tasks.[47]

SUGGESTED SOLUTION

The three lead programmers should discuss the reasons for their appointments with their teams. It would also be advisable to designate in writing the responsibilities of their new positions. Upon Ellerbrock's return, additional attention should be given to clarifying the roles of Ellerbrock and the lead programmers. All the programmers should participate in such meetings to aid in developing good relationships between the lead programmers and the others.

ADDITIONAL INFORMATION DESIRED

What was the previous pattern of leadership style practiced by Ellerbrock? Were the programmers accustomed to receiving detailed instructions from Ellerbrock, or did he permit them a high degree of freedom in the decision-making process?

Did Ellerbrock intentionally avoid, prior to going on vacation, telling the programmers about the new organizational relationship? If so, why?

We would want to know the elapsed time between Ellerbrock's telling Hall of his new assignment, and the incident between Hall and Swift. Unless this was a very short period of time, it is difficult for us to understand why the new arrangement had not been, at least, communicated via the grapevine, unless there is very limited interaction between the programmers, hence, not a highly cohesive group.

FOOTNOTES

[1]William G. Scott and Terence R. Mitchell, *Organization Theory: A Structural and Behavioral Analysis,* Revised Edition (Homewood, Ill.: Richard D. Irwin, Inc., and The Dorsey Press, 1972), p. 141.

[2]James B. Strenski, "Two-Way Communication: A Management Necessity," *Personnel Journal,* January, 1970, pp. 29–31.

[3]Jack R. Gibb, "Communication and Productivity," *Personnel Administration,* January-February, 1964, pp. 8–13.

[4]Allen Weiss, "Delegation: The Key to Success Is Participation," *Supervisory Management,* June, 1971, pp. 16–19.

[5]L. I. Gelfand, "Communicate Through Your Supervisors," *Harvard Business Review,* November-December, 1970, pp. 101–4.

[6]Donald C. Pelz, "Influence: A Key to Effective Leadership in the First-Line Supervisor," *Personnel,* November, 1952, pp. 209–17.

[7]Harold Stieglitz, "Barriers to Communication," *Management Record,* January, 1958, pp. 2–5.

[8]Dennis W. Organ, "Linking Pins Between Organization and Environment," *Business Horizons,* December, 1971, pp. 74–75.

[9]Chris Argyris, "The Organization: What Makes it Healthy," in William P. Sexton, ed., *Organization Theory* (Columbus, Ohio: Charles E. Merrill Publishing Co., 1970), p. 205.

[10]Keith Davis, "Management by Participation," in William P. Sexton, ed., *Organization Theory* (Columbus, Ohio: Charles E. Merrill Publishing Co., 1970), p. 125.

[11]Thomas H. Fitzgerald, "Why Motivation Theory Doesn't Work," *Harvard Business Review,* July-August, 1971, pp. 37–44.

[12]Robert L. Katz, "Skills of an Effective Administrator," in Max D. Richards and William A. Nielander, *Readings in Management* (Cincinnati: South-Western Publishing Company, 1969), pp. 849–65.

[13]William B. Eddy, "From Training to Organizational Change," *Personnel Administration,* January-February, 1971, pp. 37–43.

[14]*Ibid.,* pp. 41–42.

[15]Larry E. Greiner, "Red Flags in Organization Development," *Business Horizons,* June, 1972, pp. 17–24.

[16]Harold J. Leavitt, *Managerial Psychology* 2d ed. (Chicago and London: The University of Chicago Press, 1964), pp. 28–40.

[17]Robert T. Golembiewski, *Men, Management, and Morality* (New York: McGraw-Hill Book Co., Inc., 1965), chaps. 7 and 8, cited in William G. Scott, *Organization Theory: A Behavioral Analysis for Management* (Homewood, Ill.: Richard D. Irwin, Inc., 1967), p. 265.

[18]William G. Scott, *Organization Theory: A Behavioral Analysis for Management* (Homewood, Ill.: Richard D. Irwin, Inc., 1967), p. 186.

[19]*Ibid.,* p. 194.

[20]Robert L. Kahn, "Role Conflict and Ambiguity in Organizations," in S. G. Huneryager and I. L. Heckman, *Human Relations in Management* (Cincinnati: South-Western Publishing Company, 1967), p. 645.

[21]Jack R. Gibb, "Communication and Productivity," in Huneryager and Heckman, *Human Relations* p. 521.

[22]Scott, *Organization Theory,* p. 304.

[23]*Ibid.,* p. 309.

[24]*Ibid.,* p. 310.

[25]*Ibid.*

[26]Peter M. Blau, "Critical Remarks on Weber's Theory of Authority," *American Political Science Review,* June, 1963, p. 312.

[27]Scott, *Organization Theory,* p. 207.

[28]Alex Bavelas, "Leadership: Man and Function," in Huneryager and Heckman, *Human Relations* p. 285.

[29]Frank Friedlander, "Motivations to Work and Organizational Performance," *Journal of Applied Psychology* 50 (1966): 143–52.

[30]E. Lawler and L. W. Porter, "The Effect of Performance on Job Satisfaction," *Industrial Relations* 7 (1967): 20–28.

[31]John W. Slocum, Jr., "Motivation in Managerial Levels: Relationship of Need Satisfaction to Job Performance," *Journal of Applied Psychology* 55, no. 4 (1971): 312–16.

[32]For an excellent discussion of merit and bonus systems, see Timothy W. Costello and Sheldon S. Zalkind, "Merit Raise or Merit Bonus: A Psychological Approach," *Personnel Administration,* November-December, 1962, pp. 10–17.

[33]Alfred E. Schaub, "Managerial Facades," *Personnel Administration,* October, 1971, pp. 33–37.

[34]See Thomas J. Von der Embse, "Critical Factors in Organizational Commitment and Performance," *Bulletin of Business Research,* Ohio State University, Center for Business and Economic Research (June, 1972), pp. 4, 7–8.

[35]Douglas T. Hall, Benjamin Schneider and Harold T. Nygren, "Personal Factors in Organizational Identification," *Administrative Science Quarterly* 15 (1970): pp. 176–90.

[36]Robert T. Golembiewski and Stokes B. Carrigan, "Planned Change in Organization Style Based upon the Laboratory Approach," *Administrative Science Quarterly* 15 (1970): pp. 79–93.

[37]John R. Maher and Darrell T. Piersol, "Perceived Clarity of Individual Job Objectives and of Group Mission as Correlates of Organizational Morale," *The Journal of Communication,* June, 1970, p. 132.

[38]For an extensive development of project and hierarchical authority, see David I. Cleland, "Understanding Project Authority," *Business Horizons,* Spring, 1967, pp. 63–70.

[39]Michael J. Misshauk, "Supervisory Skills and Employee Satisfaction," *Personnel Administration,* July-August, 1971, pp. 29–33; especially, pp. 30–31.

[40]Bruce C. Wheatley, "Leadership and Anxiety: Implications for Employer/Employee in Small Group Meetings," *Personnel Journal,* January, 1972, p. 20.

[41]See Keith Davis, *Human Behavior at Work* (New York: McGraw-Hill Book Company, 1972), p. 439; also, Robert F. Bales, *Personality and Interpersonal Behavior* (New York: Holt, Rinehart and Winston, Inc., 1970).

[42]Paul G. Adams III, and John W. Slocum, Jr., "Work Groups and Employee Satisfaction," *Personnel Administration,* March-April, 1971, p. 39.

[43]*Ibid.,* p. 42.

[44]W. S. Hall, "Lessons from a Communication Blunder," *Supervisory Management,* December, 1971, p. 16.

[45]Don H. Scott, "Are You a Communications Cop-Out?" *Sales Management,* April 10, 1971, p. 40.

[46]William Blackie, "Authority," *S.A.M. Advanced Management Journal,* October, 1971, pp. 47–48.

[47]Robert J. House, "Role Conflict and Multiple Authority in Complex Organizations," *California Management Review,* Summer, 1970, pp. 53–60.

STATUS AND ROLE

Incident	Page
THE RESEARCH TECHNICIANS	85
Robert A. Byrum	
Analysis 1	86
Analysis 2	89
THE DESK ENGINEERS	92
M. E. Brickson	
Analysis 1	93
Analysis 2	96
PARISH DILEMMA	99
William C. Haverkamp	
Analysis 1	100
Analysis 2	103

THE RESEARCH TECHNICIANS

The primary function of the Space and Missile Support Branch of the Air Force Materials Laboratory is to conduct research on materials that are of interest to the Air Force. The branch consists of a branch manager, ten research engineers, and five technicians.

The branch manager is a dominant individual who has a doctorate degree in engineering. He has had no formal or informal training in management.

Eight of the research engineers are military officers or high ranking civil servants while the other two are first term sergeants. Each of these engineers has, at minimum, a master's degree in engineering. None of these engineers has any management training so they have adopted the branch manager's style of leadership and communication in dealing with the technicians.

All of the technicians have had between two and four years of college education, but none of them has a degree. They represent a wide range of ages, interests, backgrounds, etc. For example, two of the technicians are retired military master sergeants, while two others are young enlisted men and part-time college students. These differences have often caused conflict and hostility among the technicians in the past.

The planning and decision making are done by the branch manager and the ten engineers. Each engineer (including the branch manager) then selects research projects and uses the technicians to implement these projects. The technician's job is to set up the apparatus and to record the data.

Just recently the branch manager has been informed by an outside source that his technicians have lower job satisfaction and productivity than the technicians from other branches. He wonders how and why this can be true when none of his technicians have discussed this with him.

ANALYSIS 1: *The Research Technicians*

STATUS AND ROLE PROBLEMS

Apart from its simple structure as outlined in the incident, it appears that the Air Force Materials Laboratory is a polyglot in terms of the lack of commonalities among the research technicians. Small groups tend to form among people of common interests and backgrounds and the positive function of these associations seems to have been precluded by the makeup of this unit. Although the status and competency of the branch manager and eight of his research engineers are clear by virtue of their similar background and qualifications, this is not so apparent among the technicians and two of the research engineers. In what is normally a highly structured organization, i.e., the military, it is difficult to visualize retired, senior noncommissioned officers docilely accepting instructions from enlisted-grade research engineers of grade lower than the former had previously enjoyed. Having previously held rank and authority equal to that of at least two of their superiors, it is not inconceivable that the retired noncommissioned officers might be experiencing displeasure over the apparent status inconsistencies involved. Certainly the presence among the technicians of college-age enlisted men with comparable educational background would do nothing to enhance the role and status of the senior career men.

As for the other younger research technicians, who presumably have less working experience in formal organizations, it is quite conceivable that these workers, some of whom may hold considerable aspirations consistent with their college backgrounds, might well be frustrated by the apparent absence of any opportunity to participate in determining their activities or anything that might have an influence on them. They may look at their position as being transitory in that they are not planning on a military career and, therefore, have no incentive to excel in this organization. Effectively, several of the technicians may simply be marking time until they return to civilian life, complete their college education, or pursue some other career.

For both the retired senior noncommissioned officers, and the younger enlisted man in a research technician's position, there appears to be little in the framework of this particular unit that would afford either tangible opportunities for achievement or personal self-actualization. By virtue of the academic credentials necessary for promotion to research engineer or branch manager, it is apparent that promotions within the unit are virtually closed to the research technicians. Their status could be regarded as being terminal unless they should choose to leave the organization. In order for aspirations to stimulate achievement, there must exist an opportunity for rewards which will attain some level of satisfaction. March and Simon's model describes this well in terms of the search process leading to satisfaction and levels of aspiration.[1] Perhaps workers do not consciously plot out their strategies for seeking need satisfaction. Nevertheless, one could expect that these technicians would have certain heuristically-determined career objectives and it is obvious in this situation that they are frustrated in achieving them.

Those who support the idea of job enrichment would probably view the formal structure of the organization and the directive style of leadership as being among the root causes of the problems indicated in the incident. As already noted, there is substantial reason to believe that the unit's structure effectively retards any upward aspirations or participative activity on the part of the research technicians.[2]

MOTIVATION

It is obvious that motivation factors are almost nonexistent here. Not that these are always important to the worker, but there is sufficient evidence to indicate that technicians tend to respond very favorably to attempts at giving them more responsibilities and greater variety of work.[3] Aside from some of the more drastic revisions attempted by firms such as Non-Linear Systems, Inc.,[4] it is not imperative that tasks and relationships be entirely restructured in order to accomplish a satisfactory degree of "enrichment."[5] For example, in the incident it may be possible to have the technicians perform the same work; e.g., setting up the apparatus, testing and recording the data, but with greater responsibility for planning the tests and for reporting and interpreting results.

The point is that the engineers obviously show little regard for the technicians. This peon treatment might bolster the status of the engineers, but it will hinder them in getting productivity from the technicians. One of the Harvard cases, the United Diesel Company, illustrates this problem in considerable detail. Although it concerns relationships between engineers and draftsmen, the analogy appears quite valid. In that situation, the interaction between groups of engineers and draftsmen broke down due to confusion over the mutual expectations of the respective groups. The engineers, much like those in this incident, saw their roles as planners, initiators and final decision makers and that of the draftsmen as following orders. Yet, the draftsmen saw themselves in a more innovative role, not as subordinates to the engineers, but as experts who could take engineering ideas and convert them into practical designs.[6]

A factor compounding the status problem in our incident is the military rank situation. With two exceptions, the engineers have a defined superordinate position because of their military and civil service ranks. Therefore, unlike engineers in industry, they need not earn the respect of technicians in order to maintain status in the hierarchy. This could, of course, be advantageous in that the technicians know where they stand in the command structure. But this would assume that other status factors are consistent, which they are not in this incident. The fact that the technicians have not resolved the status differences among themselves makes it even more difficult for the manager to mitigate the intergroup frictions. In relation to the motivation factors discussed earlier, any attempts at enriching the work of the technicians might require an individualized approach, tailored to the background and interests of each technician.

COMMUNICATION AND LEADERSHIP

Reference is made in the incident to the fact that the branch manager was unaware of any problems concerning job satisfaction or productivity among his technicians. The description alluded to what might be called a directive or more authoritarian approach to his management responsibilities. Both of these circumstances are consistent with the idea that communications within the Air Force Materials Laboratory was probably one way, descending from above. Interpersonal communication vertically may have been reduced to order-giving messages with feedback limited to test results. Too, there is a distinct possibility that the disparity in role and status may have restricted informal communications, more so than one might anticipate between the research engineers and the research technicians in an organization of this limited size. Communications may possibly have also been hindered by the dissimilarity in backgrounds and interests of various types of personnel used as research technicians. The impact here would be especially great on horizontal communications.

Concerning the branch manager's leadership style, one should be careful to not generalize too broadly by reference to the autocratic caricature of military leadership. Studies conducted by one of the authors strongly indicate that leadership styles in the military are not significantly more directive than in other organizations. In fact, in Air Force research-oriented units, which comprised a large segment of the sample, the leadership styles were comparable to those of their R&D counterparts in civilian life.[7] Thus, the branch manager should not be categorized into a mythical organizational model, but rather viewed as a person who undoubtedly has considerable latitude in his leadership approach. Perhaps his failure to achieve flexibility of style is due in greater part to his lack of managerial training rather than to compelling factors related to the climate at his level in the organization.

ADDITIONAL INFORMATION NEEDED

One of the first questions that arises relates to the statement above; namely, what is the climate of the Materials Laboratory? What does the chief expect? How does he relate to the branch manager? Also, what personnel policies exist to develop and exploit the human resources and potential exemplified by the research technicians? Certainly, opportunities for training would exist in this type of organization, both for managers and for technicians. How are technicians classified? In other words, what considerations are given to the diverse backgrounds that exist in this incident? It is difficult to conceive of an organization such as this assigning people at random with no regard to common interests and background. Finally, what is communicated to the technicians with respect to the objectives of the projects? Generally, there are specifications which outline the dimensions in great detail, including the particular mission involved. Without an understanding of this mission or objective, other attempts to rectify the morale problems would be futile.

ANALYSIS 2: *The Research Technicians*

Role ambiguity and lack of status congruency appear to be major problems in this incident. Both the manager and his engineers are authoritarian with no real concern for or knowledge of management skills. All the planning and decision making rests squarely with the branch manager and his engineers. The technicians are not consulted in any way and are involved only in setting up the apparatus and recording data. Consideration is not focused on whether sufficient information is given to the technicians to perform their jobs effectively. As Kahn points out, "among the major sources of role ambiguity (is) . . . managerial philosophy which advocates restriction of information on the assumption that the division of labor makes broad information unnecessary for most positions."[8] Obviously, this is the managerial position in this incident. The technicians are told only as much as they functionally need to know to set up the apparatus and record the data. Argyris would agree that this managerial philosophy would hinder the growth of the individual's personality by providing nonchallenging work.[9] Thus, the reaction of the technicians to this kind of managerial policy is

perhaps predictable. As Kahn notes, "the individual consequences of ambiguity conditions are in general comparable to the individual effects of role
conflict. These include, for ambiguity: low job satisfaction, low self-confidence, a high sense of futility, and a high score on the tension index."[10]
Clearly these result in the incident. Scott would also point out that "as far
as possible, well-managed organizations spell out the functions required of
employees and make arrangements to assure that these functions are not
incompatible. Also, the principle of unity of command is framed to counter-
act the problems which would arise from a number of superiors having
different role expectations from the same subordinates."[11] Argyris would
continue this theme by pointing out that the chain of command in this
incident, and the span of control are contributing factors in the technicians'
job dissatisfaction.[12] The technicians have no responsibility in planning and
must take orders from a diverse and vague chain of command.

Further accelerating the technician's problem is the fact that he has no
informal group to turn to. Because of the varied background and apparent
hostility, informal group formation seems to be a distinct impossibility. As
Scott notes, "each individual will attempt to define the roles expected of
him. His accuracy in the definitional process can determine his satisfaction
and performance on the job. Management can facilitate this process by
defining task requirements."[13] With so many orders coming from so many
superiors, the expectations placed on the technicians tend to be too much.
Task requirements become vague and with no group norms to adhere to,
the technician becomes tense due to role conflict and lack of status congruency.

It seems quite clear that the number of bosses, the managerial policy, and
the resulting ambiguity is hardly effectual in this situation. Increased communication and enlightened management (unity of command) towards the
technicians could be a solution to increasing job satisfaction and productivity; however, prior to making specific recommendations additional information would be needed.

ADDITIONAL INFORMATION NEEDED

It would be helpful to have more specific information on the formal structure of the Space and Missile Support Branch. Are the five technicians
subject to orders from any one of the ten research engineers as we have
assumed? Or are they assigned to specific engineers? Do the ten engineers
and five technicians report directly to the branch manager?

Are there any informal leaders among the engineers or technicians?

Are the research engineers a highly cohesive group? We know that they
all have similar educational backgrounds but aside from this they differ

considerably with eight being officers and civilians and two being enlisted personnel. We would want to know more about the cohesiveness (or lack thereof) of this group before making any specific recommendations for organizational change.

THE DESK ENGINEERS

Mr. Schultz had become Chief of the Program Management Division three months ago. The objective of this division was to manage the research, development and production of various products. Mr. Schultz was responsible for the supervision and integration of the efforts of six program managers. The program managers had been in the division since its inception three years ago and had been selected on the basis of their experience in R&D, engineering, and management. The responsibility of the program managers had been: (1) the selection of the engineering departments to develop their product, (2) selection of production facilities, product testing, cost control, and (3) general overall authority and responsibility for their projects.

Mr. Johnson, one of the program managers, had learned that one of his projects in the development stage was not performing satisfactorily during testing. He visited the office of Mr. Krane, project engineer, to discuss the seriousness of the difficulties. In parting, it was agreed that Mr. Krane would have the unit modified and retested during the next month, and would inform Mr. Johnson of the design changes necessary at the end of the month. Mr. Johnson informed Mr. Schultz of the difficulties and the approach taken to solve the problems.

Shortly before the end of the month, Mr. Schultz called a meeting which he, together with Mr. Johnson, Mr. Krane, and Mr. White, the Vice-President of Engineering, attended. To begin the meeting, Mr. Schultz briefed everyone concerning the nature of the problem, and the engineering changes he desired to alleviate these problems. Mr. White agreed that they would make the changes Mr. Schultz suggested, and offered other changes to which Mr. Schultz agreed.

Mr. Johnson, taken by surprise, stated that Mr. Krane had been studying this problem for the past month and had conducted tests which had indicated a solution. Mr. Johnson stated that these modifications should be presented at this time.

Mr. Krane produced some hardware and a set of drawings and began to present what he had discovered. He was stopped by Mr.

Schultz who asked to see the hardware he had brought in. Upon examination of the hardware, Mr. Schultz and Mr. White agreed that the changes they had suggested at the beginning of the meeting would be made, and the meeting was adjourned.

Mr. Johnson was irritated by having what he considered inferior engineering decisions made summarily on one of his projects without consideration for his opinions, and discussed the situation with the other program managers. He found that they had had similar experiences with Mr. Schultz and had discussed the situation with him to no avail.

Disgruntled, Mr. Johnson returned to his office to decide what his next action should be.

ANALYSIS 1: *The Desk Engineers*

Mr. Schultz and Mr. White made design analyses and decisions which could more appropriately have been made at lower levels. Had they made the decisions with the full inputs of Mr. Johnson and Mr. Krane, the tension of the situation would have been decreased. Mr. Schultz was probably an autocratic manager, who provided for little or no communications upward before making decisions. He obviously was spending too much time on detailed engineering, a job which even his program managers did not do, and therefore was neglecting the task of integrating the efforts of his program managers.

In the search for primary and secondary issues, two issues appear to be primary. First is the effect of this incident on the communications between Mr. Schultz and the program managers in the future, and second, the role and status of the program managers as perceived by the functional groups with which they interact.

COMMUNICATIONS

Considerable filtering of the type described by Scott[14] will probably now take place in any communications traveling upward from the program managers to Mr. Schultz. In order to keep the chief from interfering in their projects the managers may not keep Schultz informed of problems. Schultz has set up a barrier to communications between himself and his people. The barriers arising from the communication atmosphere as described by Stieglitz[15] are especially evident. Therefore, Mr. Schultz's leadership effectiveness and activities that he is expected to perform in the organization will probably be decreased. This includes his abilities to integrate, communicate, organize, and evaluate.[16]

ROLE AND STATUS

This incident was probably one of many which has reduced the role and status of the program manager. A major purpose of the program manager concept is to plan, coordinate and expedite the integration of the objectives of the program so as to relieve top management from these detailed functions. Instead, Mr. Schultz is increasing his duties and not relying on the inferred authority of his program manager. This action by Mr. Schultz will probably result in reduced effectiveness; program managers will not be perceived as having top management support which is vital to program management because of the peculiar nature of the program managers' role.[17] This is also made quite clear by Johnson, Kast and Rosenzweig who state "the program manager has no line authority to act but depends on other manifestations of authority to attain the objective."[18] Even though the program manager must rely heavily on his expertise and rapport with the individuals involved with the program he must also have the support of top management. In referring to project managers Stewart states "clearly, therefore, he has a special need for intelligent support from higher management."[19] The program manager's approach must be to influence, motivate, persuade, and convince those he deals with. This is particularly true in this incident since the program manager does not have the power of "sanction." If it is known that his convictions, perceptions, and skills are not supported by upper management, but are subject to change at any moment, then his ability to perform is reduced and the total organization is weakened.[20]

Secondary issues are (1) the program managers feel a decrease in status, (2) their role expectation of the entire organization is not met, and (3) their feeling of self actualization is lost. The program managers probably enjoyed a higher status in the past because their decisions were generally influential in matters involving their projects. However, their subsequent decrease in influence has led to a decrease in their status. Their decreased influence also reflects on their subjective status as viewed by others.

The difference in perception of the program manager's role by Mr. Johnson and Mr. Schultz will probably result in role ambiguity. Ambiguity of the role Mr. Johnson is to fulfill will result in what Kahn would term as

". . . low job dissatisfaction, low self-confidence, high sense of futility, and a high score on the tension index."[21]

Mr. Johnson's motivation will decrease with his recent job reduction. This will lead to a deterioration of morale and productivity. Passivity or withdrawal may result as defense mechanisms.

As Mr. Johnson views his position there are probably four alternatives available to him. They are: (1) change Mr. Schultz's concept of management of the organization, (2) quit his job, (3) submit to autocratic management, or (4) filter and/or limit communications between himself and Mr. Schultz to keep him "out of the way."

In selecting the recommended alternative it is probably obvious to Mr. Johnson that the first alternative is really an impossible task. Therefore this can be eliminated as an alternative. None of these alternatives is really satisfactory. Mr. Johnson's temperament will probably not allow him to remain passive and submit to Mr. Schultz's autocratic type management. Continued employment in this situation, subject to constant filtering of information, is probably not satisfactory. Therefore, although quitting his job is distasteful, Mr. Johnson will probably do just that if and when the opportunity presents itself.

How could this situation have been avoided? Tannenbaum and Schmidt gave three factors that a manager should consider in selecting a management style. These factors are (1) forces in the manager, (2) forces in the subordinate, and (3) forces in the situation.[22] Mr. Schultz may have looked into the first factor, and his autocratic position may have reflected his own value system and his own leadership inclinations. However, he did not take into account his subordinates' needs for independence, their readiness to assume responsibility, their interest in the problems, their knowledge of the problems and how to deal with them, and their expectations to share in the decision making. He also did not take into consideration the effectiveness of the group in working together, and the knowledge of the group. Had he looked outside himself when deciding the leadership pattern to use, he certainly would not have selected the strict autocratic approach.

Additional information which needs to be known in this incident are (1) How satisfactory have the efforts of the program managers been in the past? (2) What type of leadership patterns were the program managers accustomed to before Mr. Schultz arrived? (3) What was the technical confidence level of Mr. Schultz and Mr. White? And (4) what type of leadership situation had Mr. Schultz been in before this assignment? If we had more knowledge in this area we would be better able to suggest solutions with respect to Schultz.[23]

ANALYSIS 2: *The Desk Engineers*

Mr. Johnson's problem is not unlike that of many individuals in a program or project management situation. Unfortunately, in this instance, the program manager appears to have little support from superiors. In fact, the superiors appear to be working at cross purposes. The incident appears to exemplify what has been generally recognized by authorities in the field: namely, project management, despite all its many advantages, is highly vulnerable to authority and role problems; and without adequate understanding of the managerial role of the project manager, serious dysfunctional consequences are possible.[24] One of the more obvious difficulties in this incident is the potential for role conflict particularly in Johnson's and Schultz's positions.

ROLE AND ROLE CONFLICT

Proceeding on the assumptions that Mr. Schultz is uncertain of what his functions are as chief, and that he has an engineering background, we might assume that he conceives of his role as that of chief engineer of the division. This would be consistent with the particularistic dimension of role, by which the individual perceives the role he is required to play, and evaluates his performance in light of this perception.[25] Perceiving his role to be that of an engineer, he has interfered in the programs under his subordinates' direction, and considers that all important engineering decisions should be made by him.

Each individual, in his role situation, however, is influenced not only by his own self-perception of the role but also by the role expectations imposed on him. In Schultz's case, role expectations were directed from the formal organization. His supervisors expect him to effectively manage the division and the projects for which it is responsible. Another dimension of role expectation is received from the program managers, who perceive the role of division chief to be one of supervision and support of, but not interference in, their projects. Schultz's internally-perceived role concepts of engineer clashed with the external expectations of him as manager and supervisor. In a sense, this led to role conflict, since Schultz was faced with two roles which were incompatible. This is consistent with Kahn's view that, of the three kinds of role requirements leading to conflict and ambiguity, one of the most critical is that which relates to responsibility for the work of others.[26]

The future implications of the role conflict are several. Actually, they have already begun, as evidenced by Schultz's curt reaction to Johnson when the latter presented the changes developed by Krane and himself. One could readily predict a further breakdown in communication as well, because Johnson's own role ambiguity is heightened by this action. This is likely to be viewed by Johnson as a crisis in understanding his own role and relationships with others. He cannot now turn to Schultz to help clarify the expectations of his role set,[27] because Schultz, by his action, has already threatened and frustrated him. This decision to go along with Schultz created a hostile environment for Johnson and Krane. One behavioral result is likely to be decreased satisfaction.

House suggests that role conflict created by a unity of command problem will likely result in lower individual satisfaction and decreased organizational effectiveness.[28] While it is not clear that unity of command has been violated, it is apparent that Johnson perceived confusion on the part of Schultz as to who should have decision authority for the modifications involved. A clarification of the nature of project authority would help Schultz and Johnson especially.

AUTHORITY AND RESPONSIBILITY

From the information in the incident, the exact formal relationships among Johnson, Schultz and White is not clear. It is safe to assume, though, that project management principles and guidelines should govern this situation. An understanding, therefore, of project management characteristics is imperative.

There is probably no one key to successful project management. If there exists a single characteristic of overriding importance, this would have to be in the area of developing expectations concerning the uniqueness of relationships involved. It follows that managers should come to expect a diffusion of authority and much more emphasis on horizontal rather than vertical relationships. The authority is temporary (for the duration of a project) and cuts across departmental or divisional lines. Therefore, it is essential that the permanent line managers share a common understanding of the project manager's assignments as well as the extent of authority inherent in those assignments. They need to comprehend, also, the importance of the project manager's *influence* in getting the resources and making the decisions necessary to produce the desired results. Their support can bolster this influence while nonsupport can render the project manager virtually impotent.[29] On the other hand, functional managers can overcome many of the role and authority problems by specifying, in advance, the relationships, objectives and accountabilities.[30]

Returning to our incident, we can readily observe that none of the parties involved, except possibly Krane, understood the nature of the structure within which they were operating. Schultz and White apparently proceeded along the premises of a traditional line organization. Supporting evidence for this observation is indicated in the remarks of other program managers. Had Schultz been aware of the widespread misgivings of the program managers, he might have taken steps to clarify their roles and authority. It is perhaps elementary, but nevertheless true, that when individuals possess greater knowledge of the intentions, beliefs and preferences of others, more effective participation is likely to result. Perhaps Schultz was not really interested in getting participation, though, for personal or other reasons.

ADDITIONAL INFORMATION NEEDED

A more complete analysis and solution will require substantial additional information. The following, though incomplete, are indicative of the types of information required and the reasons for their inclusion.

1. What is Johnson's capability as a manager? This would contribute to signing up his potential for assuming authority and responsibility.
2. What was Schultz's understanding of his and Johnson's roles? Perhaps the problem rests in this area.
3. What is the history of program management experiences in this organization? If troublesome, this would explain the apparent difficulties in the incident and would suggest considerable reorientation.
4. What is White's role as V.P. of Engineering? It would seem that his position is critical for support of the program effort.
5. What kind of training, if any, do engineers receive prefatory to relating with others in a program management situation?[31] This would be a vital factor in developing and assessing alternative solutions to the incident and could, in fact, be an underlying problem.

PARISH DILEMMA

Father Luken has been approached numerous times in recent weeks by some concerned parishioners about the current situation in Southeast Asia. He has been asked to address his sermons to the current U.S. involvement in that area. His most recent sermons have remained basically middle of the road, but private conversations, directed at key individuals in the parish, have favored military operations. These private conversations have suggested an almost fanatical belief that current military operations in Southeast Asia are righteous.

U.S. military operations in Southeast Asia have been of deep concern to Father Luken; however, he has, in the past, attempted to avoid committing himself in any way in his weekly sermons. Past sermons have been noncommittal and always humanistic in approach. They stressed the importance of human life and condemned killing for any reason.

During the past six months, Father Luken has been troubled by the financial condition of his parish. Membership in the parish has been on the decline. Many members have been coming to church sporadically and many have fallen behind on their annual pledges. The parish is small, containing approximately one hundred families. It is located near a large military establishment and 80 percent of the parishioners are military or military affiliated personnel. Of this 80 percent, the majority are officer personnel. The remaining 20 percent of the parishioners are local civilians. The parish has, in the past, always had large turnovers in the type of personnel but membership has remained relatively stable.

Recent diocesan newsletters and pamphlets have condemned military policy in Southeast Asia and have suggested that all priests take a firm stand by favoring the denunciation of all military Southeast Asia operations.

ANALYSIS 1: *Parish Dilemma*

There are a number of personal and interpersonal conflicts observable in this incident. One of the areas of prime importance relates to Father Luken's role as a priest, on one hand, and as a private person, on the other. The approach we will follow in this analysis is first to examine the relevant concepts regarding role behavior and theory as they apply to the incident, then look at other secondary but important topics and, finally, identify the investigatory areas which would lead to further analysis and problem solving.

ROLE AND ROLE CONFLICT

It appears that Father Luken is forced to function in a role which may be in conflict with his moral values as a person. The pressure by a certain group, although not overtly verbalized, plus the added feeling for the need of financial security, may be causing Father Luken to conform to certain behavior which violates his personal beliefs. The belief that this conflict does exist is based upon an evaluation of overt behavior and norms of people functioning in this type of profession. It would be a mistake to discount the existence of this type of conflict.

In addition to the above person-role conflict, the inter-role conflict must also be considered. As viewed by Kahn, inter-role conflict occurs when a decision situation involves choosing between divergent expectations of groups in the role-set environment. The choices may be nearly equally desirable from an opportunity cost standpoint, but even that does not diminish the effects of the conflict on the person.[32] It is obvious that a priest or minister is confronted with this type of situation almost continuously. The safest approach, whenever possible, is the middle of the road. However, because of these particular circumstances, it becomes very difficult to place the issue aside. The problem is compounded by the fact that 80 percent of the parishioners happen to associate with a particular group and perhaps the feeling is that Church and State affairs should remain separate. The attempt of Father Luken to appease both groups might not be the answer to this conflict. His personal actions lean toward the congregation's sentiments rather than towards those of the diocesan hierarchy.

This incident also suggests the presence of an avoidance-avoidance conflict. This conflict is experienced by the person who is confronted with a decision to submit to pressures from one source or else lose certain benefits.

Although Father Luken may not want to acquiesce, he is, in a way, forced into submission by the fear of being reassigned or censored in some way.

The diocesan pressure is not overt at this point nor would it be so visible as in other institutions; nevertheless, its presence would be felt by the pastor in the form of financial and other support by the diocese. The possibility of more subtle forms of reprisal by the diocese only serves to compound the problem for Father Luken, because he is unable to articulate to his friends and parishioners the possible consequences of openly sympathizing with their views.

One must try to empathize, too, with Father Luken's frame of reference as a confessor-confidant-counselor to his congregation. It is not uncommon for priests to eschew complete openness for fear of alienating the brethren. Use of instruments such as the Johari Window would very likely show areas of concealment from others of their true feelings on matters such as these.[33] The above observations reflect directly upon the role perceptions of priests such as Father Luken in that open reconciliation of his personal views and role expectations is not possible as it might be for individuals in other professions.[34]

AUTHORITY, POWER, AND INFLUENCE

There is little question but that Father Luken's degree of power in relation to his diocese and bishop will depend in some part on the financial situation of the parish. It may appear cynical to suggest, but it is all too true, that the mystical body thrives on economic sustenance. On the other hand, the existing financial and membership conditions may be attributed to the pronouncements of the diocese. In other words, Father Luken's position might be strengthened by openly supporting parishioner's views despite the loss of economic power, if it can be shown that the diocese is responsible for the parish's financial troubles.

From an organization theory perspective, there is ample opportunity to relate major conceptual areas, such as authority, power and influence. The latter, power and influence, are viewed for our purposes as identical, similar to the French-Raven analysis of social power; i.e., power is treated here as a social force which stimulates compliant behavior in others.[35] Authority will be treated as the formally-designated right to obtain compliance.[36]

The major authority question evolves around its origins in this incident. If the origin can be determined, then accountability relationship would be clarified. Church hierarchy would suggest that ministerial authority ultimately stems from the Deity and intermediately through the bishop. But the people are not in the formal ecclesiastical hierarchy insofar as specific directives are concerned. The relationship between bishop, priest and congregation is similar to that of doctor-patient. It is prescriptive rather than compulsory, because the clergy cannot force compliance nor can it punish personally (except in rare instances of excommunication) for deviations from prescribed behavior. The traditional punitive control has been through reference to the heaven-hell consequences, substituted in the modern church by appeals to individual conscience. The latter makes the accountability to oneself rather than to an established hierarchical body. It also leads to the belief that the Church exists to serve individual spiritual needs rather than vice versa.

By the above rationale, Father Luken should act in service to his congregation rather than to his superiors. This is another way of invoking the acceptance or consent theory of authority, a tempting and very possible application in this situation. The ministerial relationship fits quite neatly into the concept and flow of consent authority.[37] In the Protestant churches, for example, ministers are assigned, for the most part, only upon prior approval of the congregation. This is not the case in the Catholic Church, but even there some type of review process is utilized.[38] The ongoing clergy-parish relationship depends very heavily upon the parish's acceptance of the clergyman's behavior and his pronouncements.

Father Luken, therefore, derives his priestly authority largely through the acceptance of his actions by the congregation rather than through the directives of his bishop. Returning to the medical doctor analogy, it would be interesting to conceptualize the bishop-pastor relationship in a manner similar to the chief medical officer–staff physician relationship in a hospital. While the chief provides support, coordination, and review control over the staff physician's actions, the TV-glamorized directive relationship is probably more fiction than fact. (Not even in the entertainment programs would the chief interfere with the physician-patient relationship!) In all fairness, bishops rarely interfere with the proprietary duties and relationships of pastors, either, so one is then compelled to question why the diocesan officialdom should attempt to control the views of pastors on highly volatile issues such as the Southeast Asia question. The staff physician is entitled to render a medical judgment; why should not the pastor have the right to give a theological judgment, provided it is offered as his own rather than that of the official church? In other words, the top-down flow of authority in this incident is in conflict with the acceptance of "bottom-up" flow. This would certainly account in large measure for the decline in parish membership.

The power-influence question relates very closely to the authority issue. For example, were Father Luken to express his personal views publicly, his influence in diocesan circles would undoubtedly wane. But, at the same time, his influence with parishioners would increase because of the commonality which would develop. The congregation might, therefore, increase financial contributions, restoring fiscal soundness and improving Father Luken's stature in the diocese.

ADDITIONAL INFORMATION NEEDED

A more complete analysis of the power-influence question, as well as others discussed above, requires that additional critical information be obtained. For example, what caused the initial decrease in financial support? Did Father Luken convey the impression, through his humanistic importunities, that he was highly critical of the Southeast Asia policy?

There is a major philosophical question in the eyes of this analyst: was the issue actually a theological one and, therefore, within the competency of the Church to legislate? Could it be that Father Luken is aware of the pitfalls of venturing into volatile political arenas, especially where his theological credibility might be jeopardized? It would be important, also, to know which group, military or civilian, showed the greatest decrease in support. Were there other possible causes of the decline in membership, such as demographic shifts (e.g., age, social-economic background, race, education) or cultural and attitudinal factors which may be reflective of general societal changes?

Finally, what were the actual hierarchical relationships with the diocese and bishop? What was the extent of diocesan authority in pastoral matters? The terminology suggests a Catholic Church situation, but do not some other religions use these expressions? It would make quite a difference to know exactly which religion is involved.

ANALYSIS 2: *Parish Dilemma*

It is assumed that Father Luken personally approves of military operations in Southeast Asia, but does not approve of killing for any reason. This assumption is based on the fact that his private conversations favor military operations but his sermons have always stressed the importance of human life and condemned killing for any reason.

The major causes of the problems facing Father Luken result from role conflicts. One role conflict is closely related to Scott's description of an avoidance-avoidance conflict[39] and Kahn's inter-role conflict.[40] Father Luken is confronted here with a dilemma between two threats. On the one hand, the pamphlets and newsletters from his superiors have said that he should denounce current operations in Southeast Asia. In contrast, his congregation being composed mostly of military personnel want him to speak favorably of such action. As we have seen, this conflict has, so far, gone unresolved. Father Luken has taken a middle-of-the-road policy. The threat comes into view by the fact that if he indeed did what his superiors wanted, many more of the parishioners may leave his parish. On the other hand, if he does not denounce this action in Southeast Asia as indicated by his superiors, Father Luken may have action taken against him by his church superiors.

Another type of conflict, based on our assumptions, would be similar to what Kahn would describe as person-role conflict.[41] Father Luken favors military operation (partially because of role pressures from his parish) but at the same time the killing in Southeast Asia violates his moral values.

Individual perceptions are related to the role conflicts. The military personnel probably perceive the Southeast Asia conflict as one that is necessary to defend our country. On the other hand, the church and Father Luken believe that killing is something that should be condemned, and the importance of human life is foremost. By his humanistic approach in sermons, his parishioners perceive that he is condemning the Southeast Asian conflict. So, little by little, membership in the congregation is decreasing and the parish financial situation is getting worse. Of course, we have assumed that the majority of military personnel in the parish favor the Asian conflict. Certainly it could be said that the members are not hearing what they want to hear from Father Luken. One of the barriers to communications is individual differences. Father Luken certainly does not have the same background training as his congregation. His opinions as to the nature of war may be quite different from military personnel. His members are listening to his sermons with a "selective" ear, in fact so much so that some find no reason to come to his services any longer. Gibb might say that Father Luken is using the persuasion approach to communication.[42] By taking the middle-of-the-road stand, he is trying to influence his members to stay in his church while at the same time trying to satisfy both his own and his church's beliefs. We see that this is not working. Resistance among the members has built up and they are leaving; therefore, his approach has been ineffective in accomplishing the goals of larger church membership and financial security. We could say that Father Luken is regulating the communication flow to suit the purpose of his parish, but the members' distrust is high because of what he is saying; they want to hear only what they want to hear.

ALTERNATIVES FOR THE SOLUTION

Father Luken has a number of different solutions that he could consider to correct this problem of reduced membership and financial troubles. Should he stay "noncommittal" on this issue, as he is doing now? We have already seen that this is solving nothing. It is not only inconsistent with the goals of his church but the killing is incompatible with his value system. In addition, members are still leaving and financially the situation is worsening.

Secondly, Father Luken could agree with his parishioners and use his sermons to speak of the "righteous" war in Southeast Asia. Certainly, this is probably what the majority of the members want to hear, and in fact it may even bring some of them back to his services. However, as mentioned before, this is inconsistent with the goals of the church, and not entirely compatible with his own convictions.

Thirdly, Father Luken could flatly come out and say that he is wholly opposed to the Southeast Asia conflict. This is consistent with his church's views but will probably result in other members leaving the parish.

A fourth solution would be an approach similar to what Gibb's calls the Problem-Solving approach,[43] or a more sophisticated problem-solving approach such as that advocated by Blake, Shepard and Mouton.[44] Using a problem-solving approach Father Luken would have to show openness and trust along with interaction among his members in solving this problem. One could say that this is too much the "ideal" and would not, because of human differences and convictions, bring about the needed solution. However, this may be the only practical or workable solution. Through openness and trust with his members, whether through sermons or committee or individual conferences, Father Luken must present his and his church's views on the subject of war, killing and the Southeast Asia conflict. This is not to say that he will flatly deny the thoughts and feelings of the majority of his church members. Under the above circumstances, it might be found that the two sides are not so far apart in their thinking as they once thought. In essence, each point of view would be aired in its true light with neither point being denied flatly. Father Luken would be providing the openness, trust and interaction that is needed to solve problems of role-conflict.

ADDITIONAL INFORMATION NEEDED

Did these "key" individuals leave the church? How much influence do these "key" individuals have on the entire membership of the congregation? Do the majority of these church members, regardless of being in the military, think the church and Father Luken should agree with the killing in Southeast Asia? What were the views of the 20 percent of the church members who were not affiliated with the military?

FOOTNOTES

[1] James G. March and Herbert A. Simon, *Organizations* (New York: John Wiley and Sons, 1958), p. 49.

[2] Chris Argyris, "Personality and Organization," in D. R. Hampton, C. E. Summer and R. A. Webber, *Organizational Behavior and the Practice of Management* (Glenview, Ill.: Scott, Foresman and Company, 1968), p. 155.

[3] William J. Paul, Jr., Keith B. Robertson, and Frederick Herzberg, "Job Enrichment Pays Off," *Harvard Business Review*, March-April, 1969, pp. 61–78.

[4] Arthur H. Kuriloff, "Management by Integration and Self-Control," in Paul R. Lawrence and John A. Seiler et al., *Organizational Behavior and Administration* (Homewood, Ill.: Richard D. Irwin, Inc., 1965), pp. 792–804. However, recent developments indicate that the Non-Linear Systems program had mixed success. The company abandoned it. See *Wall Street Journal*, December 13, 1971, editorial page.

[5] The term "enrichment," now popularized to the extent that it is an industry "buzz word," is attributed to Herzberg, "Job Enrichment." Even under job enlargement, which simply adds more duties in contrast to enrichment, which heightens responsibility, modest changes can result in greater satisfaction. See Ronald C. Bishop and James W. Hill, "Effects of Job Enlargement and Job Change on Contiguous but Nonmanipulated Jobs as a Function of Workers' Status," *Journal of Applied Psychology* 55, no. 3 (1971): 175–81.

[6] See the United Diesel Corporation Case, in Lawrence, et al., *Organizational Behavior*, pp. 473–81.

[7] Norman George and Thomas J. Von der Embse, "Six Propositions for Managerial Leadership," *Business Horizons* (December, 1971), pp. 33–43.

[8] Robert L. Kahn, "Role Conflict and Ambiguity in Organizations," in S. G. Huneryager and I. L. Heckman, *Human Relations in Management* (Cincinnati: South-Western Publishing Company, 1967), p. 650.

[9] Argyris, "Personality," pp. 146–47.

[10] Kahn, "Role Conflict," p. 650.

[11] William G. Scott, *Organization Theory: A Behavioral Analysis for Management* (Homewood, Ill.: Richard D. Irwin, Inc., 1967), p. 197.

[12] Argyris, "Personality," pp. 146–47.

[13] Scott, *Organization Theory*, p. 196.

[14] *Ibid.*, p. 304.

[15] Harold Stieglitz, "Barriers to Communication," in S. G. Huneryager and I. L. Heckman, *Human Relations in Management* (Cincinnati: South-Western Publishing Co., 1967), p. 563.

[16] Scott, *Organization Theory*, p. 214.

[17] For an excellent discussion of the role of the project manager see John M. Stewart, "Making Project Management Work," in William P. Sexton, ed., *Organizational Theories* (Columbus, Ohio: Charles E. Merrill Publishing Co., 1970), pp. 354–66.

[18]Richard M. Johnson, Fremont E. Kast, and James E. Rosenzweig, *The Theory and Management of Systems* (New York: McGraw-Hill Book Company, 1967), p. 148.

[19]Stewart, "Project Management," p. 356.

[20]*Ibid.,* p. 357.

[21]Kahn, "Role Conflict," p. 642.

[22]Robert Tannenbaum and Warren H. Schmidt, "How to Choose a Leadership Pattern," in D. R. Hampton, C. E. Summer, and R. A. Webber, *Organizational Behavior and the Practice of Management* (Glenview, Ill.: Scott, Foresman and Company, 1968), p. 501.

[23]Daryl G. Mitton, "The Dimensions of Leadership Style," *Management of Personnel Quarterly,* Winter, 1971, pp. 9–12.

[24]Stewart, "Project Management," pp. 354–66.

[25]William G. Scott and Terence R. Mitchell, *Organization Theory: A Structural and Behavioral Analysis* Revised Edition (Homewood, Ill.: Richard D. Irwin, Inc., and The Dorsey Press, 1972), pp. 205–6.

[26]Kahn, "Role Conflict," pp. 650–52.

[27]*Ibid.,* p. 645.

[28]Robert J. House, "Role Conflict and Multiple Authority in Complex Organizations," in Harold Koontz and Cyril O'Donnell, *Management: A Book of Readings* (New York: McGraw-Hill Book Company, 1972), p. 408.

[29]The above treatment of project management is based partly on the following: David I. Cleland, "Understanding Project Authority," *Business Horizons,* Spring, 1967, pp. 63–70; David I. Cleland, "Project Management," in David I. Cleland and William R. King, *Systems, Organizations, Analysis, Management: A Book of Readings* (New York: McGraw-Hill Book Company, 1969), pp. 281–90.

[30]An interesting account of effective implementation of project management is given in Per Jonason, "Project Management: Swedish Style," *Harvard Business Review,* November-December, 1971, pp. 104–9.

[31]See, for example, the TRW Systems, Inc., experience as reported in: "Teamwork Through Conflict," *Business Week,* March 20, 1971, pp. 44–50.

[32]Robert L. Kahn, "Role Conflict and Ambiguity in Organizations," *The Personnel Administrator* 9, no. 2 (March-April, 1964): 8–13.

[33]See J. William Pfeiffer and John E. Jones, *A Handbook of Structured Experiences for Human Relations* (Iowa City, Iowa: University Associates Press, 1969), 1: 66–70.

[34]The religious literature, in recent years, has given major attention to the conflicts and problems described. See, for example, J. H. Simpson, "Reducing Conflicts and Tensions in the Parish Ministry: An Interpersonal Approach," *Journal of Pastoral Care,* June, 1966, p. 81; and Anthony Del Vecchio and William Mahen, *Interact* (Washington, D. C.: National Council of Catholic Men, 1970).

[35]J. R. P. French, Jr. and Bertram Raven, "The Bases of Social Power," in Dorwin Cartwright, ed., *Studies in Social Research* (Ann Arbor, Mich.: Institute for Social Research, 1959), pp. 150–67.

[36]Longenecker defines authority as the capacity to make decisions, based upon formal position. Justin G. Longenecker, *Principles of Management and Organizational Behavior* (Columbus, Ohio: Charles E. Merrill Publishing Co., 1964), pp. 348–49.

[37]Chester I. Barnard, *The Functions of the Executive* (Cambridge: Harvard University Press, 1939), especially chap. 12.

[38]The authors are not acquainted with the process involved for assigning rabbis; they are therefore excluded from the example not from oversight, but due to lack of information.

[39]Scott, *Organization Theory,* p. 79.

[40]Kahn, "Role Conflict," pp. 8–13.

[41] *Ibid.*

[42] Jack R. Gibb, "Communication and Productivity," *Personnel Administration,* January-February, 1964, pp. 8–13.

[43] *Ibid.,* p. 9.

[44] Robert R. Blake, Herbert A. Sheppard, and Jane S. Mouton, *Managing Intergroup Conflict in Industry* (Houston: Gulf Publishing Co., 1964). Even though the model presented by these authors is couched in terms of resolving conflict in an industrial setting, it is believed that many aspects of their problem-solving strategy would be applicable to the conflicts evident in this incident.

GROUP BEHAVIOR AND CONFLICT

Incident	Page
RESEARCH AND DEVELOPMENT SURVEY	110
Jay M. Meiselman	
Analysis 1	111
Analysis 2	114
THE NEW FOREMAN	117
Thomas M. Carlisle	
Analysis 1	118
Analysis 2	120
THE SEPARATED SUPERVISOR	124
Thomas M. Oleksy	
Analysis 1	125
Analysis 2	128

RESEARCH AND DEVELOPMENT SURVEY

The Long Range Planning Group (LRPG) of the Ajax Company's staff had decided that the company should more closely reevaluate its position on research and development for the upcoming fiscal year planning and budgeting cycle. Preliminary studies on their part of the group had indicated that fairly large sums of money had been invested by the company over the past five years in research and development activity, but little in the way of profitable results had materialized. The payoffs that had been realized seemed to come from low risk, product improvement type research as opposed to high risk innovative new product research. The LRPG recognized that the lack of immediate results and the high number of failures in the new product type work was to be expected because of its very nature (i.e., innovative) but felt that if high risk R&D was to be pursued in an area, a correspondingly high rate of return should be demanded by the company. It was with this understanding that LRPG decided to study the total research and development program at Ajax.

The LRPG decided to initiate a survey of all the R & D activities within the company. This survey was to be carried out by sending a questionnaire and evaluation form to each of the company research groups. There were ten research groups with approximately ten scientists in each. Each group was to answer the questions along with the evaluations requested for each of the independent research areas, about two per group.

The questionnaire and evaluation totaled twenty-six pages. The questions asked were such as: "What new product would this research develop?" "What was the potential profitability of the results of the research?" "What kind of risks could be assigned to the research?" "How much was it going to cost?" "How long would it take?" The questionnaires were placed in the company mail system on the tenth of the month with instructions for their completion. The forms were required back by the LRPG on the twenty-fourth of the month.

110

When the ten research group leaders received the questionnaires they were immediately incensed. "Who do those long range plans people think they are?" "What is the purpose of all of these questions?" "How do I know what the payoffs will be?" "How do I know when it will be done; if I knew that I probably would not be doing the work!" "I've been here twenty-five years and all of a sudden those young staff guys are trying to do my job!" These were typical of some of the comments emanating forth from the R&D leaders.

Fourteen days later, the LRPG had received responses from only four of the research leaders. The others had various excuses such as having more important things to do and not understanding the instructions. Those that were returned reflected greatly differing interpretations of the questions, obvious exaggerations as to risk and profitability, and a great deal of ambiguity.

ANALYSIS 1: *Research and Development Survey*

The predominant emphasis in this incident could very well highlight either group behavior or the organizational role of the Long Range Planning Group (LRPG). Similar to a number of other incidents in this text, the problems involved defy a precise topical identification and definition. Nevertheless, and if only for pedagogical purposes, this analysis will focus primarily on group behavior with related but secondary consideration given the role of the LRPG.

Before examining the behavior of the engineering group, some overall comments are forthcoming. The LRPG developed what they considered to be an important issue confronting the organization. It was their decision that the Research and Development activities be studied and evaluations made, based again on their studies. In other words, they unilaterally decided the evaluation was necessary and set about devising a procedure to accomplish it. Consequently, the LRPG planned, by means of a survey, to make a plan, but apparently neglected how to properly secure the information necessary to make their evaluation. It would appear that, instead, an effort should have been made to devise a plan of operation that would gain support from the participants themselves.

Considering the necessary data required for the evaluation, the LRPG should have considered the best communication approach as well as the behavioral aspects of their request and the interpersonal relationships of the research group. The organization status of a unit such as the LRPG is frequently ambiguous, a situation which compounds the problem of interacting with such a group. There are, of course, many unanswered questions in the incident. These will be raised in the context of the discussion.

GROUP AND INTERPERSONAL RELATIONSHIPS

Generally speaking, research scientists are "cosmopolitans" as opposed to "locals," in the terminology first attributed to Gouldner and later applied more extensively by others.[1] This is interpreted to mean that the scientists tend to identify more with the profession than the organization. The values and goals of the scientist might very well be quite distinct from those of the organization. The implications concerning group behavior are several. First, a "cosmopolitan" group will tend to have strong professional ties with groups outside the organization. Interactions will likely be related to their disciplines and tasks, rather than to nonwork activities. There is likely to be little self-initiated interaction with administrators, except on work-related matters. In fact, a general skepticism toward administrators pervades the scientist's culture.[2]

It is not known, of course, whether the present scientific group shares this attitude, but their reaction to the questionnaire indicates that they are highly negative in their feelings toward the LRPG, possibly due more to the perceived status of the LRPG than to merely the tactless imposition shown in requesting completion of a 26-page questionnaire. The latter alone would be sufficient to antagonize most groups, let alone the initiation of such a request by a nebulous staff group far removed from the respondents' situation. True, the R&D groups were probably not engaging in high-payoff, high-risk projects, but it should be management's responsibility rather than that of an advisory staff body such as a planning committee, to inform them of this. While the planning staff's role will be assessed later, it is apparent that whatever the focal role of LRPG as perceived by the scientists there is an obvious discrepancy in the expectations of the two groups.

Lack of participation by the research groups is, of course, an academically obvious shortcoming in the LRPG's approach to their survey. Perhaps it is not so much the participation as such that is important, but rather the development of a working relationship between the two groups through collaboration and consultation. It has been shown, for example, that both the organization and the individual stand to benefit through this mode of interaction.[3]

In order to more fully develop working hypotheses about the groups involved, there are a number of areas where information is needed. What, for example, is the history of LRPG? What have they contributed at this point? To whom does this group report and in what kind of relationship? Advisory? Prescriptive? Organizationally, in what way is the LRPG expected to relate to R&D—in an advisory capacity, an audit role, as a liaison between R&D and top management? This last category of questions leads to another topic evident throughout the incident—communication.

COMMUNICATION

The LRPG used primarily a vertical channel of communication. However, it has been shown that horizontal, interpersonal channels are generally more appropriate in this type of situation.[4] Possibly, coordination of the LRPG could have been enhanced with verbal communications, prior to the questionnaires being sent out to the various research groups, which would have given the justification and their involvement in the program. The LRPG group could have improved its plan by attempting to develop internal social relationships with the group in order to improve the flow of information.

Participation, mentioned earlier, relates particularly to this question of interpersonal channels. This communication approach would especially augment the opportunity for the R&D group to voice their views and contribute to the development and use of the survey. Planning is an activity which is highly suitable for a participative approach. The nature of the planning function is such that it directly affects the future and expectations of others in the organization, and without the endorsement of important groups such as R&D, the objectives involved would be virtually unattainable. With reference to planning, Welsch makes the point that the participative process described above is vital to insuring the quality of the plans themselves.[5]

ROLE BEHAVIOR

Any discussion of role must take into consideration the major concepts associated with roles; e.g., role set, focal person, role stress, conflict, role expectations and the evolution of the role itself. Broadly speaking, role refers to the set of behaviors and patterns of interaction necessary to the performance of a function.[6] The LRPG was obviously expected to proceed in a certain manner in carrying out the planning function. All indications are that this group was responsible for recommending future courses of action to line management. What might not be included in the position description (if such a description exists) is the approach and relationship to other organization units. Obviously, a consultative approach is necessary in this situation, but the LRPG might perceive its interaction with R&D in terms of an audit relationship and thereby pattern its initiatives around the traditional superior-subordinate accountability model.

Concerning role-set, the particular configuration is not certain from the incident, but it is apparent that a group such as this would be highly ambient; i.e., it would have an extensive environmental orientation, interacting with a variety of other organization units. Organ refers to this as a "boundary agent."[7] This situation can readily lead to a problem of role conflict, in which diverse and competing expectations are made of LRPG.

To put it another way, the LRPG is the focal "person" in an intricate web of expectations, of which planning is the central area of responsibility. Other groups are most likely depend upon the LRPG to spearhead the long-range planning function, but in full consultation with the other units. This would suggest that the LRPG should be capable of responding flexibly to a plurality of needs. In this respect, it is not surprising that the R&D group leaders reacted negatively to the questionnaire request.

ANALYSIS 2: *Research and Development Survey*

An analysis of this incident must orient itself to an attempted understanding of what happened in an intergroup, or interdepartmental, context. As we analyze the events of the incident under several conceptually drawn frames of reference it might be well to realize that perhaps the same principles or theories might be as relevant for individual-to-individual, or individual-to-group, situations as for our present group-to-group situation; this appears especially applicable to our considerations of problem-solving behavior, communication and role and status.

PROBLEM-SOLVING BEHAVIOR

In pursuing this analysis we could marshall a multitude of references pertaining to the process that individuals or groups go through in the identification and resolution of problems. We would like to propose that the concept of participative management contains the spirit, intent and identification of process that might have been well applied in the incident.

Scott and Mitchell indicate that participative management ". . . is a state of mind, . . . supported by organizational philosophy, that people do better, are happier, and goals met more effectively, if participants have something to say about matters which affect them directly."[8] They further state: "In its broadest sense participation implements the aims of democratic administration by enhancing the degree of self-determination had by people in organizations. It is a reaction to repressive autocratic leadership."[9] If we were to postulate that the research and development groups may believe that the Long Range Planning Group (LRPG) is attempting to assume itself as a "centralized authority-power center," then the analogy or pattern seems to fit well. Certain actions of the LRPG are salient: not contacting the R & D department to solicit their cooperation and input; defining the "problem" as LRPG saw it and asking R&D to furnish substantial data imput directed toward this perspective of identification. It would indeed appear that the LRPG may have violated at least the spirit of participative management.

COMMUNICATION

From the incident we quote: "The questionnaire and evaluation totaled twenty-six pages. . . . The questionnaires were placed in the company mail system on the tenth of the month with instructions for their completion. The forms were to be returned to the LRPG by the twenty-fourth of the month." A statement by Evan and Black that deals with success factors related to staff proposals is appropriate here: "The task of the line manager or staff specialist who generates a new idea is to communicate the essence of the idea and to demonstrate its utility in light of the goals of the organization. This process invariably involves efforts at education and persuasion as well as elements of bargaining in order to receive a sympathetic hearing and to elicit actions calculated to implement the new idea. Apart from problems of education, bargaining, and persuasion, there is the common problem of establishing the relevance of the new idea for the goals of the particular organization as well as the feasibility of implementing the proposal in question."[10] It may be simply said that in an effort directed toward finding a solution to the problems inherent in this incident, factors of communication might well be significantly involved.

ROLE AND STATUS

We now turn our attention from processes to other factors related to intergroup or interdepartmental relations. With regard to our two groups or departments in the incident, what unique perspectives of role or function, as based upon perceived place in the organization or their professional orientation, may have implications in our analyses? Corwin discussed the factor of specialization in generating organizational conflict: "Specialization has the effect of accentuating differences among employees and delineating group boundaries. It seems reasonable to assume that specialists are more likely than nonspecialists to develop vested interests and monopolistic claims over certain spheres of work, which they are then ready to defend from encroachment."[11] This may give an additional view on the R & D department.

One specific comment on status is appropriate here. Status considerations are closely related to role and function in the organization. If one department in dealing with another in the organization does not honor status differentials, there is cause for friction. A suggestion that status might be involved is given by the comment in the incident from the R&D man: "I've been here twenty-five years and all of a sudden those young staff guys are trying to do my job!"

If we identify the LRPG as representing an "organizational" orientation, and the typical person in R&D as a "professional," we have sufficient basis for understanding how the conflict developed.[12]

ADDITIONAL INFORMATION REQUIRED

To provide for a more accurate identification of the problems in the incident, additional information is needed. Some of the major items of information required are:

1. What is the composition, charter, and formal authority of the LRPG?
2. What measures did the LRPG use to appraise the value of past research?
3. What type of company is it; what function does R&D have in the industry, in the market, for company image, and the like?
4. What have been the past interactions between the LRPG and the R & D department?
5. How similar or different are the backgrounds and experiences of the members of the LRPG and members of the R&D group?

THE NEW FOREMAN

John Adams, a recent college graduate in engineering, had
accepted as his first full time job the position of foreman at a
local auto parts manufacturing division of a national
manufacturing corporation. After a brief two week training
program, he was assigned as a foreman trainee to a production
department. This department included about forty-five production
employees. Adams soon noted that the department was fairly
efficient with the exception of one small group of younger male
employees. This group was made up of six employees and had an
indirect influence over a fringe group of about six more. The
main problem causing the inefficiency was the amount of time the
employees in this group spent off the job in nonwork related
activities.

Correcting this problem would be difficult due to the
Union-Management Labor Contract. In effect, it read that the
employees would not be held responsible for a specified number
of units per day, but were expected to remain on the job except
for reasonable personal delays. No specific times for rest breaks,
rest room, etc., were spelled out. It was up to each employee to
fairly set his own break time. Adams decided to attack the
problem in the following manner. He picked out the worst
offender in the group and noted his time off the job for a twelve
hour period. The time off the job amounted to not quite four
hours. Armed with this data and the fact that the employee had
been verbally warned twice before, Adams issued a written
reprimand to the employee. The employee requested and received
aid from the union steward. As a result, a written grievance was
filed charging Adams with discrimination against the employee
because he was singled out from the others. The next day, at the
start of the shift, the remainder of this employee's peer group,
plus the aforementioned fringe group, all requested aid from the
union steward. They numbered about ten employees in all.

For three more days, these ten employees and the union
steward subjected Adams to mental pressure and harassment in

an effort to have him remove the reprimand from the employee's work record. The reprimand was not removed. Oddly, however, though the production output of the eleven employees directly involved fell drastically, the remainder of the employees in the department continued at about average rate of output. Also, on several occasions, Adams received verbal support and encouragement from these employees.

ANALYSIS 1: *The New Foreman*

Adams, the new supervisor, identified what appeared to him to be a problem —a small group of production employees were not performing on the same level of acceptable efficiency as other members of the department. It can be assumed that the reprimand action which he had taken was an effort to solve this difficulty and improve efficiency. Adams apparently has not, however, achieved this objective. On the contrary, he is now faced with a situation where the output level of the workers in the group has decreased rather than increased. These same employees collectively began by various means to pressure Adams into withdrawing the disciplinary action that he had taken. It then appears, at least at this point, that Adams has not succeeded in solving the problem.

SMALL GROUP

It is apparent that the negative response of the ten production employees represents a combined effort on their part to combat an action which they regard as a threat. As Scott states, "a group tends to resist those changes which are perceived as threatening to its survival."[13] They are then to be regarded as a group with its own distinct characteristics, norms and perceptions.

LEADERSHIP

Adams, in his initial expression of leadership style, chose to be somewhat autocratic. He made no attempt to determine the reasons behind the group's already low output before he began to force his will upon them. Leavitt points out the folly in this approach when he states,

If it is true that people behave on the basis of the perceived world, then changing behavior in a predetermined direction can be made easier by understanding the individual's present perception of the world. For if there is any common human-relations mistake made by industrial superiors in their relations with subordinates, it is the mistake of assuming that the 'real' world is all that counts, that everyone works for the same goals, that the facts speak for themselves.[14]

PERCEPTION

Leavitt also states that

If one's concern as a supervisor . . . is to try to effect some change in the behavior of other people, . . . then it is critical that one seek to understand their perceptions if one is to understand the circumstances under which their behavior might change.[15]

Without such advice Adams would continue to bear the risk of serious error in his attempts to increase the group's efficiency. In fact, the group now regards Adams as a threat and his circumstance is even more difficult. Likert advises on how such a situation should be approached when he states that

Two conditions appear to be necessary for a subordinate to react favorably to his supervisor's attempts to influence his behavior. First, the influence attempts should be ones which he has reacted favorably to in the past—that is, they need to be familiar. Second, the influence attempts, as seen by the subordinate, should be supportive rather than threatening.[16]

Although Adams may not have had the advantage of knowing what occurred in the past, he might well have pondered the supportive idea and devised possible solutions as alternatives to a reprimand.

CONFLICT

These ten employees are faced with a role conflict in which they are confronted with incompatible roles—maintain output or receive a letter of reprimand.[17] (Of course the degree of role conflict experienced by the group would depend on the strength of the union.) Groups tend to control the behavior of their members by applying pressure to insure that each conforms to the norms established for the entire group. But, the organization may also apply different and sometimes opposing pressures on the individual according to its value system. When this occurs, conflict results. In this incident the group members agreed or consented to output restriction despite the possibility of receiving a reprimand.

NEED SATISFACTION

Maslow provided for the response taken by these ten employees when he set forth his preconditions for basic need satisfaction. He held that "... freedom to defend one's self, justice, fairness, honesty, orderliness in the group are examples of such preconditions for basic need satisfaction. Thwarting these freedoms will be reacted to with a threat or emergency response."[18] Had Adams attempted to understand and accommodate the needs of the work group, their reaction to his effort might have been different.

Maslow would probably also define the characteristics and norms of this group as an effort on the part of its individual members to satisfy their needs. Having joined together as a cohesive group they achieved a position of strength. The reprimand not only threatened the existence of all this, but revived their safety need.

ADDITIONAL INFORMATION DESIRED

It would be helpful to know the attitude of top management. Is top management in support of their foremen? Do the foremen have the authority to hire and fire or do these types of decisions rest at higher levels of management? Does top management consider their foremen as managers or workers, or neither?[19]

What are the differences between the ten employees who are restricting output and the other thirty-five who are not? If we knew more about the norms, sentiments and values of these two groups, we could more thoroughly analyze group and intergroup behavior.

It would be desirable to know who issued the two verbal warnings and what the reactions were to them. With this information we could possibly predict the outcome of a written reprimand such as used by Adams. It would be beneficial to know more about the employee who received the written reprimand; if this employee was the informal work group leader, he could perceive the reprimand as a challenge to his status and therefore, react to assure that he would not lose subjective status as granted him by his group members.[20]

ANALYSIS 2: *The New Foreman*

A fundamental issue in this incident is that of group behavior. While there are other salient areas, the concerted reaction of the work group to the new foreman's initiatives is central to explaining the behavior involved and the application of behavioral concepts.

OVERVIEW AND QUESTIONS

In sizing up the situation, there are a few characteristics which are somewhat puzzling from both sociological and managerial standpoints. For example, a department of forty-five workers would most likely have more than one informal group of six workers. If so, what was the nature of these other groupings? Also, the union steward presumably represents all forty-five employees. Yet, he appears to be preoccupied with protecting a group that other workers probably refer to as malcontents. Is the union steward's influence dependent upon satisfying the members of this group even at the expense of others?

Another area of interest is the union contract. Apparently, this union has been able to negotiate significant alterations in the work environment by reducing the structure of break periods, output requirements and individual mobility in general. Do employees also punch time clocks? If not, this would be a logical next target for increasing personal liberties.

Regardless, this flexible work situation shifts much of the responsibility for productivity onto the worker and raises the question as to whether the workers, particularly this small group mentioned in the incident, are really prepared for the consequences. The cultural pressure for minimizing structure typically comes from the younger workers—yet, the young workers in this instance were apparently the ones who abused the system. Why? What kind of orientation did they receive? Could they have been dispersed by management and assimilated into groups of older, more experienced workers who would coach and guide them in learning and adjusting to the work system? These and various other unknowns would require investigation in order to make appropriate recommendations. However, the incident provides an excellent opportunity for examining some of the contemporary behavioral concepts involved.

GROUP BEHAVIOR

This situation is obviously not typical of those we often encounter in the social science literature. The employees here obviously have more freedom and responsibility than most in this industry. The task orientation of managers appears to be lower than the "straw man" often portrayed in automotive-related industries. There is little grist here for either camp of the humanistic a scientific management controversy.[21] Some softening of traditional managerial control orientation is a fait accompli. There is obviously elbowroom for social interaction and individual self-determination. Granted, the work is probably of a routine nature and is not in itself challenging, but the same could be said of the work in the classic Hawthorne studies as well as in numerous other studies in which social conditions were a major concern.[22] What is especially notable in this incident is the reaction of the work group to Adams's approach in identifying the inefficient workers. One could explain this behavior by alluding to the potential threat as needing satisfaction from the new foreman. Yet the apparent satisfactions are likely dysfunctional by comparison with those of other workers. There is another consideration. From a managerial viewpoint, this small group of workers had exploited the situation to the detriment of the company. From the group's standpoint, management was discriminatorily invading their territorial prerogatives, if one perceives it for the moment in the light of recent developments in the sociology of space and possession.[23] Until these phenomena are more fully understood, no amount of factual data will suffice to mollify the group's opposition to the reprimand.

There is yet another facet not frequently considered but nevertheless present. If one accepts Whyte's observations regarding the entry of college-educated foremen into departments previously managed by noncollege foremen, there is a distinct possibility that workers will perceive this as a career-blocking move. Moreover, following Whyte's research, a change in worker-management relationships is likely to follow. One consequence is that the perceived barrier to advancement will lead to greater identity with the group rather than with management or the organization.[24] Whyte refers to this as a shift from vertical to "horizontal integration."[25] In the present situation, it could imply that this group of young workers saw the advancement route closed upon hiring the college graduate. Consequently, their response was predictably to seek out alternate forms of satisfaction which derive from membership in the informal organization. The fringe group, moreover, could be ambivalent on this issue, but at the same time lean toward the group's sentiments as opposed to the organization's. One could argue, as indicated earlier, that this strategy is basically defensive and dysfunctional, but few would deny, since the time of Pareto, Mayo and Barnard, that work group behavior is or even should be logical in the conventional sense. What is important is that, to the members of the group, the new foreman constitutes a threat to their future while the preoccupation with nonwork activities serves as an outlet to reduce and channel frustrations experienced as a result. The foregoing is speculative, of course, but merits consideration in exploring ways of handling this situation.

ORGANIZATIONAL CLIMATE

Another approach to the situation is to examine the organization climate itself—the work system, type of supervision, attitudes, and expectations of management. Because of its pervasive nature, climate as such is difficult to identify. However, the components of climate—management attitudes and policies, personnel practices, work system design and procedures—can be observed and analyzed. There is little information given regarding company policies or working conditions, layout or technology. There is evidence, however, that the managerial philosophy permits alternate structures based upon individual and group discretion. This observation leads again to the behavior of the informal group.

Unlike recent industry situations, such as the General Motors Lordstown affair, there is little in the present climate to suggest rigidity of production goals and methods.[26] Thus, it is obviously not a situation of youth rebelling against stifling working conditions, but more a response to a real or imagined threat to group norms—or else, at the risk of appearing perversely unscholarly, an instance of unwarranted goldbricking by a group of malcontents who have not yet understood and internalized the meaning of work.

There is further evidence to suggest that the climate was considered favorable by most employees. The fact that Adams' action was supported by others in the department indicates that, outside of this small group, the worker-management relationships were somewhat amicable.

LEADERSHIP

Little has been said yet about Adams, his role, and his approach to handling this situation. As a foreman trainee, his credibility and influence are likely not as great as that of more experienced foremen. There is often an unwritten understanding in situations such as this which gives a new foreman immunity from recrimination and criticism by superiors, peers and subordinates. But, in return, during this indeterminate period of grace, the foreman is expected to devote his attention to learning the job and not to make sweeping changes or high-risk decisions. Adams apparently violated this custom when he decided to seek out and reprimand the laggard employees. Perhaps what he did was necessary but his approach was that of a neophyte.

The whole area of alternate approaches to discipline is, of course, a controversial one. Viewpoints range all the way from no negative disciplinary action to classic overkill; e.g., attacking a nest of wasps with a Sherman tank. However, the "hot stove" rule appears to have some advocates among proponents from both sides.[27] Briefly, this "rule" endorses an immediate, impersonal, and uniform response by the supervisor whenever an infraction occurs. In Adam's situation, though, as a new foreman, he would need to first develop expectations by group members, were he to adopt this policy. He would also need to gain prior support from his superiors and from the union for this or any disciplinary action. The union may already be sympathetic toward taking punitive measures with this group. Given time, the grapevine might transmit this sentiment to the offending group, obviating the need for direct supervisory intervention.

THE SEPARATED SUPERVISOR

Mr. Ken Fowler of the Hayson Manufacturing Company was supervisor of fifteen engineers who were located in the company's two buildings in different parts of town. Although the duties, needs, and responsibilities of the engineers in each of the two groups were very similar, Mr. Fowler spent a much greater percentage of his time in that office where his own supervisor, as well as the entire company administration, was located. In this manner, Mr. Fowler felt that he could be more cognizant of company problems and subsequent need for the services of his department. When such a need did arise, Mr. Fowler would personally decide on the course of action required, and then assign the detailed development work to one of his engineers. After this work was completed Mr. Fowler would then present the results to the proper staff personnel.

After working for Mr. Fowler for ten years, Mike Johnson, a respected employee, decided to accept a position in a small family business. Before leaving, however, he met with Ken Fowler to relate what he felt were problems of the department. In this discussion, Mike told Mr. Fowler that the morale of all employees was very poor, especially those not in the administration building office. Further, Mike described how the engineers in one office exhibited extensive inactivity, and conducted personal business all while Fowler was in the other office.

After discussing this surprising information with his own supervisor, Bill Mann, Fowler decided to promote the senior member in each office to a semisupervisory position. These men would coordinate the work activities of other office employees and report directly to Mr. Fowler. All other engineers would report to their respective coordinators, except in matters of salary and vacation which would still be Mr. Fowler's responsibility. Fowler felt that such action would promote communication and also enable him to devote more time to a new product planning committee on which he had just been placed by Bill Mann.

124

Within a week of the announcement of this action, four of the engineers in Fowler's group asked for an immediate transfer.

ANALYSIS 1: *The Separated Supervisor*

In this incident one man, Mr. Fowler, was the supervisor of two physically separated groups of engineers. When he learned that the group which was physically separated from him was experiencing morale problems and misusing their time, he appointed semisupervisors in each of the two departments. Within a week after this appointment four engineers in Fowler's group requested transfers.

The areas for consideration in this discussion are formal organization, professionalism, communication, role conflict-perception, status, and leadership-motivation.

ORGANIZATION

According to Lawrence and Seiler,

> If the interaction pattern imposed by the formal organization keeps these technically interdependent individuals and groups apart rather than bringing them together, consequences of social dissatisfaction, disintegration, conflict, and technical inefficiency will result.[28]

The physical separation between the groups and particularly the separation of the group and its supervisor are significant considerations in establishing the problem background.

In this incident, the orientation of Mr. Fowler toward the organization rather than his engineers probably created the split within the group, resulting in the actual formation of two separate groups within the division. Mr. Fowler's tendency toward directive leadership emphasized the split even more and reduced, or eliminated, the flow of information between Fowler and his engineers.

PROFESSIONALISM

While the scientist/engineer is, above all, an individual person who must be treated as such, there are certain personality traits characteristic of the group. They are intellectually curious and professionally sensitive. They require a creative environment in which they can develop their professional personality. Individuality is essential to their work. This unique combination of curiosity, creativity, individualism, and sensitivity requires special management techniques emphasizing operational freedom.[29]

Roman states, "Generally, the managers in scientific organizations are also scientists who are more alert to technical than to management problems."[30] Even though Fowler may have shared the engineers' perspective when he was at their level, he ignored his previous experience and also failed to manage the situation. Fowler appears to be more involved in solving engineering problems than he is in solving the problems of managing his engineers. His solution of appointing senior engineers to semisupervisory positions was probably arrived at with a minimum of time and trouble on his part.

There is another, more abstract, definition of "professional" which perhaps should be mentioned here. According to Sinnett, "Professionalism starts with the individual in his thoughts and actions . . ."[31] and education is not the sole criterion of professionalism, but rather the professional must be capable of dealing with people in a professional manner. In this incident it is not apparent that Fowler was willing or capable of devoting the time and effort necessary to manage the professional personnel, the engineers.

COMMUNICATION

There is no indication that Fowler had any regular contact with the separated group of engineers. When the problem with Johnson arose, he appointed semisupervisors to manage the situation. The lack of communication channels is illustrated by the fact that Fowler was unaware of Johnson's problem and those of the other engineers. Upon receiving the communication from Johnson, rather than consult with the engineers, he took immediate action to appoint "semisupervisors." A more appropriate approach would have been for Fowler to interact with the engineers to determine if Johnson's assessment was valid before instituting any change.

ROLE CONFLICT—PERCEPTION

Role conflict is quite common in management involving engineering.[32] The supervisor has two sets of principles. He must serve both higher management, emphasizing the business aspects, and his engineers, emphasizing the technical aspects. This difference in philosophy between managers and technical personnel is the source of much conflict.[33] This role conflict led

Fowler to choose the management role over the engineering role. He sought to remove himself from the engineers by establishing the semisupervisory position. Since he essentially ignored the engineers, they had little opportunity to assess what he was doing for them. Studies have shown that there is a correlation between group satisfaction and the ability of the manager to use his upward influence to gain recognition for the group.[34] With no means of perceiving this upward influence, group satisfaction of the engineers was low. Studies also reveal that effective (as rated by upper management) supervisors generally draw favorable comments from their subordinates when relationships are free and open and the supervision is general in nature.[35] Fowler, of course, ignored this contact although his supervision was only of a general nature. Thus, the engineers probably perceived him to be an ineffective manager who had little or no concern for them.

Fowler's perception of his role is also somewhat vague. An individual in an organization seeks to define his place in it by the process of role definition. This definition integrates the individual's personality, self-esteem, career objectives, and his motivation.[36] Fowler appears to be career-oriented in that he uses this situation to establish himself on a firmer basis with his own supervisor. He sought to upgrade his position by establishing closer ties with Mr. Mann while further removing himself from the engineers.

STATUS

The request by the four engineers for transfer shortly after Fowler instituted the semisupervisory position was probably because the engineers perceived a change in their status. Under the original situation the group members had essentially the same status. However, the intermediate position gave more status to the semisupervisors and less status to the others. In the case of technical people the status of an individual is not due entirely to an artificial position but also to the individual's standing within the group. This standing is a function of technical competence and esteem of his colleagues and the scientific community.[37]

LEADERSHIP—MOTIVATION

The engineers who requested transfer were apparently no longer motivated to continue their work. Generally, such motivation is instilled through contact with a leader. Fowler is not demonstrating effective leadership qualities. His actions are particularly in conflict with Stogdill's definition of leadership "... the process (act) of influencing the activities of an organized group in its efforts toward goal setting and goal achievement."[38] By being an absent leader to the engineers, he was not performing his role as a leader. When he announced the semisupervisory positions he also ignored the principles of participative management by not consulting with the engineers to hear them out on their views of the situation.[39]

CONCLUSIONS

In principle, we cannot disagree with Fowler's choice of action since it may well be true that the nature of his job did not allow him time to deal directly with fifteen individuals. However, we can be critical of "how" he made the decision. His lack of consultation with those involved and his choice of men for these semisupervisory positions may well have turned an unmanageable situation into an impossible one.

ADDITIONAL INFORMATION DESIRED

It would be helpful to know more about Mr. Fowler's educational background. If he did not have education and training in engineering and management, it is quite possible that he did not have a full appreciation of the responsibilities for managing professional personnel.

We would also want to know more about the communication system that prevailed prior to this incident. For example, how much feedback was built into the system? Did the engineers know why and how their work tasks fitted into the overall goals of the organization?

ANALYSIS 2: *The Separated Supervisor*

This incident raises several important but unresolved issues. One of these concerns the location of a manager in relation to subordinates. The physical proximity of a manager to the unit supervised will affect relationships, communication and identification patterns of both managers and operatives. For example, the manager whose office is located in an administrative building but whose unit is in another building will most likely identify with those with whom he/she interacts most frequently—presumably, other managers. It is a not-so-subtle managerial strategy to effect loyalty, interaction and, frequently, surveillance through spatial arrangements. In universities, for instance, it is a matter of continued debate whether to locate deans and chairmen together or disperse them with the units they administer.

There are several advantages and corresponding disadvantages associated with each alternative. Discussion of their respective merits is beyond the present scope, but the basic rationale suggests that locations will be determined in accordance with the desired role of the manager or administrator.

A second important consideration is the behavior of the group or groups supervised. How, in other words, will they respond, given a set of conditions in which they are physically separated from their titular leader? Miller, for example, would identify certain coordinative problems with the geographical dispersion of organization units under a common head. Thus, the groups might become autonomous, differentiated to the point that the leader is coordinating "aggregates" rather than cohesive units.[40] The manager, in this case, faces the alternatives of either reducing the geographical distance, decentralizing authority or strengthening the intergroup bonds through communication and/or group dynamics processes.

GROUP BEHAVIOR

In order to understand why the engineers reacted so badly to the action taken by Fowler to remedy the situation, we should first examine the work situation as it was before the change. Fowler did not allow his men to participate in the decision-making process. He alone had access to the information concerning the needs of his department, and he alone decided on the work to be done. The engineers were involved only to the extent of developing the details of Fowler's work assignments. When their work was completed, he presented the results to the staff personnel himself. No apparent effort was made to involve the engineers in their work, neither in the planning stage nor in the presentation stage. Increased participation in these levels would have led to improved morale in the department.

Perhaps the activities of the "separated" engineers came as a surprise to Fowler, but in the light of sociological theory, the situation should probably have been expected. Productivity information is not given, except that the group in question engaged heavily in nonwork activities. Regardless, one could predict that perceived status would be lower in the separated group than in the headquarters group. This would likely produce a status anxiety among the group members inasmuch as their perceived status is not consistent with their expected status as determined by their qualifications and role in the organization.[41] Under these circumstances, the morale problem among the separated engineers would be quite predictable.

Consistent with the above observation is the reaction of the engineers to the new supervisory arrangement. The actions by Fowler served to create an additional organization level and further removed the engineers from interaction with himself. The hierarchical problem in itself is sufficient to reduce the perceived status of the engineers, to say nothing of the communication barriers which are created by interposing another supervisory position.

Some of the newer models of organization which apply especially to professional personnel stress the importance of role congruity in organizational support of individual activities. This role congruity may be viewed in terms of a perceptual agreement between the professional's autonomous role and the organization's attempts to "naturalize" the professional to become an organization citizen. Wade has suggested what is called a "neoteric" model, with reference to an organization which is composed largely of professionals who identify more with specialized disciplines than with the organization.[42] While this model might apply more to university professors whose work can be performed autonomously,[43] it is possible that engineers and scientists also share similar work patterns within business organizations. In other words, the engineers are quite likely identified with their professional groups to a greater extent than with the large organization. This would suggest that management's role should be more supportive in the sense of providing the kinds of conditions which augment rather than hamper individual professional development.[44] There is the possibility— not known from the information given—that the engineers in question are what Barnes refers to as "socials" or "organizationals" rather than professionals, but regardless Fowler's managerial behavior is such that even those interpersonal relationships which would characterize the "socials" is not particularly encouraged.[45] Until the important status problems are resolved, it is likely that the engineers will experience frustration in their work relationships and the level of interaction will tend toward nonwork activities or toward complete disintegration should the role and status matters not be clarified in the near future.

MOTIVATION

Fowler failed in several ways to motivate the engineers in their work. The work itself was not satisfying because it consisted primarily of carrying out the details of Fowler's instructions. The men were given no responsibility for making the decisions. Recognition and sense of achievement accrued tend to be absent in the motivation system. However, the work did not contain sufficient dissatisfiers to cause the men to leave the department. Fowler's habit of being away from the office much of the time made it possible for the workers to pursue their social needs through informal interaction. This loose supervision promoted a relatively open work situation but at the expense of productive effort.

There are several models of motivation which might be applied to this situation. One of the most popular is the Maslow model which is explained in different sources given in these analyses. A related concept is the Herzberg motivation-hygiene model, also referenced in these pages. The Herzberg model is, in fact, one that is especially applicable to engineers in that this profession comprised a large segment of Herzberg's research sample. Among engineers, for example, the dual factor motivation-hygiene thesis was highly relevant.[46] In other words, factors such as responsibility and interesting work are of high importance to engineers. Fowler's approach did not encourage a positive interest in the work itself, nor did it foster commitment and responsibility. What his approach did from the standpoint of dual-factor theory was to fixate the behavior of the group at a hygiene level.

Clark's model is especially relevant here because of its dynamic quality.[47] Clark extends the Maslow hierarchy to include conditions associated with shifts from one level to another. Applying this model to the present situation, there were several conditions present in the work group's environment prior to the change:

a. Low perceived contribution opportunity
b. accommodative leadership
c. high status congruence
d. high interaction opportunity
e. high employment security

Given these conditions one would find members' safety and membership needs relatively satisfied, but their self-esteem and status-prestige needs somewhat frustrated. Productivity meets minimum requirements and turnover-absenteeism is average.

When Fowler promoted the two senior men to semisupervisory positions, however, the conditions in the work group's situation changed for the worse. Not enough information is provided in the incident to enable specifying the exact change that took place, but we can safely infer a shift to the left on Clark's model, which implies low status congruence and frustration of interaction opportunity. The new supervisors probably exhibited more production-centered leadership and close supervision, which severely frustrated employees' status-prestige and interaction needs. There is nothing in the incident to suggest that Fowler either anticipated these results or took measures to avoid them, which would indicate a lack of empathy on his part.

Edgar Schein described the above in terms of a psychological contract entered into by employees and the organization.[48] The key feature of this contract is the set of expectations the employees have about the organization and the set of expectations the organization has about its employees.

Past experience on the job and interaction between the engineers and the organization's management had developed among the engineers the expectation of fairly loose supervision, implying trust consistent with their esteem needs. But when Fowler promoted the two men to supervisor, the employees perceived this action as a change inconsistent with their psychological contract. Once the company violated its obligation to provide the engineers the benefits negotiated by past experience, there was a breakdown of shared expectations and instability set in. Here again, there is nothing in the incident to suggest that Fowler either anticipated the engineers' reaction or attempted to influence them towards a more favorable attitude to the change. For example, he merely announced the change, allowing the engineers to interpret it any way they were inclined. A manager with a keen faculty for sensitivity, unlike Fowler, would not have been surprised when several engineers requested immediate transfers from his department. This raises the question of leadership and supervision, topics which have not yet been elaborated upon, but which are observably significant.

LEADERSHIP AND SUPERVISION

One of the outstanding features of this incident is the separation of Mr. Ken Fowler from the group of fifteen engineers he supervises. This separation appears to be caused by two factors. First, the engineers are located in two different buildings in different parts of town. Second, Fowler habitually spends a disproportionate amount of time at the company's administration building because of his desire to keep in closer touch with company needs for engineering services. One cannot argue with the former because it is impossible to be in two different places at the same time, but the latter raises a serious question. Is Fowler really interested in being informed of company problems in order to enhance his department's service to the company, or merely to further his personal interests and career goals? The fact that he wants to devote more time to a new product planning committee when problems within his department require attention supports the view that Fowler's main concern is not with representing his constituency.

If, indeed, his primary interest is not supervisory, three important implications should be considered. First, research findings indicate that supervisors who regard supervision as the most important part of their work and spend most of their time on it tend to elicit higher productivity than those who do not.[49] There is no information in this incident concerning a lack of productivity except for Mike Johnson's description of extensive inactivity and conduct of personal business during Fowler's absence. These nonproductive activities would not have been so prevalent had supervision been more effective. Second, his lack of interest in supervising his department may have been perceived by his men and interpreted as an indication that Fowler was "pulling for himself,"[50] which could have negative effects on employee morale. Third, Fowler's lack of interest in supervision resulted in his taking inappropriate action to remedy the problem that Mike Johnson had brought to his attention. He was unwilling to devote more of his time and effort to supervising, so the alternative of increasing direct supervision of his men was not adopted. Instead, he chose to promote the senior man in each office to a semisupervisory position reporting directly to him. In this way, the engineers would be more closely supervised by someone else, and Fowler could still spend his time on the other matters that interested him. These three considerations raise serious questions with regard to Fowler's leadership abilities.

ADDITIONAL INFORMATION NEEDED

The body of this analysis contains several suggestions concerning information missing in the incident which would add to our understanding of the underlying causes. One additional point needs to be mentioned here. What were the forces in the engineering group? Did the engineers discuss among themselves the change in supervision and reach a group decision to protest it by requesting transfers from the department? Bennett has shown that such a decision process, when accompanied by both a decision regarding a future action and a high degree of actual or perceived consensus regarding intention to act, leads to high probability that the act will be executed.[51] It seems likely that such a decision process may have occurred since (as suggested earlier) the change in supervision probably lowered the group interaction thereby depriving the members of a source of satisfaction.

FOOTNOTES

[1]Alvin W. Gouldner, "Cosmopolitans and Locals," *Administrative Science Quarterly* 2, no. 3 (December, 1957): 282–92.

[2]Wendell French, *The Personnel Management Process* (Boston: Houghton Mifflin Company, 1970), pp. 525–27.

[3]John D. Avam, Edward S. Esbeck and Cyril P. Morgan, "Relation of Collaborative Interpersonal Relationships to Individual Satisfaction and Organizational Performance," *Administrative Science Quarterly*, September, 1971, pp. 289–97.

[4]Richard L. Simpson, "Vertical and Horizontal Communication in Formal Organizations," in Donald E. Porter, Philip B. Applewhite and Michael J. Misshauk, *Studies in Organizational Behavior and Management* (Scranton, Pa: Intext Educational Publishers, 1971), pp. 520–27.

[5]Glenn A. Welsch, "Some Behavioral Implications on Profit Planning and Control," *Management Adviser,* July, 1971, pp. 21–27.

[6]The author's definition of role. Related definitions and discussion of role concepts appear in Daniel Katz and Robert L. Kahn, *The Social Psychology of Organizations* (New York: John Wiley and Sons, Inc., 1966), pp. 47–49; and Joseph A. Litterer, *The Analysis of Organizations* (New York: John Wiley and Sons, Inc., 1965), pp. 55–56.

[7]Dennis W. Organ, "Linking Pins Between Organizations and Environment," *Business Horizons,* December, 1971, pp. 73–80.

[8]William G. Scott and Terence R. Mitchell, *Organization Theory: A Structural and Behavioral Analysis,* Revised Edition (Homewood, Ill: Richard D. Irwin, Inc., and The Dorsey Press, 1972), p. 274.

[9]*Ibid.,* p. 275.

[10]William M. Evan and Guy Black, "Innovation in Business Organizations: Some Factors Associated with Success or Failure of Staff Proposals," *Journal of Business,* October, 1967, p. 520.

[11]Ronald G. Corwin, "Patterns of Organizational Conflict," *Administrative Science Quarterly,* December, 1969, p. 508.

[12]For a comprehensive coverage of how conflict develops and the accommodations that are necessary in organizations which employ large numbers of professionals, see Fremont E. Kast and James E. Rosenzweig, *Organization and Management: A Systems Approach* (New York: McGraw-Hill Book Co., Inc., 1970), chap. 17.

[13]William G. Scott, *Organization Theory: A Behavioral Analysis for Management* (Homewood, Ill.: Richard D. Irwin, Inc., 1967), p. 96.

[14]Harold J. Leavitt, *Managerial Psychology* 2d ed. (Chicago and London: The University of Chicago Press, 1964), pp. 30–31.

[15]*Ibid.,* p. 35.

[16]Renis Likert, "Motivation and Increased Productivity," in S. G. Huneryager and I. L. Heckman, *Human Relations in Management* (Cincinnati: South-Western Publishing Co., 1967), p. 373.

[17]Robert L. Kahn, "Role Conflict and Ambiguity in Organizations," *The Personnel Administrator,* March-April, 1964, pp. 8–13.

[18]A. H. Maslow, "A Theory of Human Motivations: the Basic Needs," in D. R. Hampton, C. E. Summer and R. A. Webber, *Organizational Behavior and the Practice of Management* (Glenview, Ill.: Scott, Foresman and Company, 1968), pp. 34–35.

[19]L. A. Dale, "The Foreman as Manager," *Personnel,* July-August, 1971, pp. 61–64.

[20]Scott and Mitchell, *Organization Theory,* pp. 196–97.

[21]The argument is debated in the following: Chris Argyris, "A Brief Description of Laboratory Training," George Odiorne, "The Trouble with Sensitivity Training," and Chris Argyris, "In Defense of Laboratory Education," all in Ernest Dale, *Readings in Management: Landmarks and New Frontiers* (New York: McGraw-Hill Book Co., 1965), pp. 282–90.

[22]Two excerpts on the Hawthorne Studies appear in the following: Paul R. Lawrence and John A. Seiler, et al., *Organizational Behavior and Administration* (Homewood, Ill.: Richard D. Irwin, Inc., 1965), pp. 165–83.

[23]Robert Ardrey, *The Territorial Imperative* (New York: Athenium Press, 1966). Also, see E. T. Hall, *The Hidden Dimension* (Garden City, N.Y.: Doubleday and Company, 1966).

[24]William F. Whyte, *Organizational Behavior: Theory and Application* (Homewood, Ill.: Richard D. Irwin, Inc., 1969), pp. 446–47.

[25]*Ibid.,* p. 446.

[26]See Barbara Garson, "Luddites in Lordstown," *Harper's Magazine,* June, 1972, pp. 68–73; also, "The G.M. Efficiency Move That Backfired," *Business Week,* March 25, 1972, pp. 46–48.

[27]William F. Dowling, Jr. and Leonard R. Sayles, *How Managers Motivate: The Imperatives of Supervision* (New York: McGraw-Hill Book Co., 1971), pp. 135–37.

[28]Lawrence and Seiler, *Organizational Behavior,* p. 569.

[29]Daniel D. Roman, *Research and Development Management: The Economics and Administration of Technology* (New York: Appleton-Century-Crofts, 1968), pp. 268–301.

[30]*Ibid.,* p. 287.

[31]Chester M. Sinnett, "What is Professionalism?" *Research/Development,* January, 1972, p. 17.

[32]Louis B. Barnes, "Engineering Supervisors in the Middle," in Lawrence and Seiler, *Organizational Behavior,* pp. 439–42.

[33]Robert D. Best, "The Scientific Mind vs. the Management Mind," *Industrial Research,* October, 1963, pp. 50–52.

[34]D. C. Pelz, "Influence: A Key to Effective Leadership in the First Line Supervisor," *Personnel,* November, 1952, pp. 209–17.

[35]Floyd C. Mann and James K. Dent, "The Supervisor: Member of Two Organizational Families," *Harvard Business Review,* November-December, 1954, pp. 103–12.

[36]Daniel J. Levinson, "Role, Personality, and Social Structure in the Organizational Setting," *Journal of Abnormal and Social Psychology,* March, 1959, p. 172.

[37]Roman, *Research and Development.*

[38]Ralph M. Stogdill, "Leadership Membership and Organization," *Psychological Bulletin,* January, 1950, p. 4.

[39]Chris Argyris, "Organizational Leadership and Participative Management," *Journal of Business,* January, 1955, pp. 1–8.

[40]Eric J. Miller, "Technology, Territory, and Time," *Human Relations* 12, no. 3 (1959): 243–72.

[41]See Harry Levinson, *Executive Stress* (New York: Harper and Row Publishers, 1970), especially chap. 5, pp. 43–55.

[42]L. L. Wade, "Professionals in Organizations: A Neoteric Model," *Human Organization,* Spring/Summer, 1967, pp. 40–46.

[43]See, for example, Louis J. Shuster, "Mobility Among Business Faculty," *Academy of Management Journal,* September, 1970, pp. 325–35.

[44]Davis gives a concise description of the supportive theory and contrasts it with others in his widely-read text. See Keith Davis, *Human Relations at Work: The Dynamic of Organizational Behavior* (New York: McGraw-Hill Book Company, 1967), pp. 5–6 and chap. 28.

[45]Barnes develops these "types" in considerable detail. See Louis B. Barnes, *Organizational Systems and Engineering Groups: A Comparative Study of Two Technical Groups in Industry* (Boston: Division of Research, Harvard Business School, Harvard University, 1960); also, Thomas E. Miller, "Building Teamwork in Organization," *Personnel Administration,* September-October, 1971, pp. 38–45.

[46]Frederick Herzberg, *Work and the Nature of Man* (Cleveland: World Publishing Co., 1966), pp. 92–98.

[47]James V. Clark, "Motivation in Work Groups: A Tentative View," *Human Organization* 19, no. 4 (Winter, 1960–61): 199–208.

[48]Edgar H. Schein, *Organizational Psychology* (Englewood Cliffs, N.J.: Prentice-Hall, Inc., 1965), p. 44.

[49]Several earlier studies yield this finding. Among these are Daniel Katz, et al., *Productivity, Supervision and Morale in an Office Situation* (Ann Arbor, Mich.: University of Michigan Press, 1950), and Daniel Katz, et al., *Productivity, Supervision and Morale Among Railroad Workers* (Ann Arbor, Mich.: University of Michigan Press, 1951).

[50]Floyd C. Mann and James K. Dent, "Supervisory Identification with Management and/or Workers," in Lawrence and Seiler, *Organizational Behavior,* pp. 431–33.

[51]Edith B. Bennett, "Discussion, Decision, Commitment and Consensus in Group Decision," *Human Relations* 8, no. 3 (1955): 47.

AUTHORITY

Incident	Page

THE TASTY BAKERY   138
Gail Rouch
Analysis 1   138
Analysis 2

THE RADIO COMMUNICATIONS GROUP   144
Haskell R. Scheimberg
Analysis 1   145
Analysis 2   147

THE NITROUS-OXIDE INCIDENT   151
Peter Benham
Analysis 1   151
Analysis 2   153

THE TASTY BAKERY

The Tasty Bakery employs two waitresses, Jane and Helen, on the 5:00 a.m. to 2:00 p.m. shift. These two waitresses handle the entire restaurant operation during these hours. This includes taking orders, cooking, serving, operating the cash register, and clearing tables. They also help with the baking as well as serving the bakery customers.

Most of the customers are men working on construction of an interstate bypass nearby. The same men patronize the bakery every day for breakfast, lunch, and coffee breaks.

Edith, the owner's wife, is generally in the store while Jane and Helen are working. She has no specific duties. She actually does little work. She usually "supervises" the activities of the employees.

One morning Jane noticed that Edith was removing tips from tables before they had had a chance to clear the tables. Because tips accounted for a substantial part of their take-home pay, Jane and Helen were naturally upset. They approached Homer, the owner, with their problem. He was sympathetic but said there was little he could do except suggest that they collect their tips as quickly as possible.

They tried to do this, but were unsuccessful. Edith continued to collect their tips. Rather than approach Homer again, Jane and Helen decided to handle it themselves. As the customers (the regular ones) paid their bills that day, the girls explained the situation and suggested that if the customers would like to leave a tip they should hand it to one of the two of them personally.

ANALYSIS 1: *The Tasty Bakery*

An initial review of this incident leads one to describe Edith's behavior as blatantly unethical. She appears to be stealing tips from employees. However, before prematurely condemning Edith, it is necessary to examine the underlying behavioral factors. For example, perhaps Edith is entitled to some share of the tips because of her effort in serving customers. Or maybe the policy on tips was never clearly defined. It could be, also, that Edith wanted to expedite the clearing of the tables and consequently removed the tips in order to prepare the tables for other customers. The incident does not indicate that Edith kept all of the tips; it is left to the reader to assume that she did. Nor is the base pay mentioned. Perhaps this was adequate, from Edith's standpoint, to warrant collecting the tips for the "house." So much, though, for speculation on the rationale for Edith's behavior. The fact is that she violated a long-standing norm among waitresses (and proprietors) in the restaurant industry; namely, that tips, or at least some proportion thereof, are the inviolable property of the waitresses or waiters.

There are various behavioral implications in the incident which broach several topical areas such as perception, leadership, communication and group behavior. But one area that especially predominates is that of authority. We have already discussed the ethical implications of the incident. In relation to this is the issue of rights—involving both the tips and the decision-making prerogatives of Homer, the restaurant-bakery owner.

AUTHORITY, RESPONSIBILITY AND ACCOUNTABILITY

The authority question is perhaps related more to management theory than to organizational behavior. Nevertheless, it is virtually impossible to make the separation in practice because of the behavioral ramifications of management practices. In classical management terms, Homer possesses authority to enact and enforce the policy on tips. But, in modern organization concepts, authority alone is not sufficient to effectively conduct the business at hand. Homer personifies the Etzioni model of headship, as contrasted with formal and informal leadership.[1] That is, Homer appears to have neither formal nor informal power, at least in relation to his wife who is apparently second-in-command formally and first-in-command informally.

It is not unusual to find problems of this nature appearing in small, family-operated businesses.[2] But, usually the authority matters are resolved (a) by one of the combatants leaving, (b) through informal agreement or compromise, or (c) by edict. Alternative (c) is probably impossible as far as this incident is concerned, unless the positions of Homer and Edith are reversed, placing Edith in the top management position. Alternative (a) is possible but not probable, unless combined with alternative (b), informal discussion and compromise. In other words, the probability of Homer or Edith leaving the business would depend largely upon mutual arrangements which can be made through meaningfully discussing the problem.

The authority problem is complicated by the fact of Edith's position as supervisor. She apparently assumes that it is within her rights to determine how the tip money should be distributed. Jane and Helen, on the other hand, assume that the tips are their property, in the form of compensation. However, the waitresses evidently did not confront Edith and, therefore, bypassed the so-called normal hierarchy. Even if Homer had taken the necessary corrective action with Edith, the waitresses would be saddled with a situation of working with Edith and would probably find her more contemptuous than before. On the other hand, it is possible that the practice of asking customers for handing them the tips could alienate the clientele and adversely affect the overall business—and future tips. Therefore, Homer's suggestion is self-defeating.

One cannot overlook the question of competency in this incident. The ineptitude of both Homer and Edith is rather obvious. Lane Tracy, in an interesting sequel on the Peter Principle, refers to the use of what he calls "parahierarchies" and "horizontal hierarchies" to maintain organizational vitality while preventing the Peter Principle from reaching its logical conclusion; i.e., all positions in an organization hierarchy being staffed by incompetents.[3] There is little in either of the above sources that would apply directly to a very small enterprise, since the Peter phenomenon appears to afflict larger, bureaucratic organizations. Nonetheless, the parahierarchy idea is intriguing in the light of this situation. Briefly, the parahierarchy concept refers to those parallel channels which supplement and complement the command hierarchy. It consists primarily of workers whose upward mobility is blocked by reason of their educational background, the type of work, or some other factor—perhaps even, as Tracy suggests, sex and racial bias. Thus, nurses in a hospital, blue-collar workers in an industry, secretaries in an office, or waitresses in a restaurant could fall into this category of people who are highly competent and cannot move upward easily.[4] Retrogressing further, it has been suggested facetiously that the janitors and the secretaries run a university.[5] Whatever its merits, this observation at least intuitively recognizes the nature of the distinct academic and nonacademic hierarchies in a university and the impossibility of cross-over between them.

The immobile employees in this incident are Jane and Helen. Most likely, the business is able to survive because of their capabilities. It is apparent that Edith contributes little and that Homer's primary involvement is his financial investment in the firm. The bakers and cooks are not mentioned, but it is assumed that they are reasonably capable employees. If the above speculations are accurate, it would appear that Edith should either reverse roles with one of the waitresses or else remove herself completely from the business.

There is a third alternative, of course, and that is to train Edith in the supervisory role. But, from the information given, it is difficult to be optimistic over this choice, because improvement through training of any sort depends largely on the individual's desire to grow and to become more effective.

ANALYSIS 2: *The Tasty Bakery*

There are five areas relevant for an analysis of this incident. The areas are perception, communication, authority, leadership and small groups.

PERCEPTION

The perceptions of the two waitresses most likely differ rather drastically from that of Edith or Homer. Perhaps Homer has failed to change (or even try to change) Edith's behavior because he does not understand her perception of the situation and those involved. Edith's perception of the tips includes the belief that she has a right to share in them. As Leavitt said, "the world as it's perceived is the world that is behaviorally important."[6] However, there was no indication in the incident that either Homer or the waitresses tried to understand the way Edith may be looking at the situation. Of course, it would be helpful to have additional information on the various relationships that exist between and among these four people. Such information might enable one to make more definite statements about the perceptions, and how well these perceptions are understood and accepted by the others.

COMMUNICATION

There seems to have been a breakdown in the communication process in the bakery. Stieglitz defines communication as "the interchange of information and ideas among all individuals in the enterprise."[7] This interchange is not taking place. Edith was not included in any of the communications about the situation. Additionally, Jane and Helen decided, after their initial communication with Homer, not to participate in an interchange with him.

Without more detailed information about the bakery, it is impossible to state definitely the cause(s) of the breakdown. However, it is possible to set forth some likely causes from those discussed by Scott.[8] One cause may be distortion which is a problem of semantics in which the sender(s) and receiver(s) are not precisely transferring their ideas to the other. Filtering in which there is conscious manipulation in the upward flow may also be present. In this incident, the filtering would be done by Jane and Helen in the communication to Homer. Homer may be experiencing a communication overload in which there are more communications coming into him than he can effectively handle. We would need more information before this could be established as a cause. A fourth cause could be one of timing. Perhaps Jane and Helen chose a poor time to approach Homer with their problem, thus causing the breakdown. Lack of acceptance by Homer of the communication from Jane and Helen could be another cause.

Stieglitz also suggests a list of causes, of which some are appropriate to this analysis.[9] Individual differences can cause breakdowns in communication because people assign different meaning to words and actions and because interests among people vary. Homer may not have taken the meaning of the communication to be as serious as Jane and Helen meant it. He may not have been interested in how much the girls made from tips. The top man in the organization (Homer) himself can be a barrier to communication. Homer does not seem to be willing to communicate because perhaps he fails to understand the need for communication. Homer may be afraid of exposing himself to criticism because he does not seem able to influence his wife.

AUTHORITY AND LEADERSHIP

Authority and leadership form another area for analysis. According to Presthus, authority is a crucial element in overcoming individual goals in favor of organizational goals.[10] He goes on to define authority as the "capacity to evoke compliance in others."[11] Homer does not seem willing or able to do this with the three people involved.

Is Homer's authority (if indeed he has any) legitimate? Presthus makes the statement that "authority seems to grow out of a dynamic, reciprocal relationship between the leader and the led, in which the values, perceptions, and the skills of followers play a critical role in defining and legitimating the authority of organizational leaders."[12] From the information that is given in the incident, this dynamic relationship does not seem to exist at the Bakery. It appears likely that Homer has little authority at his own bakery.

Is Homer a leader? Homer did not provide for much assistance to Jane and Helen when they needed to choose a way to resolve the situation. Homer does not seem to exhibit any particular leadership pattern. Perhaps he purposely did not offer a solution because he wants them to arrive at a choice on their own. Still Homer is making a mistake because if he wishes to adopt this type of leadership pattern he should join the two waitresses in arriving at the solution.

SMALL GROUPS

There is at least one dyadic group (Jane and Helen) operating in this incident, and there may be another composed of Homer and Edith. Without additional information it is impossible to state any other informal relationships that may exist within the bakery. This incident does, however, illustrate the strength that a small group may possess. Jane and Helen have formed an influential group that is able to resolve the situation without following formal lines of authority. They are able to correct the situation by gaining the cooperation of another group (that is, the customers).

THE RADIO COMMUNICATIONS GROUP

A2C Alvin Jones was assigned to a thirty-man group of highly trained Air Force enlisted personnel involved in monitoring foreign radio communications at a small base in remote Eastern Turkey. With the exception of Jones, every member of the group was an NCO. Jones was well liked by the members of the group and respected as an expert, not only in his assigned specialty, that of a Russian linguist, but for his detailed knowledge of operating procedures. Members of the group frequently asked Jones for his advice, both on matters pertaining to the job as well as on personal matters, much to the chagrin of Sergeant Otis, the group's supervisor. Sergeant Otis often commented to members of the group that Jones, who was awaiting reassignment to officer training school, was "playing officer" or "passing out bad advice."

When the group was assigned to the midnight shift, it was Sergeant Otis's policy to allow small groups of men to have the night off when he felt that there was not enough work to keep them busy. It was the custom of the men to go to the NCO lounge and have a few beers when they had the night off. Jones, as the group's only airman, could not go into the lounge. When he had the night off, he either went to the base movie or stayed in the operations area to study emergency operating procedures. On one midnight shift, Sergeant Otis, together with a few of his men, went to the NCO lounge after he determined that it would be a slow night. Sergeant Keets was left in charge with instructions to call Otis if anything developed.

A short time after Otis had left the operations area, Jones called to Keets, "I have just intercepted critical information. We have just a few seconds to get it off!" Critical information refers to information that must be relayed within two minutes to various high ranking officials for action. Unit operating procedures designate what type of information is considered critical.

Panic crossed Keets' face. "Are you sure?"
"Yes."

"I'll get Otis," replied Keets weakly.

"There isn't time. You'll have to sign the message."

"What if you're wrong, Al? Let's get Otis."

"I'll send it on my signature. The guys in the comcenter never look to see who signed a message. You call Otis."

Sergeant Otis returned ten minutes later and discussed the matter with Sergeant Keets. When he was finished, he called for Jones.

"Jones, I want you out of this operations center now!" he screamed. "I leave for just a few minutes and you screw things up. I let you read a few of my procedural manuals and you think you know it all. I hope they court-martial you for exceeding your authority. Now get out of here."

ANALYSIS 1: *The Radio Communications Group*

As with many other incidents, it is difficult to pinpoint the major topical areas involved. The situation concerns group behavior but also influence, authority, role behavior, leadership and communication. However, because of the question of legitimacy which appears to underlie the action of Jones and the reaction of Sergeant Otis, the approach here will center on the issues related to authority.

AUTHORITY

Sergeant Otis is the leader of the group mainly because of his position in the organizational structure. That is, he is the titular head of the communications group. The group held Otis in the position of work leader and to some extent, informal leader, at least before Jones's arrival.

Jones has undoubtedly supplanted Otis in some aspects of informal leadership. By reason of his expertise, Jones had gained a degree of influence which eroded the formal authority of Sergeant Otis. Not that this is necessarily undesirable. Mary Parker Follett argued very strongly for expertise as a basis of authority back in the pioneering era of management theory.[13] Contemporary organization theory tends to lean toward nonformal and informal bases of authority, and expertise is one of the underlying determinants.

Jones obviously possessed the personal characteristics which relate to informal authority.[14] As a recognized expert, his opinions and advice were respected by the group members. As a candidate for officer training, he had demonstrated his potential for handling greater responsibilities. As an Airman 2/C, he appears to interact well with NCOs of superior rank. In fact, the factor of not being permitted to visit the NCO club probably works in his favor. The NCOs tend to compensate for the loss of social interaction by establishing closer relationships at work.

In the situation where Jones signed the emergency message, the authority issue is not clear. Keets should have signed it, since he was left in charge of the operation, but Otis apparently did not formally delegate authority to Keets for this action. One question relates to whether authority in this instance would be understood because of the physical impossibility of Otis signing it within the two minutes allotted. In other words, do the demands of the situation supercede the hierarchical procedures in situations such as this? The two-minute limitation was established by a higher authority than Otis. The lives of millions of citizens could be at stake. In this perspective, it is obvious that the national fate should not rest in the hands of a sergeant who is reluctant to delegate necessary authority to meet the crisis.

Otis should have thanked Jones rather than reprimanding him, because Otis blundered by leaving the operations area. Had Jones followed Otis's orders to the letter, Otis would have probably been reprimanded for not following operating procedure in getting the message out in time. But Otis was obviously blinded by his dislike for Jones and his vengeance for Jones's undermining his influence. Keets, being somewhat neutral in this personal conflict, could likely have signed the message with impunity.

OTHER SALIENT TOPICS

Sergeant Otis demonstrates the traits of the nonleader as defined by Tarnopol.[15] A nonleader tends to be unsure of himself. Any change in his position, the attitudes of subordinates toward him, or in the task, leads to hostility toward what he perceives to be the cause for the change. He can also become highly vengeful about the situation. Any challenge to his leadership or supervisory position is perceived by him as a threat. The first such hostility shown by Otis is his remarks about Jones. Even though the operations orders state the procedure to be followed in emergencies such as this, Otis used the situation to unleash his hostility toward Jones. Perhaps one reason for this is that he blames Jones for a loss of informal leadership, and Otis must now struggle to maintain respect by emphasizing his role as formal leader. Formal position can be used as a crutch in this respect and to the authoritarian leader this is often the only perceived alternative to protecting his/her ego. In contrast, the situation here obviously called for what is known as "expressive" leadership; relationships orientation on the part of the supervisor, especially because of the high job demands and pressures.[16]

RELATED QUESTIONS AND CONSIDERATIONS

It would aid the solution of the above issues to know more about the message procedures. Surely, the manuals would spell out the requirements and authorizations involved. Also, how did the interpersonal conflict develop between Otis and Jones? To what extent was Jones responsible by his actions? Did Jones encourage the group to turn toward him rather than towards Otis, knowing that this would create hostility in Otis? Spontaneous and natural affiliation cannot be prevented, but by giving advice within the organization channels, he might have befriended Otis rather than alienating him. It is this analyst's view that too little attention is given in current organizational behavior literature to the responsibilities of the individual in making the organization work effectively. In other words, individual needs tend to be deified at the expense of individual obligations.

While it may be desirable to think in terms of adapting structures to these individual needs, managers are also individuals and their strengths and shortcomings should be considered in the equation. Surely this is not to suggest an obsequious deference to formal leaders, but, as Jennings points out, based upon his studies, the road to promotability is not paved by making the boss look like a buffoon.[17] Rather, it is both wise and humane for a subordinate to bolster the superior's strengths rather than to exploit his/her weaknesses. Conversely, it is the superior's responsibility to promote the type of conditions which encourage cooperative behavior between subordinates and superiors.

ANALYSIS 2: *The Radio Communications Group*

To the casual observer, Sergeant Otis appears to have reproached A2C Alvin Jones for his disobedience in "exceeding his authority." However, Otis intended to do more than merely correct Jones's behavior. He clearly indicates his desire to arrange to have Jones court-martialed. He has elected to employ a power act designed as a reprisal. This means it is more important to Otis that Jones be punished than that the task be accomplished.[18] Such a preference points to the existence of some sort of conflict between the two men. We shall begin this analysis with an investigation of the underlying causes of this conflict.

STATUS AND EGO CONFLICT RELATIVE TO AUTHORITY

This incident contains sufficient evidence to support the inference that Otis perceives Jones as a threat to his personal status in the work group. In terms of Etzioni's dual leadership concept,[19] Otis is the designated head with positional authority but lacking in personal acceptance, whereas Jones is the informal and natural leader. This is evident from the fact that the other members of the group liked Jones, respected him as an expert, both in his specialty, and for his detailed knowledge of operating procedures, and frequently asked his advice both on military and personal matters. This fact was probably a constant source of annoyance and disappointment to Otis, who wished to be the one whom the others consulted.

The tendency of the others to consult Jones, a person of lesser military rank, on matters pertaining to the job tempts us to infer that they did not regard Otis as highly competent. Their lack of confidence in Otis deprived him of a major source of legitimate authority.[20] He tried to compensate by striving for popularity by allowing his men to have the night off, and by going with them to the NCO lounge. We can speculate that these attempts had enjoyed a limited degree of success. When Otis noticed Jones emerging as an informal leader, he probably felt socially insecure and disliked Jones for his popularity. In terms of Maslow's hierarchy,[21] Otis was probably operating at the social needs level. His unsatisfied need for social acceptance influenced his perception of Jones. As a result, Otis perceived Jones to be a threat to his social status in the work group.

According to Leavitt's concept of perception, we perceive what we hope, fear, and expect.[22] Otis's social needs greatly influenced his interpretation of Jones's behavior. When Jones exhibited unusual interest in studying emergency operating procedures, Otis interpreted this behavior as "playing officer." The others in the group accepted Jones's special interest and respected his expertise in operations, but Otis alone saw this as something to be discouraged. Otis did not like Jones to read his procedural manuals because this was depriving Otis of his special status as the group's expert on procedure.

Once Otis perceived Jones as a threat to his social status in the work group, he made comments to other members of the group designed to decrease Jones's social status. Otis knew, (perhaps not consciously) as espoused by Turner, "the extent to which a group member upholds group norms helps define his . . . social standing in the group."[23] In his comments Otis emphasized that Jones was "playing Officer" and passing out bad advice. By trying to convince others that Jones did not embody the group's norms, Otis hoped to relegate Jones to a deviant's standing. In the doing, Otis hoped to restore himself to a higher relative social status. These attempts probably were not successful. Then, when Otis learned that Jones had signed the critical message and sent it on, he interpreted this action as an intolerable personal affront and a personal threat. He wanted the source of the threat (Jones) removed if possible by means of court-martial, or at least punished; and he wanted the event publicized in order to make Jones look bad to the work group.

ROLE CONFLICT AND AMBIGUITY

Another approach to this incident is in terms of role conflict and ambiguity. There is no evidence in the incident to indicate that either Keets or Jones had ever been specifically instructed on what to do if they received a critical message when Otis was absent. Therefore, both Keets and Jones were faced with having to decide whether to call for Otis, thereby delaying the message ten minutes or to send the message at once and comply with the two-minute operating procedure. Jones was the focal person in a conflict situation of the inter-sender type.[24] The norms of his small work group dictated that he should delay and call Otis, but the norms dictated by the larger military organization (as stated in the Emergency Operating Procedures) required him to act immediately. Jones was forced to choose between two contradictory roles from two different senders. In making his decision to act, Jones would inevitably violate the norms of one or the other role-sender, thereby risking some form of unfavorable sentiments or punishment being directed against him.[25]

Jones' eventual decision to sign the message and send it on immediately is in harmony with the hypothesis stated by Barnes. ". . . an individual behaves in accord with the values and norms of his dominant reference group."[26] It is apparent from the incident that Jones had never become a full member of the work group because he never completely embodied the required norms. First, he was unable, due to his rank, to go with the others to the NCO lounge and had therefore nearly become an isolate going to movies and studying emergency operating procedures alone during his time off. Second, he was looking forward to being reassigned soon to officer training school. Both of these factors helped to diminish the influence of his work group and to make the larger military organization his dominant reference group. Considering these factors, Jones was destined to choose the role of immediate action. Little attention was given to the possibility of a reprisal, so severe that it might lead to a court-martial.

ADDITIONAL INFORMATION DESIRED

First, it would be helpful to know the relative social standing of Jones and Otis in order to predict the reaction of the work group to Otis' action.

Would they side with Otis or with Jones, making Jones a martyr-hero and lowering Otis's standing in the group?

Second, was part of Otis's motivation a fear that his superiors would blame him for being absent during the crisis? Was he scapegoating in the hope of avoiding personal blame in the event the message was not in the critical category?

Third, it would be helpful to know more about Keets. We can assume from the incident that he is probably an indecisive and weak supervisor; or, on the other hand, we can assume that he fears Otis to the extent that he would not make any decision without first consulting Otis.

Fourth, it would be desirable to know more about the norms and values of the higher management personnel (above Otis) within the unit. If their norms were congruent with those of Otis, we could predict subsequent actions that would be taken in this incident.[27]

THE NITROUS-OXIDE INCIDENT

As an orderly in a local hospital, Jack Coons's duty was to clean and prepare the maternity ward and delivery rooms. Jack's supervisor was the head nurse in the maternity ward on night duty. She in turn reported to the head nurse for that wing of the hospital.

After working several months in this area, Jack detected great hostility between the ward head nurse and the staff physicians. The head nurse was a strict disciplinarian and closely followed all hospital rules and regulations.

Over a period of time, it became evident that the head nurse disliked Jack's running errands for the doctors. She even went to her supervisor with the complaint that the staff physicians were using her subordinates and that she could not allow this to continue.

One evening this entire matter came to a climax when a doctor sent a nurse out of the delivery room for nitrous-oxide. The anesthetist had exhausted his supply and only the head nurse could authorize getting more. The head nurse was nowhere to be found so the doctor authorized the delivery room nurse to tell Jack to get the nitrous-oxide without the head nurse's approval.

Under great anxiety and frustration Jack secured the nitrous-oxide. Shortly afterwards, the head nurse learned of Jack's actions and reprimanded him for not getting her approval. She later complained directly to the head nurse of that wing about the staff physician's actions.

ANALYSIS 1: *The Nitrous-Oxide Incident*

In this incident Jack was experiencing role conflict. Because of unclear job definitions and an ambiguous chain-of-command relationship, role conflict was caused by the line-staff relationship of the doctors with the head nurse. Jack probably perceived the doctors as having legitimate authority and this caused organizational tension, resulting from the interplay of two authority types. Staff physicians usually have functional status with no authority over head nurses. The head nurses usually have scalar status and the right to supervise.

Due to Jack's status judgment and perception of legitimate authority of the doctors, he was in conflict with the head nurse. In a Weberian sense, the nurse held traditional hierarchical authority. This took the form of coercive power in that she could reward or punish Jack on the basis of his following or not following the orders and rules of the formal organization.

The status-ego threat between the head nurse and staff physicians probably caused faulty communication in the ward. Because of faulty communications, Jack's responsibilities were probably ambivalent. This status-ego threat undoubtedly led some doctors to communicate directly with Jack.

In analyzing this incident we can rely on some research discussions of the bureaucratic model as it relates to a hospital. Studies of the bureaucratic model emphasize the purposive nature of organizations, defining them as social units deliberately constructed and reconstructed to achieve specific goals. Such groupings are characterized by: (1) deliberately planned divisions of labor and communications; (2) one or more systems of authority; and (3) "substitution of personnel" whereby unsatisfactory members may be replaced.[28] In dealing with perhaps the most outstanding point in Weber's model, that of authority and authority relationships, many recent authors have begun to differ from the more traditional notions. Weber argued that bureaucratic authority is based upon technical knowledge and training, whereas more recent authors point to the inherent contradiction between technical expertise and disciplined compliance.[29] This dilemma is best exemplified in Etzioni's discussion of authority relations between professionals and nonprofessionals in an organizational setting such as a hospital.[30] In this type of organizational setting, it would appear that the basic principles of administrative and professional authority are incompatible. The ultimate justification of the latter is that a given act is, to the best of the person's knowledge, the right act; of the former, that the act is in line with the rules and regulations of the organization. [31]

The bureaucratic model allows for only one line of authority, but in the general hospital there are several lines of authority.[32] Because of these several lines of authority we would suspect that low-level personnel are subject to more than one system of authority at a time, as was the situation in which Jack found himself.[33]

The position of nurses in the hospital lies between that of full professionals (i.e., doctors) on the one hand and employees on the other. Nurses are, Etzioni contends, more "semi-professionals"—they apply knowledge, but they have less training than a physician. They are not officially responsible for life-death decisions, although they do affect them. Thus, nurses have less autonomy than physicians, are more subject to daily regulation and close supervision, and have more highly specified duties. Most of their supervision, however, is performed by other semiprofessionals (i.e., nursing supervisors) and by professionals.[34]

A major issue in employment of professionals is the portentous instability in these groupings. Etzioni and others have pointed to increased tension and conflict in those organizations encompassing large numbers of both professionals and bureaucratic employees.[35] Often friction incidents and role conflicts are associated with the positions of members of an organization, the diversity of their backgrounds, and differences in the bureaucratic characteristics of the organization.

ADDITIONAL INFORMATION NEEDED

Did the other orderlies in the hospital obey doctors' orders as sort of an unwritten code of conduct? Did the staff physicians thus maintain authority and power over the nonprofessional employees? By trying to please the head nurse and also the doctors, Jack could possibly be experiencing avoidance-avoidance conflict.[36]

Did the staff physicians, as perceived by the orderlies, possess greater status in the maternity ward than the head nurse?

ANALYSIS 2: *The Nitrous-Oxide Incident*

This incident exemplifies a dilemma that has been difficult to resolve throughout the development of organization theory; namely, effectively integrating the needs of the administrative hierarchy with those of the professional hierarchy in organizations where the dual hierarchies are required because of the nature of the work within the institutions. Hospitals and universities are types of organizations where this dual hierarchy situation has traditionally existed and will continue to remain in the foreseeable future.[37] The problem can be viewed from different perspectives, but it tends to basically focus on authority.

AUTHORITY

There are various "understandings" in a hospital organization which defuse the authority issue to some extent. Patient care is generally considered the primary objective in a hospital and the physician is directly and ethically responsible for the patients' welfare.[38] The hospital administration hierarchy clearly recognizes the physician's functional authority in decisions concerning the medical care of patients. References cited in Analysis 1 of this incident suggest, too, that organization theorists are working toward developing a fuller understanding of the managerial and behavioral issues involved.[39]

Conflicts of status and authority, therefore, are not prevalent where the physician-patient relationship is the focal concern. Thus, the physician's authority to prescribe certain treatment is not questioned by other hospital employees. But, when the treatment must be facilitated through the administrative structure, problems of authority, power, role and status can often arise.

We will elaborate later on these areas, especially the authority and status questions, but first there are certain areas in which the information given is either puzzling or incomplete. For example, it is difficult to imagine the head nurse alone having authority for procuring medication, or in this instance, chemicals needed by the anesthetist. Certainly, she would be aware of the urgent nature of the physician's request. In a pathology lab, for example, emergency tests, called "stat" orders, can circumvent any routine administrative procedure, unless, of course, the procedure affects the quality of the test itself. In this incident, were it an emergency, it seems clear that the physician could authorize the acquisition of the nitrous-oxide.

The terminology is unclear, also. *Anesthetists* are not ordinarily physicians; *anesthesiologists* are. For our purposes we will assume that he/she was an M.D. or O.D., depending on the type of hospital involved—another area of missing information. It would also be helpful to know whether the head nurse had an assistant who could authorize the request in the head nurse's absence. Similar to the Radio Communications Group incident in this section, the individual in charge should have made arrangements in advance to accommodate decisions which cannot be delayed. Of course, we do not know if the nitrous-oxide situation was, in fact, an emergency but we can safely assume that maternity does not fit into the category of elective surgery (in which case a delay would be more defensible). In addition, nitrous-oxide, known to the layman as "laughing gas", is very frequently used and, unlike narcotics, the control would not need to be so stringent.

Perhaps the statement that the head nurse is a strict adherent of policy and procedure is something of a "red herring." She was evidently out of bounds in requiring her permission for obtaining the nitrous-oxide. This incident was described to practitioners (an M.D. and a nurse) by the author and the consensus was that authority resides with the physician in this type of situation. The reason is basically that the physician has authority to prescribe the treatment and to determine when the medication is to be administered. The head nurse in this instance works in a service relationship, arranging for use of the operating room and the supplies and equipment needed. It was the nurse's responsibility to supply the nitrous-oxide in the first place and in this incident she was delinquent by reason of not having done so. Perhaps this is the reason for her apparent defensiveness over what she perceived as an orderly circumventing her command. It is a common practice in hospitals for orderlies to take directives from various individuals. Obviously, this head nurse was atypical in her reaction to staff physician's use of her subordinates.

There is in many respects a similarity here to a project management situation. In a hospital, though, because of the urgency of many of the activities, the "project manager," or physician, has less difficulty in wielding influence to obtain the needed resources. Not that the problems are less serious, though. There are still egos involved, as this incident clearly demonstrates, and in order to work harmoniously under these circumstances, a great deal of interaction, mutual consultation and diplomacy are necessary.[40] This is another way of saying that flexibility is essential in the on-going relationships between those who report in the hierarchical structure and the specialists (physicians) who use the resources provided by the formal organization.

Finally, there may appear to be a violation of the single accountability principle, but this should not be alarming in itself. There is a superordinate principle involved, that of unity of objectives, which supercedes and integrates the common hierarchies.[41] Viewed in this perspective, it is apparent that the patient care objective is primary and structural considerations secondary in the incident.

FOOTNOTES

[1]Amitai Etzioni, "Dual Leadership in Complex Organizations," *American Sociological Review,* October, 1965, pp. 688–98.

[2]For an informative discussion of behavioral problems in family-owned businesses, see Harry Levinson, "Conflicts that Plague Family Businesses," *Harvard Business Review,* March-April, 1971, pp. 90–98.

[3]Lane Tracy, "Postscript to the Peter Principle," *Harvard Business Review,* July-August, 1972, pp. 65–71; and Laurence J. Peter and Raymond Hull, *The Peter Principle* (New York: William Morrow and Company, Inc., 1969).

[4]Tracy, "Postscript," pp. 65–71.

[5]This is not so far-fetched, either, as the author sees it.

[6]Harold J. Leavitt, *Managerial Psychology* 2d ed. (Chicago and London: The University of Chicago Press, 1964), p. 35.

[7]Harold Stieglitz, "Barriers to Communication," *Management Record,* 20, no. 1, January, 1958: p. 2.

[8]William G. Scott, *Organization Theory: A Behavioral Analysis for Management* (Homewood, Ill.: Richard D. Irwin, Inc., 1967), pp. 301–14.

[9]Stieglitz, "Barriers," pp. 2–5.

[10]Robert V. Presthus, "Authority in Organization," in William T. Greenwood, *Management and Organizational Behavior Theories,* (Cincinnati: South-Western Publishing Co., 1967), p. 514.

[11]*Ibid.,* p. 515.

[12]*Ibid.,* p. 524.

[13]Mary Parker Follett, *The New State* (London: Longmans, Green and Co., Ltd., 1920); also Mary Parker Follett, "The Illusion of Final Authority," in Lyndale Warwick, ed., *Freedom and Coordination: Lectures in Business Organization* (London: Sir Isaac Pitman and Sons, Ltd., 1949), pp. 1–10.

[14]Justin G. Longenecker, *Principles of Management and Organizational Behavior* (Columbus, Ohio: Charles E. Merrill Publishing Co., 1964), pp. 350–58.

[15]Lester Tarnopol, "Personality Differences Between Leaders and Non-leaders," in William T. Greenwood, *Management and Organizational Behavior Theories: An Interdisciplinary Approach* (Cincinnati: South-Western Publishing Co., 1965), pp. 719–24.

[16]Robert D. Rossel, "Instrumental and Expressive Leadership in Complex Organizations," *Administrative Science Quarterly* 15 (1970): 306–16.

[17]Eugene Emerson Jennings, *The Mobile Manager* (New York: McGraw-Hill Book Co., 1967), especially chap. 4.

[18]Herbert Goldhammer and Edward A. Shils, "Types of Power and Status," in D. R. Hampton, C. E. Summer, and R. A. Webber, *Organizational Behavior and the Practice of Management* (Glenview, Ill.: Scott, Foresman and Company, 1968), p. 481.

[19]Etzioni, "Dual Leadership," pp. 688–98.

[20]Chester I. Barnard, "The Theory of Authority," in Hampton, Summer, and Webber, *Organizational Behavior,* p. 451.

[21]A. H. Maslow, "A Theory of Human Motivation," *Psychological Review* 50 (1943): pp. 370–96.

[22]Leavitt, *Managerial Psychology,* p. 31.

[23]Arthur N. Turner, "A Conceptual Scheme for Describing Work Group Behavior," in Paul R. Lawrence and John A. Seiler et al. *Organization Behavior and Administration* (Homewood, Ill.: Richard D. Irwin and The Dorsey Press, 1965), p. 157.

[24]Robert L. Kahn, "Role Conflicts and Ambiguity in Organizations," in S. G. Huneryager and I. L. Heckman, *Human Relations in Management* (Cincinnati: South-Western Publishing Co., 1967), p. 645. Co., "Conceptual Scheme," np. 161–62.

[26]L. B. Barnes, "Organizational Systems and Engineering Groups: A Comparative Study of Two Technical Groups in Industry," in Lawrence and Seiler, *Organization Behavior,* p. 199.

[27]Turner, "Conceptual Scheme," pp. 154–64.

[28]Amitai Etzioni, *Modern Organizations* (Englewood Cliffs, N.J.: Prentice-Hall, Inc., 1964), p. 3.

[29]Peter M. Blau and W. Richard Scott, *Formal Organizations: A Comparative Approach* (San Francisco: Chandler Publishing Co., 1962), pp. 33–36.

[30]Etzioni, *Modern Organizations,* pp. 76–78.

[31]*Ibid.,* p. 77.

[32]Fremont E. Kast and James E. Rosenzweig, *Organization and Management: A Systems Approach* (New York: McGraw-Hill Book Co., 1970), p. 542.

[33]Etzioni, *Modern Organizations,* p. 86.

[34]*Ibid.,* pp. 88–89.

[35] *Ibid.,* p. 75; Kast and Rosenzweig, *Organization,* pp. 544–45.

[36]Scott, *Organization Theory,* p. 79.

[37]The dimensions of the issues involved are outlined and discussed in Robert J. House, "Role Conflict in Complex Organizations," *California Management Review,* Summer, 1970, pp. 53–60.

[38] *International Code of Medical Ethics* (London: World Medical Association, 1949); also, *Principles of Medical Ethics* (Chicago: American Medical Association, 1955). The co-author is indebted in this analysis to his wife's M.A. thesis: Allecia R. Von der Embse, "An Analysis of Ethics for Medical Experimentation," M.A. thesis, University of Dayton, 1970.

[39]For a discussion of the power dimensions related to a physician's role, see Amitai Etzioni, "Organizational Control and Leadership," in William P. Sexton, *Organization Theories* (Columbus, Ohio: Charles E. Merrill Publishing Co., 1970), pp. 350–51.

[40]See David I. Cleland, "Understanding Project Authority," *Business Horizons,* Spring, 1967, pp. 63–70.

[41]This observation is based upon integrative approaches to objectives discussed in: Stanley E. Seashore, "Criteria of Organizational Effectiveness," *Michigan Business Review,* July, 1963, pp. 26–30; and Peter F. Drucker, *The Practice of Management* (New York: Harper and Brothers, 1954).

POWER

Incident	*Page*
AMERICAN HARVESTER COMPANY	159
Wayne Fields	
Analysis 1	160
Analysis 2	162
THE STAFF MAN	167
Robert E. Reed	
Analysis 1	167
Analysis 2	170
THE ABSENTEE SECRETARY	174
Lon Comomile	
Analysis 1	175
Analysis 2	178

AMERICAN HARVESTER COMPANY

In June of 1968, the American Harvester Company, located in the Midwest, hired several college graduates with degrees in business administration. One of them was a young management major from a state school who had graduated with honors. He had been very active in college and was highly recommended by the professors of his major. Although he was rather boyish in physical appearance, he exuded a feeling of self-confidence and pride in his intellectual abilities. Also, top management had great hopes that someday he would prove to be a fine upper level supervisor for them, and his progress was closely watched.

The young graduate was started as a production foreman in a section where work was done in assembling the American Traveler. It was in his area of the department that the main Traveler body, that is, the flooring, the sides, the top, and the front end were assembled. The stamped parts that made up the front end and the flooring were spot welded in this same area. A supply of all the necessary stamped parts that the section needed to do their job was kept here, coated with a preservative grease. Some of the new foreman's men were responsible for steam cleaning these parts, which were then taken by the stock boys to the area of assembly. In addition, he also supervised a lift driver, two parts supply men, and a parts salvager. These twenty-five subordinates all belonged to a local of the UAW, which had considerable influence over the local management of this particular A. H. Plant.

This section of the Traveler department was very important because it was the starting point of the whole assembly line process that resulted in the complete production of the Traveler station wagon. They had to work closely with the section adjacent to them, as it placed doors, etc., on the Traveler shells. This section was almost exclusively an assembly line process and was run by an older man who had risen to his foreman's job from the ranks, as had the foreman that the young graduate had replaced. From the very beginning of his new job, the young foreman seemed to experience difficulty in relating to the men about him, even though the general manager, and others, consulted with him at least once a day.

The young supervisor's subordinates began to deride him behind his back and nicknamed him "Lt. Fuzz." They appeared to resent his authority and paid little heed to anything that he might tell them. He was the object of most of their discussions and none of them were flattering. Soon the insults, hostility, and lack of respect led to work stoppages and sabotage that created a lot of down time. As a matter of fact, "down time" became the motto of the section, especially when someone of importance was nearby. All of these problems led to a low productivity for the section, which in turn created low productivity for the whole Traveler department. The continued low output made top management realize that something had to be done to solve the problem.

ANALYSIS 1: *American Harvester Company*

The problem of making changes in management personnel is often over-looked or at best given only slight attention in industry. Top management usually performs extensive analysis on projects related to procuring and installing capital equipment, but when human "capital" is involved, these same companies tend to balk at spending more than minimal time and money.[1] The problem in this incident seems to meet this description. The work stoppages and sabotage are apparently related to the change in fore-men. The cause, however, is not necessarily the new foreman himself nor the company, but a combination of factors, some controllable by manage-ment and some not.

In relation to the new foreman, the incident excludes some very necessary information. He is described as being capable in the academic arena but nothing is said about his specific actions as a foreman. In most cases, the actions of the supervisor play a large part in determining supervisor-subor-dinate relationships. This type of information would be of value in deter-mining the root of the problems in the incident. Nothing is mentioned, either, about training for new foremen. Presumably, there is some type of training, since this company participates in a supervisory training program sponsored by a local university; but apparently, the young graduate in our incident had not yet experienced the training.

POWER AND INFLUENCE

Wilson equates the situation of a new supervisor with that of Joe Namath, quarterback for the New York Jets.[2] It will be recalled that Namath was originally signed for what was considered an astronomical salary at the time. At first, Namath's new teammates resented and disliked him as a rookie whom they considered overpaid. Compounding the problem of Namath's acceptance was his attitude—humility had never been considered one of Namath's virtues. Yet, when he proved that he could handle the quarterback position better than anyone else on the club (and as he claims, in the league), he became accepted and respected by his teammates.

There are differences, though, between our young supervisor's situation and that of a football quarterback. For one, the quarterback's position power is such that leadership can be demonstrated very quickly. Noncooperation by teammates will show very clearly in the films of practices and games, so even though the players may dislike the quarterback, they are compelled to give him a chance if the coach sends him in. The plays are set, and deliberate errors by teammates can be quickly observed if they attempt to sabotage the quarterback. Ability in passing and play-calling is readily observed, also, and success of a play brings immediate satisfaction which can dispel previous antagonistic feelings simultaneously. In addition, there is the cultural sentiment developed at all levels of the game toward giving a person a chance to prove himself, regardless of how others might feel about the individual.[3]

The foreman's situation, by comparison, is more difficult. The factors which demonstrate his/her capability are not so explicit as on an athletic team. Workers do not always share the ethical standard of cooperating in order to give the new foreman a chance. Often the foreman's introduction to the work group dooms the relationship from the beginning. If, for example, the workers perceive that the foreman has little interest in their welfare, the foreman will be branded as a management man.[4] Or if the foreman historically had little influence with his/her own superiors, it will be difficult for the new foreman to gain the respect and cooperation of employees. One argument might point to the young foreman's lack of experience and relative immaturity in explaining his relative ineffectiveness. Yet, as Fiedler's studies have shown, experience is not a factor in supervisory effectiveness and in fact is negatively related in some organizations.[5]

As mentioned earlier, the new foreman may not be the principal cause behind the development. The incident states that the foreman of the adjacent section and the new foreman's predecessor had both come up through the ranks. If this type of promotion had been a company policy, the new action could be perceived as a threat to existing foremen. They might feel that their only means of advancement was being shut off; therefore, the actual problem might be this perceived threat and not the inability of the new foreman.

OTHER SALIENT AREAS

Role behavior is another area observable in the incident. Unlike other incidents in this text, this would appear to be one situation where the role expectations are highly defined and prescribed. Nonetheless, there is the possibility for a person-role conflict related to the divergent expectations of the young foreman on the one hand and the prescribed role behavior on the other.[6]

The supervisor's role-set is generally complex. He/she interacts with staff specialists, superiors, other supervisors, workers, and union representatives, among others.[7] Our young foreman might be proud of his intellectual accomplishments, but he could also alienate others by trying to impress them through his language and mannerisms. Were he interacting only with staff specialists, this approach might be acceptable, but as it is, the role-set is much too diverse. In other words, the young foreman will have to become highly flexible in his relationship with significant others in his environment.

Motivation is another area of importance in this incident. Assuming that the young foreman is somewhat achievement-oriented, it would follow that he will want to participate meaningfully in the decisions which affect his section. He will also want to obtain productive effort from his employees. Under present circumstances, neither of these accomplishments appear likely until there is greater organizational support in terms of resources, encouragement, and cooperation. These conditions are essential for motivating at the achievement level.[8] Elaborating further on an earlier point, it will be necessary to bring the new foreman along gradually through training, orienting other supervisors and workers toward preparing them for a "new breed" of foreman, and preparing top management for providing increased delegation and support as well as expecting certain shock waves from new foremen with fresh ideas.

ANALYSIS 2: *American Harvester Company*

Indications are that the group primarily resents the fact that the new foreman was brought in straight out of school, and they feel the job should have gone to someone who worked his way up through the ranks. The problem is probably worsened by the fact that the new foreman is highly self-confident, and top management has great plans for him. The situation has presently deteriorated to the point where the subordinates resent the young supervisor's authority, ignore his orders and at every opportunity try to make him look bad to his supervisor.

Additional considerations are (1) that the group works closely with another section that is supervised by an older foreman who came up through the ranks, (2) the foreman's supervisor stops by daily, and (3) any problem in the section affects the whole department.

PERCEPTION

A study reported by Misshauk reveals that "high" producing assembly line workers perceived significantly greater degrees of technical and administrative skills in their supervisors than did the "low" producers.[9] It appears that this technical skill may be considered important to assembly line workers because they look to the foreman to solve job-related problems that arise from the work environment. Misshauk points out that while the key factor influencing both performance and satisfaction levels for employees is the perception that they have of their supervisor, this perception may not be based on fact. An article by Sorcher points out that the expectations and perceptions of work groups depend upon the perceptions of the groups' own roles within the organizations.[10]

Considering the above two concepts, we observe that the previous foreman was an older man who had come up through the ranks. It is quite easy to see that the group probably perceived that they had some influence in the way the previous foreman managed the section. They probably believed that the old supervisor would be more receptive to their opinions and suggestions because he could understand the position of the members of the work group, having been a member himself.

The incident also points out that the local union had considerable influence in the plant. It may well be that the employees perceived a threat to this influence with the appointment of a college trained foreman.

The Misshauk study illustrates the fact that if a supervisor is perceived to have little technical competence, the more likely it is that the employees will be dissatisfied.[11] In this incident, the new foreman was perceived as having little technical skill, as evidenced by the attitude of the employees. In addition, the other foremen are perceived as having technical skill because of their experience in the job, and their age. The fact that the new foreman's supervisor stops by daily to check on the progress of the group probably reinforces the employees' perceptions that the new foreman is technically and administratively incompetent.

The group may also have perceived a threat to their status because a nontechnical man with no experience was brought in to head the department. This would imply that the work done in the section was less complex than in other sections. According to Argyris, in order to defend themselves, group members can deny or destroy whatever is threatening them.[12] In this incident the work group is obviously attempting to "destroy" the new foreman by making him look bad. They want to prove that the job is too complex for an inexperienced, nontechnical man, and in this way regain their lost status.

POWER AND AUTHORITY

This incident clearly reveals that the new foreman lacks power and authority. It appears that he has not been able to establish any source of power and therefore is unable to exercise effective control. If we consider the five sources of power (reward, coercive, legitimate, referent and expertise) espoused by French and Raven,[13] there is no evidence that the new foreman is perceived by his subordinates as having any influence or power. This incident would also seem to verify Barnard's acceptance theory of authority, whereby the authority resides with the persons to whom it is directed and not with the supervisor.[14]

MOTIVATION

A study involving personnel officers revealed several reasons why companies should not hire college graduates as foremen; these reasons are summarized as: (1) loss of morale in the organization, because employment of college graduates cuts off the only promotion opportunities for the shop workers; and (2) the type of education received by the typical college graduate is neither necessary nor desirable for foreman type jobs; technical training is more directly related to the job.[15]

We have also observed from other studies that promotion opportunities are a strong motivating force. In studies conducted by Hilgert, lack of advancement opportunity was a dissatisfier and presence of advancement opportunities provided for motivation.[16] In this incident, the new foreman, brought in from outside the company, effectively blocked all promotion opportunities for the employees in the group. Before this happened, they may have had reason to believe that the next foreman would be one of their members. From the studies discussed above, we can see where action to hire an outsider would be resented by the group resulting in dissatisfaction and loss of motivation. In addition, as previously discussed, the new foreman had no technical skills which caused further group dissatisfaction because the employees now have no one to consult on technical problems.

LEADERSHIP

The previous foreman (because he was once a member of the work group) probably took a more active interest in the group than does the new foreman. He probably shared his ideas with others and gathered ideas and suggestions from others. By inviting participation, he was able to motivate those responsible for carrying out the work. Productive participation demands a permissive climate and willingness to credit others for their contributions. Having been one of the work group, the old foreman was probably better able to communicate with and accept advice from the work group than is the new foreman.

The new foreman, just out of school and full of confidence, probably thinks he can handle the job by himself, and sets out to prove it. His leadership style is not directly discussed, but we might suspect him to be autocratic. This drastic change in leadership style no doubt causes resentment in the employees, because, as discussed above, they perceived themselves as no longer being involved in the decision-making process. Again, this threat in loss of influence may have caused the employees to resist the new foreman.

GROUP BEHAVIOR

A new manager for any position is generally selected, or should be selected, on the basis of outstanding achievement. The skills which led to his success may be quite different from those needed for his new position. Having earned a reputation, the manager is given a new challenge and expected to excel. This transition, however, does not always place the new manager in a friendly environment. According to Uyterhoeven, "he may find that his promotion has caused resentment."[17] Some may consider themselves better qualified, because of age or seniority; or they may resent the new manager because he represents an "educated elite."

We realize from the study of group behavior that groups normally maintain a certain level of cohesion, loyalty and cooperation among the members. Any deviates incur the penalties of nonconformity, which may range from their being made the butt of jokes to receiving verbal abuse. In the incident, we see what appears to be an entire group effort concentrated in opposition to the foreman. As suggested by Uyterhoeven, we see sabotage taking place in response to the resentment; and, according to Uyterhoeven, it should have been expected.[18]

CONCLUSION

The basic problems in this situation appear to be:

1. The selection of the new supervisor has blocked promotion opportunities with a loss of motivation.

2. The new foreman is perceived to be lacking in technical competence, which has lowered the perceived status of the work group.

3. The group is reacting to uphold their status in the eyes of their peers.

4. The group perceives a threat to their influence in the section, and thus additional loss of status.

ADDITIONAL INFORMATION NEEDED

To adequately evaluate this incident, the following information would be needed:

1. Why did the old foreman leave, and what was his relationship with the work group? If the old foreman was replaced by top management against the desires of the work group, the members of the work group could easily resist the change because of a fear of the unknown. This would be especially true if the old foreman possessed norms, sentiments and values which were congruent with those of the work group.

2. How does the work group under consideration relate to other work groups? For example, if their norms, sentiments and values are strongly consistent with those of other work groups, they could perceive themselves as possessing considerable power and could therefore more readily ignore the new foreman.

3. What actions has the new foreman taken, if any, since he assumed his new position? Again, if he demonstrated norms entirely inconsistent with the work group, his failure could easily have been predicted.

4. Why did the general manager consult daily with the new foreman? If this consultation was obvious to the work group, they could perceive that the general manager did not have confidence in the foreman, and there is some research to indicate that where this type of condition exists the subordinates will lack respect for their superior.

THE STAFF MAN

Tom Peterson is manager of the technical publications department of a medium sized manufacturing firm. He has been with the company twenty years and has worked himself "up through the ranks."

Bob Hanna occupies the newly established position of systems analyst, a staff position within the department, reporting directly to Peterson. Hanna is responsible for improving and developing systems for the distribution of the publications. The nature of his job requires that he have several meetings with Peterson each week. Hanna has a good personality and is well liked. He is also well-educated and holds several degrees.

The department is divided into three sections with approximately eight employees in each section. However, all three sections are located in one large office area with no partitions separating the three sections. Bob Hanna is located near the center of the office at a desk vacated by a recent retiree.

More and more of the employees were going to Hanna for advice, even though it was not his job. At first the advice was of a minor nature, but eventually the situation developed to the point where Hanna began not only to advise but to direct the work of the employees as an assistant department head would do. When Peterson became aware of the situation he became enraged and recommended to his own boss that Hanna be fired and the position abolished.

ANALYSIS 1: *The Staff Man*

There are several concepts and forces such as power and influence, authority, communications, status and leadership applicable to this incident.

POWER AND INFLUENCE

Scott defines social influence as ". . . a behavioral transaction in which a person or group is induced by another person or group to act in conformance to the influencing agent's objectives, values, norms or standards."[19] Obviously Hanna is an influencing agent over the other employees since they conform to his advice and direction. The question to answer is *"Why is Hanna an influencing agent?"*

As stated by Scott, "Sources of influence can be found in status, possession of information, access to communication channels, and personality."[20] One source of Hanna's influence is his own personality. He is well liked by the employees and thus able to better communicate with them about their problems. Mechanic[21] refers to this as attractiveness and as a source of power. We can conclude that Hanna possessed power over the employees. This power could be shown to result from Hanna's personality, his associates, and his expertise. However, if we also accept Weber's definition of power as ". . . a form of domination" and ". . . an individual's ability to impose his will on others despite resistance . . ."[22] we would be forced to say that Hanna does not possess the ability to reward or punish the employees; and therefore, if the employees decided not to comply with Hanna's decisions, he would have little power to make them conform.

AUTHORITY

Even though Hanna had no formal authority, he possessed authority over the employees and helped defend it by showing that his authority was legitimate on the basis of charisma. Charisma is defined by Scott as being possessed by ". . . an individual who has the personal ability to produce support of followers who believe in his goals."[23]

COMMUNICATION

Hanna is in a unique position since he has access to several communications channels. Again, Mechanic refers to this as a source of power.[24] He is located near the center of an open office and has access to information flowing between the employees and might become a focal point in the transmission of much of this communication. He also has a great deal of communication with Peterson and is able to learn of new developments in the department and the company before many of the other employees. Thus, Hanna is a vital link between the employees and Peterson.

Hanna possesses a great deal of information which is of vital importance to the employees and their jobs. In addition, Hanna possesses a great deal of information about the job itself. He is probably considered somewhat of an expert in his area, and thus, the other employees would tend to be influenced by his knowledge.

STATUS

At first, we might think that Hanna has limited status in the department since he is seated at a similar desk with the other employees and lacks the usual status symbols. However, as Scott defines status, there are two connotations:

> In the objective sense, status is considered as a position involving rights and duties arranged in a structure of human interrelationship . . . The subjective aspect of status concerns how people make status judgments of others.[25]

Hanna lacks the objective type of status, since he is not in an organizational position which gives him these certain rights and duties over the employees, nor the status symbols associated with such a position. However, he does appear to possess a high degree of subjective type status. Hanna's lack of status symbols might actually have added to his ability to influence the employees. The employees might have felt more at ease talking to him.

LEADERSHIP

As stated by Scott, leadership activity supplies structure, by crystallizing goals and objectives.[26] Hanna seems to have performed this function possibly where Peterson failed to do so. Hanna is more of a natural leader while Peterson is the designated leader. As stated by Scott, "The natural leader achieves this role primarily as a result of group consensus . . . The designated leader is one who is appointed to serve in a formal capacity as an agent of the organization."[27]

ALTERNATIVES

1. Fire Hanna and hire another man. This would stop the conflict, but it would probably arise again with the new man. In addition, Hanna appears to be a valuable employee.

2. Give Hanna formal authority by making him assistant department head. This would have to be accepted by Peterson (which might be difficult) and this solution would burden Hanna with several administrative tasks that he probably does not want.

3. Hire an assistant department head (preferably someone within the department) who would handle administrative affairs and would work with

Hanna on technical problems. One drawback to this solution is the additional cost involved in hiring the assistant.

4. Establish a program within the company to improve communication between supervisors and employees. It would appear from the facts in this incident, together with the analysis, that Tom Peterson has not been effectively communicating with his subordinates.[28]

CONCLUSIONS

The first three alternatives mentioned above have certain drawbacks as noted. And alternative 4 appears to be the best, based on the concepts involved in the incident.

ADDITIONAL INFORMATION DESIRED[29]

1. It would be helpful to know the ages of Hanna and Peterson, since the latter might be jealous or suspicious of a younger man who might take over his job in the future.

2. Even though Peterson worked himself "up through the ranks," we do not know his educational background. If his education is less than Hanna's, this might cause some of Peterson's resentment for Hanna.

3. It would also be helpful to know the amount of education, experience and skill of the other employees in relation to both Peterson and Hanna. The employees would tend to respect someone possessing greater knowledge than themselves and would be more greatly influenced by that person.

4. Finally, it would be helpful to know the relationship existing between the employees and Peterson. If the employees were afraid to talk to Peterson, or if Peterson never made himself available for consultation with the employees (which is assumed for purposes of analysis), this would tend to cause them to turn to Hanna for advice.

ANALYSIS 2: *The Staff Man*

Bob Hanna's job as a systems analyst probably requires the writing of procedures and the educating of people on any system which he implements or changes. If a situation develops which is not clearly explained in the system's procedures, or was unforeseen when the procedures were written, the systems analyst is often the best source of advice, for seldom does anyone else know the system better. One would expect a systems analyst to be closely acquainted with the activities related to systems modified or installed by the analyst.

Before examining the major topical issues in the incident, it would be helpful to spell out those areas where information is required to improve the identification and solution of the problems. For example, who made the decisions to establish the position and to hire Hanna? It appears that Peterson's control over these matters is limited. How well was Hanna performing in his primary role as systems analyst? How familiar is Peterson with the work of the systems analyst? Did Peterson confront Hanna about the situation prior to recommending his dismissal? What is Hanna's work experience and educational background? What reason(s) did Peterson present to his boss in order to have Hanna fired? All of these questions relate to sizing up the behavior of the characters involved and to understanding the underlying problems. The information sought would also assist in evaluating alternative solutions.

POWER AND INFLUENCE ISSUES

The fact that Bob Hanna gradually expanded his activities to approximate those of an assistant department head is not unusual. This phenomenon would indicate that a need for daily direction was present, and that the people in the department gradually chose Hanna to fill the need. Hanna could have filled the void for any of several reasons. His formal educational background is probably more extensive than that of others in the department. Expertise is a source of power and influence, and some recognition of capability would accompany his level of formal education. An individual who is capable of waging an intelligent debate or one who possesses an attractive personality also possesses power. These were probably additional sources of power for Hanna.[30]

In the process of system design, a systems analyst must study the operations of the current systems in great detail in order to determine where improvements may be made. In this process, Bob Hanna may have acquired an excellent understanding of the department's operations, perhaps even a better knowledge than Peterson. Hanna's knowledge of the department's operations would serve to amplify technical expertise. Moreover, once he has mastered his technical duties, one could expect a diffusion of his talents.[31]

Hanna's location in the middle of the department would make him much more accessible than Peterson, if Peterson has a private office or a desk outside of the department. If the firm is highly bureaucratic, and Peterson's reaction indicates that it is, the people in the department would probably feel more reluctant to seek advice or direction from Peterson than they would under a more open work system.

The fact that Hanna reports directly to Peterson gives him a higher perceived status than most other people in the department, assuming that supervisors head up each of the sections. Since Hanna's job probably takes him into the realm of all three sections in the department, he may be perceived as having a higher status and a more important role than the section supervisors. If the section supervisors seek out his advice, this perception would tend to be strengthened. His level of satisfaction would also be high, partly because of the variety and diversity of interaction in his role.[32]

The preceeding factors are some of the reasons for Hanna's power and influence. Hanna has been elected the "unofficial" leader of the department. Now the question remains: "What, if anything, should be done about it?"

One would need to know a little more about Mr. Peterson before recommending a specific course of action. Since Peterson asked his boss to fire Hanna, Peterson probably didn't hire him. If Hanna was placed in Peterson's department without Peterson understanding the nature of the systems analysis activity, Peterson may be afraid that Hanna is being trained to either spy on him or, worse yet, replace him. Peterson may, in fact, be a good manager who is simply afraid that his job is in jeopardy. On the other hand, Peterson may be jealous of Hanna's education and his ability to get along with and direct the people in the department. Peterson may be a traditional bureaucratic manager who believes his territorial rights are being violated.

OTHER SIGNIFICANT AREAS

There are obvious motivational implications in this situation. Peterson could be experiencing a self-esteem crisis in that Hanna's presence was embarrassing, educationally. The "up through the ranks" avenue of promotion suggests that Peterson's educational background might be quite limited. The resulting threat of inadequacy would not prompt him to select a man who was his very antithesis. It is likely, then, that Peterson would have been critical of whoever was selected. His disdain for the position and/or the man is illustrated by the fact that the staff systems analyst was casually assigned to an available desk in the common office area.

Then, too, there is the related factor of Peterson's leadership style. The open office area suggests that Peterson prefers to observe the interactions and activities of subordinates. This layout could unintentionally encourage interaction, but could also stifle creativity. The symbolism, too, is one of low status in this type of arrangement.[33]

In conclusion, the forces working in the situation indicate that the systems analyst position installation was doomed to failure from the start. Peterson's values, his general lack of confidence in his subordinates and his autocratic inclinations coupled with his apparent feelings of insecurity were in direct opposition to the expectations of Hanna. Hanna was obviously willing to assume responsibility and, in general, appears to require considerably more freedom than the situation would permit. Both individuals may have been effective in their appropriate environments, but neither showed much of an inclination towards accommodation in this situation. If one follows Labovitz's thesis, Peterson's strategy was suitable for a stable, traditional environment, but not for the newer, more dynamic setting that is evolving in this incident.[34]

THE ABSENTEE SECRETARY

Mrs. Cleo Barton, age 57, is secretary to both Albert Saxton, a middle-age executive, and Jim Grant, his young assistant. The majority of her time is spent doing work for Mr. Saxton, who has delegated many of his routine responsibilities to her. The nature of Mr. Grant's work does not require the services of a full-time secretary.

Mrs. Barton obtained permission from Mr. Saxton to use her vacation days at will rather than in a consecutive two-week segment. Often Mr. Saxton spends part of his week out of town. Mrs. Barton uses her vacation days during Mr. Saxton's absence. A review of her attendance record reveals that days absent due to sickness coincide with Mr. Saxton's trips.

On several occasions Mr. Grant has had to obtain the assistance of other secretaries to handle urgent matters. His routine correspondence is often delayed. When he discussed this problem with Mrs. Barton she adopted a vigorous defensive attitude. In two separate conferences Mr. Grant brought this situation to the attention of Mr. Saxton. Each time Mr. Saxton said he would take care of the matter.

During Mr. Saxton's last trip, Mrs. Barton returned from her Tuesday lunch two hours late and intoxicated. She immediately left for a "coffee break" with two girls from the secretarial pool. Mr. Grant, who was in another part of the building at the time, was informed of this incident one-half hour later by the administrative assistant to the executive vice-president. He had seen the three enter a nearby cocktail lounge.

The following day the office manager fired one of the secretaries. The other had given notice on Monday of the preceding week that she was quitting. She was not allowed to finish out the week. Mrs. Barton did not return until the following Monday.

When Mr. Saxton returned the following week, Mr. Grant informed him of the incident and recommended that Mrs. Barton

be severely reprimanded. Mr. Saxton informed Mr. Grant that
the preceding week had brought nothing but problems. He felt
that his job was now in jeopardy due to top level managerial
changes; his youngest son had just lost his job; his oldest son's
unemployment compensation had run out and he was still unable
to find work. Mr. Saxton said he would deal with Mrs. Barton.

It has now been three weeks since the incident. Mr. Grant has
not been informed of what, if any, action has been taken. Mrs.
Barton is still on the job. Rumors concerning her and Mr. Saxton
are spreading throughout the secretarial pool. Mr. Grant is
investigating the possibility of employment elsewhere.

ANALYSIS 1: *The Absentee Secretary*

Analysis of this incident reveals the existence of a number of deficiencies
in the relationship between Mrs. Barton, Mr. Saxton and Mr. Grant. The
incident indicates the presence of confused channels of command, precon-
ceived attitudes based upon past experiences, and conflicts supported by
feelings of insecurity and personal problems.

It seems obvious that some of the problems in this incident stem from the
poor channels of communication among the three parties. Definite instances
of short-circuiting are present. Mrs. Barton apparently communicates extensively with Saxton and very little with Grant. The lack of communication and understanding has resulted in Mrs. Barton not perceiving correctly
the service she is to perform for Grant. Mrs. Barton appears to be working
under the impression that she is Saxton's secretary and her only responsibility to Grant is on a self-determined basis. The lack of reliable, concrete
communication channels has caused a mismatch in perceptions between her
role as viewed by Grant and as seen by herself. Saxton's treatment of Grant
might be reinforcing these conflicting perceptions. For example, if Saxton
delegated very little meaningful authority to Grant in his absence, Mrs.
Barton would perceive Grant as unimportant and feel free to do as she
pleased.

At this point, it is necessary to question just what assistance was given
to Mrs. Barton by Mr. Saxton which would have helped her function
successfully in her role. It is apparent that Saxton is quite concerned with
his personal goals and for this reason it is doubtful that any constructive
direction has been given to Mrs. Barton. It appears that Mrs. Barton has
been left to decide for herself what she can and cannot do. Mrs. Barton's

action, an example of which is mentioned in the incident when she became intoxicated, suggests that this may have been a sign that she was in need of, and was not getting, direction and recognition from Mr. Saxton. This lack of structure can lead to role ambiguity and apparently did in this incident.[35]

Aside from the aforementioned factors such as communication, role and leadership, there is another area which could be of overriding importance. This is the question of power and influence.

POWER AND INFLUENCE

The final development reported in the incident offers a clue to the extent of Saxton's power and influence in handling the Barton affair (no pun intended). The power in this situation apparently resides with Mrs. Barton, perhaps due to Saxton's sympathy for her condition, fear of retaliation should he fire her, or a more deep-seated personality weakness in dealing with women.[36] One obvious possibility is that there is some extracurricular involvement that Saxton wishes to remain secret. The more cynical observer might pounce on the coinciding absences to confirm any inference of hanky-panky.

Whether or not the rumors of a nonbusiness relationship between Saxton and Mrs. Barton are true, the important factor is that some associates perceive them to be. The members of the secretarial pool could be generating these rumors in an effort to discredit Saxton and retaliate for the apparent partiality shown toward Mrs. Barton.

These unverified rumors, along with Saxton's inaction following the Barton incident, can only serve to damage his position and reputation as an executive. Apart from any moral considerations, it is simply unwise for an executive to engage in or convey the impression of engaging in any intimate social activities of the type rumored. Many business firms have written or unwritten policies to this effect. Townsend, in his parody of organization life, gives clear and serious warning on this matter in his example of the amorous personnel manager who used the executive secretaries for other than business purposes.[37] The important point is that the executive compromises his/her position and is vulnerable to accusations of bias and injustice which could destroy one's professional career. Returning to this incident, though, there is one fact given which should help dispel any supposition of foul play: Mrs. Barton was 57 years old. While the age factor does not necessarily mean a cessation of passion, it ought to at least suggest discretion!

Saxton, because of his position as the senior executive in the office, is expected to play certain roles. He could have defined the lines of communication and responsibility. His influence, even though it may have rested on the attitudes of the individuals in his environment and the system of communication, is a self-supporting condition. Saxton could either be successful because of his influence or he could fail because he used it improperly.

Grant is the middleman in this incident. He has been unable to get results from Mrs. Barton or Mr. Saxton. He has had no feedback from his senior associate each time he has mentioned the problem involving Mrs. Barton. It can be assumed that this has been very frustrating to Grant and his perception of Mr. Saxton as a manager has been affected. Grant is faced with the dilemma of either accepting Saxton's decision, disputing it or leaving altogether.

It should also be pointed out that Grant is a victim of short-circuiting. The incident indicates that Mrs. Barton and Mr. Saxton have affected certain working agreements which were unknown to Grant. This again is the result of a poorly defined communication channel. Related to this problem, Grant is confronted with role ambiguity. He is now uncertain as to the scope of his responsibilities, the extent of his authority, his superior's criteria for evaluating performance and his advancement opportunities; in short, there is uncertainty over the major facets of his professional life which strike directly at his individual needs. In other words, there is no closely defined path to achievement.[38] Moreover, his organizational status is, in effect, lower than that of the secretary who is formally supposed to report to him. Indeed, Saxton might be protecting a loyal secretary (and himself) by ignoring her blandishments, but he is doing so at the very high cost of losing competent associates in the organization.

ADDITIONAL INFORMATION NEEDED

It would be helpful to know if Saxton had ever, in the past, had an assistant. Perhaps Mrs. Barton was quite satisfied with her position until Mr. Grant came along, and had difficulty adjusting to the presence of an assistant.

It would be good to know if Mr. Saxton had ever taken the time to explicitly tell Mrs. Barton why Grant was working as his assistant and that she should be of service to Grant whenever he needed her.[39] Also, did Saxton inform Grant of the routine tasks that Mrs. Barton was doing for him? It may be that if Mr. Saxton had taken the time to assure Mrs. Barton that her job was not going to be changed, Mrs. Barton's attitude may have been entirely different.

Information on the jobs performed by each of these individuals would be helpful for the analysis. Also, it would be helpful to know more about the top-level management changes which were disturbing Saxton. Perhaps Mr. Saxton has been having some problems which have caused top-level management to reexamine his effectiveness. Mr. Saxton may be very insecure about his status. This insecurity on the part of Mr. Saxton should be elaborated upon in greater detail.

Finally, information on top-management climate and policy would be necessary. It may very well be that these elements are adversely affecting Saxton, psychologically and physiologically. These effects can stimulate extreme introspection, raising self-doubts and causing a retreat to an autistic preoccupation with self. Compounding his problems are the needs of new associates such as Jim Grant. Perhaps this is a good occasion for Saxton to consider what Hanan calls an organizational "Bill of Rights," which would spell out the prerogatives of junior associates along with the ethical principles which will guide managerial behavior.[40]

ANALYSIS 2: *The Absentee Secretary*

Mrs. Barton neither perceives nor accepts the authority of Mr. Grant. Communication within the organization needs to be improved. Barnard says that a person will accept a communication as authoritative if he: (1) understands it; (2) believes it consistent with the purpose of the organization; (3) believes it compatible with personal interest; and (4) has the ability to comply with it.[41] There is evidence in the incident to suggest that these conditions have not been adequately met. Mr. Grant has been unable to effect communication regarding the objectives of the organization and the scope of Mrs. Barton's responsibility in meeting them. He has not offered sufficient inducement to secure commitment to work. Mrs. Barton is reacting to conflict by resorting to defense mechanisms such as conversion and aggression.

Probably more important than authority is the concept of power. Mrs. Barton probably perceives that she has more power than Mr. Grant; this perception may result from her time in the organization, position in the organization and her relationship with Mr. Saxton.[42]

The alternatives suggested are outlined below:

1. Mrs. Barton could be fired. Her performance on the job has been inadequate, she has a drinking problem, and there are rumors concerning Mr. Saxton and her. Comment: Since Mrs. Barton holds a fairly high position in the secretarial hierarchy, one must assume competence, experience, and the capability to perform adequately. Experienced secretaries of Mrs. Barton's caliber are difficult to replace. The evidence presented in the incident does not prove that a drinking problem exists. We probably should also discount the rumors about Mrs. Barton and Mr. Saxton, or at the very least, obtain additional information prior to taking any action based on these rumors.

2. Mr. Grant could intensify his search for another position. It is impossible for him to achieve rapport with Mrs. Barton. Comment: Jim Grant probably will not escape from problems by changing jobs. Grant could derive greater executive growth and fulfill his higher order needs more fully by staying in his present position, and attempting to solve the problem at hand. From a more pragmatic viewpoint, if Mr. Saxton's perceptions about the intent of top management are correct, there may be a rather attractive job opening within the organization.

3. Mr. Grant could discuss the problem with Mr. Saxton and ask for his help. Mr. Saxton needs to be made aware of the problem. Comment: While filtering may have occurred in Grant's communications with Albert Saxton, Mr. Grant has brought Mrs. Barton's behavior to Mr. Saxton's attention on three separate occasions. Mr. Saxton has chosen to ignore the matter. Since Mrs. Barton's performance for Mr. Saxton has apparently been adequate, Mr. Grant's problems do not motivate him, at this time, to take any positive action.

4. Mr. Grant could seek the assistance of top management in solving this problem. Comment: This is probably a poor solution. Top management can solve the problem for Mr. Grant, but it is a problem that Grant should be able to solve for himself. Management will realize this. Grant's opportunities for advancement could be adversely affected by such action.

5. Mr. Grant could attempt to work out a solution with Mrs. Barton through a series of face-to-face confrontations. Comment: This is considered the best solution. Ambiguity and role conflict, as discussed by Kahn, have weakened interpersonal relations.[43] Kahn says that conflict and ambiguity result in withdrawal and avoidance; these tendencies have been exhibited by Mrs. Barton and also by Mr. Saxton. Only through repeated interactions with Mrs. Barton and Mr. Saxton can Grant hopefully secure some acceptance of his authority. Mr. Grant should strive to achieve integration. An approach similar to that expressed by McGregor would appear to have some application to this incident. McGregor's four phases are: (1) clarification of the job (it must be communicated to Mrs. Barton that the work she does for Mr. Grant is also important to the organization); (2) establishment of specific targets for a limited time period (Mrs. Barton's absenteeism would be a good one); (3) supportive management during the target period; and (4) appraisal of results.[44] Likert would also probably suggest this approach; he advocates that a supportive rather than a threatening style of management increases both motivation and productivity.[45] Odiorne would also probably favor this solution.[46]

ADDITIONAL INFORMATION NEEDED

There are many factors which it would be valuable to know prior to arriving at a decision. The size and the type of organization are unknown. What is Mr. Saxton's job? Executive is an indefinite term. Much more information about Mrs. Barton would be desirable. Is her behavior of recent origin? Is she the head of a household, and how important is the job to her? If her job is not one of central life interest to her, she may feel that attempts to increase self realization would be futile;[47] this may not preclude effective performance on the job, but would require more rigid guidelines. In Kahn's terms, Mr. Saxton appears to be a focal person.[48] He may be experiencing pressures from top management, his assistant, his secretary, his family, and the office grapevine. At this point, he is certainly guilty of some degree of indecisive management.

FOOTNOTES

[1] Robert C. Wilson, "Easing the Way for the New Manager," *Business Horizons,* October, 1970, p. 53.

[2] *Ibid.,* p. 56.

[3] For a scholarly account of leadership and organizational factors in a football team, see Ralph M. Stogdill, *Team Achievement Under High Motivation* (Columbus, Ohio: Bureau of Business Research, Ohio State University, Research Monograph No. 113, 1963).

[4] See Floyd C. Mann and James K. Dent, "The Supervisor: Member of Two Organizational Families," *Harvard Business Review,* November-December, 1954, pp. 103–12.

[5] Fred E. Fiedler, "Leadership Experience and Leader Performance—Another Hypothesis Shot to Hell," *Organizational Behavior and Human Performance* 5 (1970); 1–14.

[6] Robert L. Kahn, "Role Conflict and Ambiguity in Organizations," *The Personnel Administrator* 9, no. 2 (March-April, 1964): 8–13.

[7] For an extensive treatment, see William F. Dowling, Jr. and Leonard R. Sayles, *How Managers Motivate: The Imperatives of Supervision* (New York: McGraw-Hill Book Co., 1971), pp. 269–304.

[8] Excellent discussions of motivational conditions in a more practical yet scholarly vein are found in: Saul W. Gellerman, *Motivation and Productivity* (New York: American Management Association, Inc., 1963), and Douglas McGregor, *The Professional Manager* (New York: McGraw-Hill Book Co., 1967).

[9] Michael J. Misshauk, "Supervisory Skills and Employee Satisfaction," *Personnel Administration,* July-August, 1971, pp. 29–33.

[10] Melvin Sorcher, "Motivation on the Assembly Line," *Personnel Administration,* May-June, 1969, pp. 40–48.

[11] Misshauk, "Supervisory Skills"

[12] Chris Argyris, "Personality and Organization," in D. R. Hampton, C. E. Summer, and R. A. Webber, *Organizational Behavior and the Practice of Management* (Glenview, Ill.: Scott, Foresman and Company, 1968), p. 138–49.

[13]John R. P. French and Bertram Raven, "The Bases of Social Power," in Dorwin Cartwright and A. F. Zander, eds., *Group Dynamics,* 2d ed. (Evanston: Row, Peterson and Company, 1960), pp. 607–23.

[14]Chester I. Barnard, *The Functions of the Executive* (Cambridge: Harvard University Press, 1938).

[15]Kenneth Hopper, "The Growing Use of College Graduates as Foreman," *Management of Personnel Quarterly,* Summer, 1967, pp. 2–12.

[16]Raymond L. Hilgert, "Satisfaction and Dissatisfaction in a Plant Setting," *Personnel Administration,* July-August, 1971, pp. 21–27.

[17]Hugo E. R. Uyterhoeven, "General Managers in the Middle," *Harvard Business Review,* March-April, 1972, pp. 75–85.

[18]*Ibid.*

[19]William G. Scott, *Organization Theory: A Behavioral Analysis for Management* (Homewood, Ill.: Richard D. Irwin, Inc., 1967), p. 200.

[20]*Ibid.*

[21]David Mechanic, "Sources of Power of Lower Participants in Complex Organizations," *Administrative Science Quarterly,* 7, no.3, (December, 1962): pp. 349–64.

[22]Scott, *Organization Theory,* p. 205.

[23]*Ibid.,* p. 201.

[24]Mechanic, "Sources of Power," pp. 349–64.

[25]Scott, *Organization Theory,* pp. 182–83.

[26]*Ibid.,* p. 209.

[27]*Ibid.,* pp. 214–15.

[28]An investigation revealing how communications can be improved within a company is summarized by L. I. Gelfand, "Communicate Through Your Supervisors," *Harvard Business Review,* November-December, 1970, pp. 101–4.

[29]The additional information desired is for the most part relative to status congruency as presented by George C. Homans, *Social Behavior: Its Elementary Forms* (New York: Harcourt, Brace and World, Inc., 1961).

[30]Based upon the French-Raven analysis of power. See French and Raven, "The Bases of Social Power," in Cartwright and Zander, *Group Dynamics,* pp. 607–23.

[31]Fremont Shull and Bert C. McCammon, Jr., "Adaptive Behavior in Business Organizations," in William P. Sexton, *Organization Theories* (Columbus, Ohio: Charles E. Merrill Publishing Co., 1970), pp. 402–10.

[32]Larry L. Cummings and Aly M. Elsalmi, "The Impact of Role Diversity, Job Level and Organizational Size on Managerial Satisfaction," *Administrative Science Quarterly,* 10 (1970): 1–10.

[33]See Keith Davis, *Human Relations at Work: The Dynamics of Organizational Behavior* (New York: McGraw-Hill Book Co., 1967), pp. 53–55.

[34]George H. Labovitz, "Organizing for Adaptation," *Business Horizons,* June, 1970, pp. 19–26.

[35]John R. Rizzo, Robert J. House and Sidney L. Lirtzman, "Role Conflict and Ambiguity in Complex Organizations," *Administrative Science Quarterly* 15 (1970): 150–63.

[36]See, for example, Frieda Fordham, *An Introduction to Jung's Psychology* (Baltimore: Penguin Books, Inc., 1959).

[37]Robert Townsend, *Up the Organization* (Greenwich, Conn.: Fawcett Publications, Inc., 1970), pp. 98–99.

[38]See Evans's discussion of path-goal instrumentality as related to motivation: Martin T. Evans, "Managing the New Managers," *Personnel Administration,* May-June, 1971, pp. 31–38.

[39]Although in this author's experience, the age factor would hamper adjustment to the new situation. Among older secretaries whose training and skills are limited, high dependency on the chief can develop, making life extremely difficult for the junior "intruder."

[40]Mack Hanan, "Make Way for the New Organization Man," *Harvard Business Review,* July-August, 1971, p. 136.

[41]Chester I. Barnard, "The Theory of Authority," in D. R. Hampton, C. E. Summer, and R. A. Webber, *Organizational Behavior and the Practice of Management* (Glenview, Ill.: Scott, Foresman and Company, 1968), p. 452.

[42]For a comprehensive coverage of how lower participants such as secretaries, hospital attendants and the like possess power in organizations see David Mechanic, "Sources of Power of Lower Participants in Complex Organizations," *Administrative Science Quarterly,* December, 1962, pp. 349–64.

[43]Kahn, "Role Conflict," pp. 8–13.

[44]Douglas McGregor, *The Human Side of Enterprise* (New York: McGraw-Hill Book Company, Inc., 1960), pp. 61–75.

[45]Rensis Likert, "Motivation and Increased Productivity," *The Management Record,* (April, 1956), pp. 128–31.

[46]George S. Odiorne, "Discipline by Objectives," *Management of Personnel Quarterly,* Summer, 1971, p. 13–20.

[47]Robert A. Dubin, "Industrial Research and the Discipline of Sociology," *Proceedings of the 11th Annual Meeting, Industrial Relations Research Association* (Madison: The Association Press, 1959), pp. 160–63.

[48]Kahn, "Role Conflict," pp. 8–13.

LEADERSHIP

Incident	Page
THE EXPANDED DEALER ORGANIZATION	184
Daniel M. Graves, III	
Analysis 1	185
Analysis 2	187
MONITORED PHONE CALLS	190
Allen L. Ralston	
Analysis 1	191
Analysis 2	194
THE NEW EXECUTIVE	197
T. M. Leathem	
Analysis 1	198
Analysis 2	201

THE EXPANDED DEALER ORGANIZATION

In September of 1967, the Fisher Electric Appliance Corporation franchised eight large chains, totaling over 750 stores, in order to reach a previously neglected market. This was in addition to over 14,000 existing independent dealers already selling electrical appliances. Although the general sales manager, Mr. Alderson, knew that this would create more work for the 200 salesmen, he also knew that it would help the division's profit picture. It was decided that Mr. Delaney (Mr. Alderson's old boss) would head the department. Although Mr. Delaney was nearing retirement and rarely agreed with Mr. Alderson's policies, it was felt that through his management and organizational ability, he would be able to quickly turn the department into a profitable venture.

Within six months, many of the independent dealers began to complain and threatened to cancel their franchises with Fisher. Because the chain stores were buying in quantity, they were severely undercutting the independent dealers' prices. Because of this situation, Mr. Alderson sent letters to all Fisher zone managers and personnel which in effect stated:

> "The independent dealers have built this company into what it is today. They have 'stuck with us' in both good and bad times. The future of the Fisher Corporation depends upon a strong dealer organization. Therefore, we must strive to help our dealers stay in business.

Although there was no indication of a previous problem, in June of 1969 the chain stores began to complain that they were not being sufficiently contacted by Fisher's salesmen. Mr. Delaney authorized an investigation, and within three weeks he had the results. The results showed that all stores received contact when taking on Fisher products, but only 20 percent of the stores had had at least one subsequent contact up to the time of the study. Mr. Delaney knew that unless this situation improved, the chain stores would switch to other suppliers. Therefore, he sought answers as to why the contact was so poor for the chain stores.

184

ANALYSIS 1: *The Expanded Dealer Organization*

The salient issues in this incident are in the areas of communication and leadership. These are so highly interrelated we will attempt to analyze them as integral issues as they bear on the problem.

A communication problem exists not only between Alderson and Delaney but also throughout the entire organization. The incident reads, "Within six months, many of the independent dealers began to complain and threatened to cancel their franchise with Fisher." There had to be a lack of understanding on the part of Mr. Alderson not to have become aware of this dissatisfaction.

Again, the incident reads, "Although there was no indication of a previous problem, in June of 1969 ..." This was almost two years after the change. Both Mr. Alderson and Mr. Delaney showed a lack of sensitivity to the problem to let two years elapse without recognizing that a problem could exist. There was obviously a lack of interaction with the salesmen on the part of both Mr. Alderson and Mr. Delaney. Though both apparently were in a supervisory position over the salesmen, neither knew what the salesmen were doing.

No sense of "teamwork" or participation appears to prevail in the total organization. The salesmen apparently were dissatisfied. Scott states that satisfaction depends on "perceived freedom by persons to participate in decision-making and communication activities."[1] The salesmen did not participate in much of the decision-making, at least not in this particular incident. The lack of participation combined with limited and ambiguous communication established a situation that failed to provide a supportive environment enabling the salesmen to achieve objectives.[2]

From the information given us in the incident, Mr. Alderson did not take into consideration the forces in the salesmen. Nor did he weigh the forces in the situation completely.[3] Though he did consider that "it would help the division's profit picture," he did not take into consideration what it would do to the salesmen, to the independent dealers, or for that matter, to the chain stores and future business.

Gibb mentions the difference between the persuasion approach and the problem-solving approach.[4] The persuasion approach lends itself to being authoritarian, to fixing blame, and to manipulating in order to achieve results, whereas, the problem-solving approach considers communications as a symptom of a problem existing in the organization, and thus attempts to change the organization. Rather than involve the salesmen in the decision initially, and thus eliminate some of the communication problems, Alderson made the decision on his own, thereby providing an environment that could easily result in a dysfunctional group, as we will later see. In this situation, when Mr. Alderson discovered the problem with the independent dealers, he immediately isolated the problem as it pertained to the treatment of the independent dealers. In so doing he used words that expressed favoritism, thus placing the chain stores in a different category. He did not look at the total organization nor seek ways to bring the total organization together. The problem also exists because of the favoritism shown to the independent dealers. By saying such words as ". . . the independent dealers have built this company into what it is today", "the future . . . depends upon a strong dealer organization," and the like, he can only be setting up the chain stores against the independent stores, and projecting his expectations upon the salesmen to favor the independent stores.

There may be some confusion in the chain of command, though possibly this is due to insufficient information in the incident. Is Mr. Alderson directly over the salesmen? But if the salesmen are also to sell to the stores under Mr. Delaney, is Mr. Delaney also in some way a supervisor of the salesmen? If this is the case, then the salesmen are caught in a confusing situation—do they seek to please Mr. Alderson or Mr. Delaney?

There is a lack of understanding on the part of Mr. Alderson toward his salesmen. Scott lists six guides for improving understanding. The sender of the message must consider "both his and the receiver's attitudes toward the message . . ."[5] Alderson only considered his attitude, and not that of the salesmen. Nor was there any attempt to "consider the language the receiver will understand."[6] Though Scott also lists that the sender "is constantly aware of the impact of his words on the receiver,"[7] Alderson at no point in the incident showed evidence of knowing the impact on the salesmen.

The salesmen eventually neglected the chain stores in deference to the independent stores. The incident reveals that the salesmen were suddenly confronted with more work than before; and, as Likert mentions, pressures from above tend to be resented.[8] This type of resentment could have easily existed on the part of the salesmen, since they were not consulted on a decision which directly affected them. The salesmen's choice, therefore, could have been: (1) reduce the work in both the independent and the chain stores; (2) reduce the work in only the independent stores or; (3) reduce the work in only the chain stores. Though at first they attempted to work with the chain stores, they eventually ignored them. Mr. Alderson expected the salesmen to give preference to the independent stores. This is stated very clearly. From what we can see in the line of authority (though it is ambiguous) the salesmen are staff to Mr. Alderson. Therefore, they would naturally conform to his expectation, and at the same time, reduce output.

ADDITIONAL INFORMATION DESIRED

Further information needed to more completely analyze the incident could be summarized as follows:

1. What was the organizational structure? To whom were the salesmen responsible?
2. What was the relationship between Delaney and Alderson? What prompted the previously made decision that placed Alderson in a superior position to his former boss?
3. Who made the study? Delaney authorized it, and could easily have structured it according to his perception.
4. Was there any attempt to help the salesmen understand Mr. Alderson's decision? Did he even look for acceptance?

ANALYSIS 2: *The Expanded Dealer Organization*

In introducing the new chain stores into the organization, Mr. Alderson assumed that the assumption of the added burden of servicing these accounts could be accomplished without adding any additional men to the sales force. No explanation as to their potential was stressed, only that this addition would be profitable to the firm. What was not evidently considered were the behavioral implications of this action.

First, the work content was changed, imposing a threat to the salesmen. As can be seen from the given data, each salesman now had over seventy stores to service, which required a salesman to closely watch his time. If he did not, his sales volume could decrease, making him look bad in his supervisor's eyes. Second, the work relationship as discussed could also pertain to salesmen's relationships with the existing independent dealers. Through experience and time allocation, the salesmen had probably developed a "cozy" market, regarding most dealers as friends. The new accounts meant that the market would be changed, and less time spent with each dealer. This was enough to suggest that a problem was in the making.

Although Alderson's intentions were good, the statements were not explicit, nor directed toward the problems. This left the matter wide open to speculation and personal interpretation. First, the majority of the salesmen perceived the statement to mean that Mr. Alderson was more interested in the independent dealers than in the chain stores. In other words, they felt that he ranked them higher in importance. Basically, there are two aspects to perception. The first is information which can be verified. The other involves information which can be screened and admitted as importance is felt. This second aspect is known as selective perception.[9]

At his age and in his current position, Delaney was not the person to please. Alderson was the man responsible for promoting and rewarding salesmen; therefore, the salesmen continued to channel their efforts to the independent dealers. Undoubtedly, some salesmen experienced dissonance because they were aware of the importance of chain store accounts on the one hand, but wanted also to protect their interests on the other by satisfying Alderson's requests. One might conceive of this as a double approach-avoidance conflict in that each alternative contains both opportunity losses and gains.[10] The strategy in this type of situation would be more complex than in either approach-approach or simple approach-avoidance situations. One could predict that the salesmen with lower frustration tolerance might withdraw and/or follow a compromise path at a low activity level. It is not clear that this is what occurred, but it could be expected unless the policy matter is resolved.

We have included this incident under leadership, reservedly so, primarily because of the observed leader behavior of Alderson and Delaney. Up until now, the discussion has concerned primarily perception and change. At this point, we will shift our perspective to the leadership issues in the incident.

LEADERSHIP

One obvious difficulty is that of a former boss reporting to the very individual (Alderson) who was formerly a subordinate. The situation is further compounded by Alderson's apparent reversal of a strategy promulgated by Delaney. The incident indicates another potential trouble spot, i.e., the divergence of viewpoint between Alderson and Delaney. Differences in managerial values do not suggest ineffectiveness, as demonstrated by George in his study on values among subordinate managers and supervisors,[11] but where concrete policies are involved it is likely that some conflict will result.

An item of information needed for further analysis would be a description of Delaney's strategy. From the way Delaney is characterized, it is likely that he would take a very directive approach toward shaping the sales structure in order to serve the new franchises. This observation, together with the antagonisms generated by the change in the salesmen's work system, would lead to the possibility of "malicious obedience"[12] on the part of salesmen, i.e., following instructions to the letter, knowing that this rigid adherence would cause neglect of other important responsibilities. A highly directive leadership approach by Delaney would only serve to aggravate this situation. Although one cannot generalize too broadly, marketing organizations tend to be characterized by a consultative mode of leadership and salesmen would respond more positively to this style.[13]

It would also be helpful to know how the field or district sales managers responded to the change in distribution structure. Presumably, there are managers or coordinators in the field, given an organization of this size with the number of accounts serviced. Moreover, it is not mentioned whether the

200 new salesmen have actually been hired or are about to be hired. This could make a tremendous difference in the follow-up to the incident, because they could possibly be trained and assigned to relieve existing salesmen of their added burden.

Then, there is the question of salesman compensation. It would behoove Delaney and Alderson to alter the compensation structure in order that salesmen are rewarded for servicing both types of accounts. Whether this has been considered is not known, but one would expect that they will want to re-evaluate the compensation system. It could be that salesmen perceive low commissions in relation to the chain store accounts. Or on the other hand, they might not feel adequately trained to deal effectively with the chain store buyers and, therefore, in the rewards-investments equation, disproportionately greater effort is required for a given amount of sales.[14]

Finally, training appears to loom important in the evolution of the sales organization toward more complex interactions. The change will undoubtedly move the organization into a new stage of growth. In Greiner's terms, the organization will face a control crisis because of the new complexities introduced.[15] Thus, coordination will be necessary to overcome this crisis, and it is questionable whether Alderson and Delaney are managerially tooled up for the change. It is not clear yet whether the training should follow the laboratory approach, but this has been demonstrated to be effective in improving relationships between salesmen and sales executives.[16]

MONITORED PHONE CALLS

On a Friday afternoon Gil Harris, National Insurance Regional Manager, called his accounts division manager, Earl Bennett, into his office and explained to him that he had, for some time, been considering a program which he felt could reveal any possible problems with customer service. Now he was prepared to implement it. Over the weekend the telephone company was to install new equipment allowing incoming and outgoing phone calls to be monitored. The program involved three managerial and nine clerical employees all of whom had either agent or policy holder contacts. Mr. Harris was to maintain the tapping device in his office. Not only did he wish to personally supervise the program, but he felt that employees would be enthusiastic about an opportunity to prove themselves before higher management. As Bennett attempted to express his reservations Harris ended the talk by saying that his decision was a good one and that Bennett should notify his people of it. Monday morning Bennett called the twelve employees together and told them of Mr. Harris's wishes.

The announcement was followed by a great deal of grumbling. One girl was overheard telling her co-workers, "I've always prided myself in doing a good job. We should go in there and complain, but he would probably fire the lot of us."

During the first month of monitoring, absenteeism nearly doubled, and two employees notified Bennett they wished to transfer to another section. When asked why, they replied they couldn't stand being "watched" all the time. Bennett knew he would be held responsible for this activity and didn't know what to tell Harris. His problem compounded when he received the following memo from Harris:

"Earl, it appears as though I have been successful in uncovering problem areas. Your people don't seem to spend enough time with agents or policy holders. They act as though they are in a hurry and on occasion are downright 'rude.' Be in my office at 10 a.m. tomorrow morning with your recommendations on how you are going to straighten this out."

ANALYSIS 1: *Monitored Phone Calls*

Any analysis of this incident must include an examination and evaluation of the leadership method used. We can then proceed to study the various problems that occurred within this framework of discussion.

LEADERSHIP

It requires no close examination to determine that Harris was, in the most traditional sense, a boss-centered leader. He made the decisions. Even when offered advice from a subordinate, he refused to listen. Tannenbaum and Schmidt presented what they termed a "Continuum of Leadership Behavior."[17] To the left on this scale was the boss-centered leader "who makes his decision and announces it." This description would seem to be fairly accurate of Harris's style of leadership. His control was so absolute that one employee felt that if the group were to confront him on his decision to monitor their phone calls, he would "fire" the lot of them. Goldhammer and Shils would describe the type of power used by Harris as "domination" or ". . . influencing the behavior by making explicit to others what he wants them to do (command, request, etc.)."[18]

With respect to Bennett we must conclude that he is not a leader. When he notified his employees of the new monitoring system, he told them merely of "Mr. Harris's wishes." He functioned merely as a link in the communication chain, not as a leader.

Perhaps Jennings would classify Bennett as the ultimate expression of his point of view. Jennings believes that "today's executives lack creativity" and that "present organizations kill leadership."[19] This may well be stretching Jennings's intentions somewhat, but he enlightens us to suspect that the organization must share with Bennett in the responsibility for his actions.

PERCEPTION AND GROUP BEHAVIOR

The accelerating rate of absenteeism and the transfer requests represent a concerted effort on the part of the employees to combat a practice which they regard as a threat. Or, as Scott puts it, "a group tends to resist those changes which are perceived as threatening to its survival."[20] The key words herein presented are "group" and "perceived." Whether the managers and nine clerical workers had in the past assumed group characteristics and behavior is not fully determinable. What is evident, however, is that the introduction of the conversation monitoring equipment produced responses that either created or reinforced worker cohesiveness resulting in their adopting defense mechanisms.

Harris clearly did not anticipate any negative reaction on the part of this group. He was unable to foresee the manner in which the employees would perceive what was happening. This assumption is supported by the fact that the problem facing management was not prevention, but rather, remedy. Leavitt points out the folly in the approach when he states, "For managerial purposes, the importance of the perceptual world is clear. If one's concern as a supervisor or counselor or committee member is to try to effect some change in the behavior of other people, and if in turn, people's present behavior is determined by their perceptions of their environments, then it is critical that one seek to understand the circumstances under which their behavior might change."[21] Without such understanding, management runs the risk of unanticipated and unfavorable responses. Such was the case at National. Harris even went so far as to think that these employees would react favorably and "be enthusiastic about an opportunity to prove themselves before higher management."

COMMUNICATIONS

This incident presents some serious communication problems. Gibb advocates what he terms a "Problem solving" approach to communication.[22] He indicates that in a majority of situations this approach proves most successful. However, with the type of leadership pattern at National, this approach would probably not be possible. Rather, Harris could adapt more readily to Gibb's "persuasion approach." Although Gibb lists several inherent difficulties in the persuasion method, he at no point contends that it cannot be effective when justifiably applied. Gibb states, "The persuasion manager tends to see communications as primarily an influence process . . . managers try to sell ideas, or to motivate others to work harder, feel better, have higher morale, and be more loyal."[23] At National no attempt was made to "sell" the work group on the true intention and value of the monitoring and how it might relate to their security. In fact, even Bennett had not been "sold" on the idea. Herein lies the difficulty. Proper and effective communications have been impeded by organizational barriers. Of those presented in the article by Steiglitz[24] "corporate climate and mechanical barriers" are most applicable in this incident. If Harris could not see the need for properly communicating with Bennett, then why would Bennett in turn see the need to communicate with his workers?

NEED SATISFACTION

Maslow provided insight with respect to the response taken by the employees when he set forth his preconditions for basic need satisfaction. He held that ". . . freedom to defend one's self, justice, fairness, honesty and orderliness in the group are examples of such preconditions for basic need satisfaction. Thwarting this freedom will be reacted to with a threat or emergency response."[25] When the monitoring of phone conversations commenced, the safety need of these employees was no longer satisfied. This lack of satisfaction caused feelings of anxiety. These feelings were further expressed by a high degree of absenteeism and two requests for transfer.

CONFLICT

The employees served as identification models to one another and the employees can be described as belonging to the same role set. When pressures emerged in opposition to their expectations of the work situation, a dilemma developed. Scott would describe this as "Role Conflict" which, as he says, "results when an individual is faced with two roles which are incompatible."[26] Kahn explains the employee reaction to this incompatibility when he states "the most frequent behavioral response to role conflict is withdrawal or avoidance of those who are seen as creating the conflict."[27] Certainly no withdrawal is more complete than total removal from a hostile environment.

The dilemma facing the work group can be expanded further. Rather than accept the monitoring, their reaction was that of fear; this results in lower levels of job performance and greater absenteeism. However, on the other side was a very real fear of managerial reprisals for these actions. Scott terms this an "avoidance-avoidance conflict."[28]

CONCLUDING REMARKS

Any solution to this situation becomes a direct result of the analysis. The trouble spots must be corrected. The paradox in which Bennett in particular finds himself presents a sad commentary on the company. It is interesting to consider whether Harris will blame Bennett when he comes to realize the entire situation as it actually exists. He may well do so without ever realizing that he is primarily at fault. Harris evidently did not meet his responsibility of staging the proper managerial climate and designing the type of organization that would facilitate effective communication. Yet, in the meantime, Bennett fell victim to a blind bureaucracy.

Harris must reexamine his leadership style and become more receptive to the needs of his subordinates. His autocratic methods were not the most effective. How much less autocratic he should become is not fully determinable. Possibilities range from McMurry's "benevolent autocracy"[29] (slight change) to the concepts set forth by Argyris regarding the "optimizing of an individual's needs."[30] Neither is necessarily recommended, but within this spectrum lies the optimal alternative.

ANALYSIS 2: *Monitored Phone Calls*

To analyze the incident, it would be helpful to know if there had been a problem with customer service prior to installing the monitoring system. For the purpose of this analysis, we will assume that no apparent problem with customer service was evident. Also a preliminary interpretation of Gil Harris is that he is autocratically-oriented and that Earl Bennett is a manager with at least average ability but is somewhat thwarted in his efforts by Harris.

In explaining his idea to Bennett, Harris did not allow any feedback, which implies that he is somewhat autocratic. The one-way communication did not permit Bennett to explain the possible human relations problems that would occur. Secondly, whether or not the monitoring idea was good, proper communication concerning the purpose of the monitoring was completely absent. Harris should have foreseen the problem that would occur and, to avoid it, he should have either altered his method of obtaining the information or found an adequate way to solicit support from the employees for the monitoring system. It could have at least been explained that the purpose of the monitoring was not to fire people, but to help them find more efficient methods of answering customer calls. In short, Bennett and/or Harris should have pointed out a number of employee-related benefits to allay workers' fears.

LEADERSHIP

There is ample evidence to show that Harris is an authoritarian manager. For example, Harris will not allow Mr. Bennett, the manager of the target group, to voice any reservations he holds about the project. In addition, employees were afraid to complain to Mr. Harris. Harris does the actual listening rather than Bennett, and seems unable or unwilling to allow Bennett the chance to work with his employees.

Harris seems more concerned with the job rather than the people. He is overstepping the chain of command by the use of this program. He is monitoring another manager's employees, and not allowing Mr. Bennett to participate in the study, yet will hold Bennett responsible for results. In this regard, Harris seems to share McMurry's views regarding benevolent autocracy. McMurry states the view to be that real participation is possible only at upper management levels and that the average employee is often not capable or does not want to join in participative management.[31]

A second aspect of the problem that reveals Harris's authoritarian style is his reason for proceeding with the program. It would seem logical that before a program of this type is planned, the department member involved should be consulted. He is presumably more aware of problems that exist. Moreover, research shows that where quality of work is especially important, consideration is a vital leadership characteristic.[32] It appears that Harris is more concerned with personally controlling the situation than with finding and solving problems.

In synthesizing the leadership facets of the situation, it is necessary to also attempt to understand what might be Bennett's reasons for what might be perceived as an eavesdropping, "big-brother" approach which violates a widely-accepted value of privacy in U. S. culture. In the first place, Harris most likely has his own set of pressures to which he must respond. His role-set consists of more than just Bennett's group. Perhaps he has received negative feedback on customer service pertaining to Bennett's division. Secondly, distasteful as it might appear, this type of surveillance might be defensible from the standpoint of the effects of telephone deportment on the primary service objectives of the organization. Harris may have been tactless in his introduction of the monitoring system, but that should not overshadow the possibility of needing it.

Monitoring of this sort is quite common, especially in training situations. The distinction which makes it more acceptable is that employees are generally conditioned to the practice, and the objectives are also understood, unlike the present situation. Moreover, one must discern certain differences among circumstances where monitoring is practiced. Big brotherism would, it seems, apply more to one's private life than to one's work activities. Surely, the more desirable situation is that in which trust makes any sort of surveillance unnecessary. But even where trust exists, control needs might require at least occasional checking on work activities.[33] Therefore, one could argue that Harris's objectives were appropriate, but that he blundered in his approach, primarily due to his leadership style.

MOTIVATION

This incident depicts a situation which Herzberg might call poor hygiene. According to Herzberg, hygiene factors are extrinsic conditions which surround the job. Examples are policy, supervision, salary, interpersonal relations and physical working conditions.[34] These factors do not directly affect motivation, but can cause dissatisfaction. Harris's monitoring of the telephones is an instance of this. He made the employees believe that he did not trust them and that they were being watched. This caused employee dissatisfaction.

One woman employee seems especially distraught. She had previously prided herself on her work, but now Harris seems to distrust her. This type of feeling is undoubtedly present in all employees to some degree. Another indication of rising dissatisfaction is the higher rate of absenteeism, along with the requests for transfer.[35]

These hygiene factors could also be responsible for the work performance of the department. Where before no problems were noticed, Harris has now discovered that Bennett's employees are not performing adequately. Perhaps employees appear rude over the telephone because they are in a hurry to get off the line, knowing that their calls are being monitored. It is now known which needs were most prevalent before the system was installed. However, in all likelihood, security was not an overriding need as it apparently now is. If this supposition is correct, employees have experienced a shift consistent with Clark's interpretation of the Maslow theory, from either a social or esteem orientation to a preoccupation with safety factors. The opportunity for interaction has been stymied, and employment itself threatened by Harris' actions.[36]

In conclusion, any predictions concerning Bennett's response would be purely speculative. Most likely, he will avoid a major confrontation with Harris, judging from Bennett's previous behavior. It is not known how similar situations, if any, were handled in the past. As it stands, Harris holds the evidence whereas Bennett has less conclusive proof concerning effects upon employees. Even the concrete data on absenteeism and transfer requests could be reversed by Harris into arguments in favor of the monitoring policy. In other words, Harris could say that the absenteeism and transfer requests "prove" that employees are afraid to have their calls monitored for fear of having mistakes uncovered. But, Bennett could counter, too, that employees experienced "stage fright" and, were he to have his behavioral science wits about him, might suggest to Harris that experiments be conducted to test this view. This mythical debate, though, is doomed to have dysfunctional consequences. Harris might win the battle out of sheer power, but he will not increase commitment in the process. It can only create resentment throughout the organization unless he cultivates the psychological need for commitment which most likely is already latent in the employees.[37]

THE NEW EXECUTIVE

After several years of declining profit contributions, which were characteristic of the industry, top management of the Emerald Instrument Corporation undertook various programs to eliminate unprofitable plants and businesses and to rearrange and eliminate personnel requirements. Particularly affected in the latter category were members of middle management. The district sales manager at Baltimore, William Cairns, although well liked by his office staff and salesmen, was suddenly removed in the summer of 1970. His replacement, Robert Duff, had similarly been simultaneously dropped from a very responsible sales position in higher management.

Notwithstanding the cloud that hung over these changes, but perhaps mindful of it, Mr. Duff undertook an aggressive program of reviewing office and sales practices and altering and changing procedures where he deemed it necessary or helpful. Changes effected included speeding up and increasing the number of administrative reports required of the office staff and salesmen, greater emphasis on "putting it in writing" and record maintenance, and reducing the amount of incoming phone calls from salesmen to effect economies as well as to allow the new district sales manager more time to become personally involved in the major account responsibilities handled by the individual salesmen. The new manager was more assertive in taking direct action, making rapid decisions, and relying less on individual office or sales personnel in decision making. He vigorously pressed his sales representatives for extra efforts but was not prone to make note of individual successes. He remained detached, kept his own counsel, and, unlike his predecessor who was addressed on a first name basis within the office by everyone, he was addressed as Mr. Duff by the clerks and secretary.

Unrelated promotion and retirement had resulted in the office having a new office manager and a new secretary at about the same time that Robert Duff took over as district sales manager. In addition, there were two other experienced clerks and five veteran salesmen. Apart from their normally full time assigned tasks, the office staff was called upon to generate the large amount of statistical and survey information that was needed on which to base decisions. To a lesser extent, the sales personnel were also required to prepare related information.

Although the high degree of activity on the part of the new district sales manager and the large number of changes were not without significant successes, some serious problems resulted. Unlike the district manager, the new office manager routinely worked late every night and sometimes on weekends. To a lesser extent, this was also true of the secretary. She showed considerable signs of apathy as her normal work load piled up while she devoted more time to special projects for Bob Duff. This became a sore point with the salesmen who were anxious to have correspondence and quotations expedited. Both members of the office staff and the sales force showed signs of frustration, alienation, and antagonism. Within a few months, at least two people were seriously considering leaving the company. Another very capable salesman had already accepted a position with another firm before personally being dissuaded by Bob Duff in an eleventh-hour plea.

ANALYSIS 1: *The New Executive*

In analyzing this incident, a number of factors are found to indicate that this situation could have been anticipated and avoided if certain concepts of organizational behavior and theory had been understood and applied. Each factor which is felt to have been significant in this incident will be presented and discussed, in the order of importance.

Due to changing business conditions, the company was forced to make efficiency changes which resulted in the displacement of personnel. Mr. Duff's attitude toward the way in which his office should be run was antithetical to that of Mr. William Cairns. When Duff took over the job, he reviewed office and sales practices and altered existing procedures. It is assumed that the employees were also aware of the company's program of change. Therefore, they perceived these changes as a threat to their present work situation. In effect, their work was under review and they were afraid. Their security was threatened. Not only will a perceived threat cause resistance, but it can destroy the morale of the work force.

A major organizational theory variable which comes into play is that of Duff's style of leadership. It seems that he had a strong authoritarian style, as opposed to Mr. Cairns who appeared more participative in approach.

LEADERSHIP STYLE

There are several items of additional information that would be useful in this area. First, it would be helpful to know what style of leadership the previous sales manager used. Second, it would be helpful to know what style of leadership Mr. Duff had used in the past and why he had been dropped from a very responsible sales position in higher management. It would also be helpful to know how management as well as the salesmen and clerks perceived their performance under the previous manager's style of leadership. All of the above information is highly relevant in interpreting how these indivduals will react to the new manager.

Since the previous manager was well liked, and since the autocratic tendencies of the new manager are referred to as changes, it is assumed that Mr. Cairns was very employee-centered. This means that there probably has been a shift from employee-centered leadership to boss-centered leadership.

Mr. Duff has evidently been an effective leader in the past since he has been a member of top management. This does not mean that he will be an effective leader in this situation since a leader's effectiveness depends not only on his characteristics, but also on the characteristics of the situation in which he finds himself.[38] Duff may be an effective leader in a well structured, authoritarian organization, but he is not effective in a less structured, democratic situation. Moreover, he (Duff) is individual-oriented rather than group-oriented in his decision making, an approach which is inconsistent with contemporary organizational and cultural trends.[39]

In using a boss-centered style of leadership, Mr. Duff has failed to consider the forces in the situation and the forces in the subordinates.[40] Looking first at the forces in the organization, Mr. Duff has failed to consider the type of organization that exists. Organizations have values and traditions which influence the behavior of the people who work in them. To deviate radically from what is generally accepted is likely to create problems, unless the changed styles are properly introduced.

Mr. Duff has also failed to consider the forces among the subordinates. As a result of past leadership, the subordinates have the following characteristics: (1) a relatively high need for independence, (2) a readiness to assume responsibility for decision making, and (3) a desire to participate. In sum, the subordinates expect and actually have a need to share in the decision making; thus they resent Mr. Duff's making the decisions himself.

As a result, Mr. Duff has not been able to attain the minimum act of leadership which is ambiguity or uncertainty reduction.[41] In addition, Duff has not achieved the benefits of participative management. This is the next area of analysis.

It has already been developed that the employees expect and have a need for participative management. Duff, the new manager, has attempted to reduce the amount of employee participation in all aspects of the organization's decision making and planning activities in this incident. This undoubtedly is a major cause of the problem. It is not only participation itself which is so important; it is also a matter of employees feeling important and wanted by being consulted. The latter may be more important than the resulting increase in effectiveness of the decision itself. However, effectiveness can be a positive feature of participation under certain conditions, such as where various perspectives are needed and where the group itself has achieved a level of interaction in which matters are fully discussed and deliberated.[42] It is felt that subordinates in this instance could make valuable contributions, as evidenced by their experience and level of commitment to the organization. The autocratic style of leadership along with the lack of participation relate to another problem area: communication.

COMMUNICATION

The primary communication problem is the lack of two-way vertical communication. This is a result of the directive style of leadership exercised by the new sales manager. He is actually not willing to communicate; he is not willing to listen to the ideas of his subordinates. In essence, he only practices one-way communication, which is not really communication but order-giving. The greater the understanding the more likely it is that human behavior will proceed in the direction of accomplishing goals stated by management. The antithesis of understanding is ambiguity. Ambiguity will be discussed subsequently in relation to role behavior.

Upward communication is a channel of emotional and informational expression for people down the line. It carries information such as: (1) problems on which subordinates need help; (2) suggestions for improvement; and (3) subordinates' opinion about jobs, associates, and the company. All of this information is important to the manager if he is to prevent the types of problems that have already occurred in this incident. Thus, it is essential that the manager encourage two-way communication.

ROLE BEHAVIOR

The primary cause of role conflict in this incident is what Robert L. Kahn refers to as overload.[43] Overload simply means that the individual has more demands impinging on him than he can possibly satisfy.

The secretary is involved in what Kahn called an intersender conflict, i.e., requests and commands from one role sender oppose those from another sender.[44] Mr. Duff is asking her to spend more time on his special projects while the salesmen are anxious to have their correspondence and quotations expedited. She is spending extra time at her job; however, her normal workload keeps on accumulating.

The salesmen are also involved in intrasender conflict. The different requirements from their manager are incompatible. He is asking for greater sales effort from the salesmen while at the same time he is asking for more routine paper work. For example, he has asked the salesmen to: (1) increase the speed and number of administrative reports, (2) put a greater emphasis on documentation and record maintenance, and (3) prepare some of the statistical and survey information that is needed. All of this additional paper work is incompatible with the manager's goal of increased sales effort.

In addition to the role conflicts that exist, there is also role ambiguity. This role ambiguity is a result of uncertainty about scope of responsibility, about the expectations of others regarding one's performance and about the way in which one's supervisor evaluates one's work.

This uncertainty is the result of change. First, the old, well-liked office manager has been replaced by Duff. He has a different style of leadership, a different concept of communication and a different attitude toward his subordinates.

In addition to uncertainty about Duff as an individual, there is much uncertainty about his new policies. For example, he has reduced the number of incoming calls from salesmen, which means they must make more decisions without his advice. At the same time, he is very assertive in taking direct action and making rapid decisions without the participation of his salesmen. These two policies are contradictory and would naturally lead to uncertainty. Another policy that would cause uncertainty is his failure to note individual successes. He has asked for extra efforts but when they are accomplished he fails to recognize them. Thus, the salesmen are uncertain about what is expected of them from their new boss. The linkage between management and salesmen has been severed and in order to reestablish the working relationship, the salesmen's contributions should be encouraged.[45]

ANALYSIS 2: *The New Executive*

Before addressing the basic problems of this incident, it might be well to consider, speculatively, what may have been some of the contributing factors. At the outset, we are compelled to ask how Mr. Duff perceived his new situation. Did he perceive it as temporary assignment? Were the changes in district managers made because of the personalities involved? Were the changes made because of demands by upper management or were they initiated by Bob Duff in an effort to rebuild his battered career? Although the answers to these questions and other related questions are not known, it is accurate to assume that they, in varying degrees, had a profound effect on the thinking of the sales and office staff at Baltimore.

As might be expected, reassurances given at the time to the individual employees were perceived rather thinly, and the impact on the office personnel was rather sobering. Disquieting as the management changes were, there are strong indications that the new pattern of leadership was even more disruptive. Mr. Duff represents a distinct shift to the left on the "Continuum of Leadership Behavior"[46] because of his greater use of authority and the resultant diminishing of the participative decision-making previously extended to his subordinates. As noted in the incident, he was detached, and his motives were not always known or correctly interpreted by his subordinates. Because of the company's problems, the circumstances of Duff's arrival, and his more authoritarian manner in influencing his subordinates, the subordinates perceived serious threats to such derived growth motives as security, opportunity, participation, recognition, communication and independence.[47]

There is a distinct possibility that "the characteristics of the situation"[48] may have favored a less authoritarian choice in managers; however, this was probably not the most important consideration at the time Bob Duff was shifted to his new position. As was strongly implied in the incident, Bob Duff's predecessor, William Cairns, relied to a greater extent on more participative management practice; therefore, it is not unreasonable to anticipate considerable resistance on the part of those who previously had enjoyed a greater degree of influence on matters affecting them.

There were instances of role conflict being generated as a result of Mr. Duff's assignment. The relatively new office manager and the secretary were both called upon to supply much of the statistical and study information in addition to their regular responsibilities. In varying degrees, this resulted in overload in both cases. In the particular instance of the secretary, there was a decidedly negative outlook generated. Although it may not have been perceived as such by Bob Duff, the increased demands on the sales force for added and more effective efforts, while simultaneously reducing his (Duff's) accessibility through informal phone and personal contacts, was also a source of role frustration.

The specific avoidance of encouraging remarks by the district sales manager for specific successes probably also had a disturbing effect on the sales representatives who had relied on this type of recognition in the past.

Obviously, insecurity is a motivating force. As Scott points out, a satisfied need is not a motivator.[49] To this extent, it might have been that Duff intentionally played down individual accomplishments as a means of encouraging greater efforts on the part of sales personnel to gain the needed recognition that they sought from him. Alternatively, it appears that such activity was actually perceived by some of his subordinates as removing opportunities for recognition. The increased direct participation of the district sales manager, at times without the foreknowledge of the affected salesman with key accounts, was not easily reconciled promptly to the salesmen. Even where they understood the necessity or the desire of the district sales manager to afford them greater personal support, the net effect, at times, probably gave rise to a question about the degree of confidence that Duff had in them. Additionally, the decreased role of sales and office personnel in decision making tended to cast similar doubts as to the degree of confidence they enjoyed. The change in leadership pattern, changes in the role assumed by the district sales manager, and the shift from informal communications access to a formalized system probably tended to reduce the role effectiveness,[50] at least initially, of the subordinates who had previously experienced a well established pattern of responsibilities and relationships.

One of the most apparent problems created by the incident was that of communications. Direct access to Bob Duff was discouraged, based on his desire to see more recorded communications and by simultaneous efforts to reduce telephone costs. More formalized written communications can be regarded or perceived as a means of circumventing any meaningful exchanges by subordinates who formerly enjoyed a greater opportunity to influence decision making where it affected particular accounts. There probably was a greater tendency for communication to become one-way. Of the dichotomy between persuasion and problem-solving communications techniques, Duff, consistent with his more authoritarian leadership style, relied heavily on persuasion.[51]

Apart from the barriers of communications established by Bob Duff, it was quite apparent that the subordinates would similarly establish barriers as well. There was a discernible tendency to try to anticipate what Duff had in mind in order to be able to tell him what others thought he wanted to hear. Then too there was a greater reluctance to bring some matters to the district sales manager's attention because it could expose someone in the office or sales staff to criticism. Where possible, the situation created by the incident prompted greater short circuiting among employees who were not comfortable with the situation. As noted by Gibb, "Persuasive communications tend to produce distrust, circumvention, or counter-persuasion."[52]

FOOTNOTES

[1]William G. Scott, *Organization Theory: A Behavioral Analysis for Management* (Homewood, Ill.: Richard D. Irwin, Inc., 1967), p. 98.

[2]Robert C. Miljus, "Effective Leadership and the Motivation of Human Resources," *Personnel Journal,* January, 1970, pp. 36–40.

[3]Robert Tannenbaum and Warren H. Schmidt, "How to Choose a Leadership Pattern," *Harvard Business Review,* March-April, 1958, pp. 95–101.

[4]Jack R. Gibb, "Communications and Productivity," in S. G. Huneryager and I. L. Heckman, *Human Relations in Management* (Cincinnati: South-Western Publishing Co. 1967), pp. 520–29.

[5] Scott, *Organization Theory,* p. 313.

[6]*Ibid.*

[7]*Ibid.*

[8]Rensis Likert, "Motivation and Increased Productivity," in Huneryager and Heckman, *Human Relations,* p. 371.

[9]For a concise, scientific treatise on the perception process, see Albert H. Hasdorf, David J. Schneider, and Judith Polefka, *Person Perception* (Reading, Mass.: Addison-Wesley Publishing Co., 1970).

[10]Calvin S. Hall and Gardner Lindzey, *Theories of Personality* (New York: John Wiley and Sons, Inc., 1957), pp. 446–49.

[11]Norman George, "Supervisors' Indentification With Management: A Study of Comparative Values and Effectiveness," (Ph.D. diss., Ohio State University, 1962).

[12]Defined here as following orders or procedures rigidly at the expense of other responsibilities; e.g., the machine operator who follows orders to "produce" by working as fast as he can, literally destroying the equipment in the process.

[13]Norman George and Thomas J. Von der Embse, "Six Propositions for Managerial Leadership," *Business Horizons,* December, 1971, pp. 33–43; Tosi and Carroll also note that marketing personnel perceive themselves as having considerable voice in setting objectives. See Henry L. Tosi and Stephen J. Carroll, "Some Structured Factors Related to Goal Influence in the Management by Objectives Process," *M.S.U. Business Topics,* Spring, 1969.

[14]Wendell French, *The Personnel Management Process* (Boston: Houghton-Mifflin Company, 1970), pp. 132–35.

[15]Larry E. Greiner, "Evolution and Revolution as Organizations Grow," *Harvard Business Review,* July-August, 1972, pp. 40–44.

[16]See Robert T. Golembiewski and Stokes B. Carrigan, "Planned Change in Organization Style Based on the Laboratory Approach," *Administrative Science Quarterly* 15 (1970): 79–93.

[17]Tannebaum and Schmidt, "How to Choose," pp. 95–101.

[18]Herbert Goldhammer and Edward A. Shils, "Types of Power and Status," in David R. Hampton, Charles E. Summer, Ross A. Webber, *Organization Behavior and the Practice of Management* (Glenview, Ill.: Scott, Foresman and Company, 1968), p. 480.

[19]Eugene Emerson Jennings, "The Anatomy of Leadership," in Huneryager and Heckman, *Human Relations,* pp. 259–63.

[20]Scott, *Organization Theory,* p. 96.

[21]Harold J. Leavitt, *Managerial Psychology* 2d ed. (Chicago and London: The University of Chicago Press, 1964), p. 35.

[22]Gibb, "Communication and Productivity," in Huneryager and Heckman, *Human Relations,* pp. 520–29.

[23]*Ibid.,* p. 525.

[24]Harold Stieglitz, "Barriers to Communication," in Huneryager and Heckman, *Human Relations,* pp. 563–69.

[25]A. H. Maslow, "A Theory of Human Motivation: The Basic Needs," in Hampton, Summer and Webber, *Organization Behavior,* p. 35.

[26]Scott, *Organization Theory,* p. 197.

[27]Robert L. Kahn, "Role Conflict and Ambiguity in Organizations," in Huneryager and Heckman, *Human Relations,* p. 649.

[28]Scott, *Organization Theory,* p. 79.

[29]Warren G. Bennis, "Revisionist Theory of Leadership," in William T. Greenwood, *Management and Organizational Behavior Theories* (Cincinnati: South-Western Publishing Company, 1965), p. 732.

[30]*Ibid.,* p. 735.

[31]Robert N. McMurry, "The Case for Benevolent Autocracy," *Harvard Business Review,* January-February, 1958, pp. 82–90.

[32]Robert C. Cummins, "Relationship of Initiating Structure and Job Performance as Moderated by Consideration," *Journal of Applied Psychology* 55 (1971): 489–90.

[33]Although McGregor would argue strongly for greater self-control. See Douglas McGregor, *The Professional Manager* (New York: McGraw-Hill Book Co., 1967), pp. 116–33.

[34]Frederick Herzberg, *Work and the Nature of Man* (Cleveland: World Publishing Company, 1966), pp. 71–91.

[35]Cummins studied the effects of foreman structure and consideration in similar terms, i.e., turnover. See Cummins, "Relationship," pp. 489–90.

[36]James V. Clark, "Motivation in Work Groups: A Tentative View," *Human Organization,* 19, no. 4 (Winter, 1960-61): pp. 199–208.

[37]Douglas S. Sherwin, "Strategy for Winning Employee Commitment," *Harvard Business Review,* May-June, 1972, pp. 37–47.

[38]Evidence in support of the situational view has been reported in several studies and articles. Among them are: John J. Morse and Jay W. Lorsch, "Beyond Theory Y," *Harvard Business Review* (May-June, 1970), pp. 61-68; Robert Tannenbaum and Warren H. Schmidt, "How to Choose a Leadership Pattern," *Harvard Business Review* (March-April, 1958), pp. 95–101; Fred E. Fiedler, *A Theory of Leadership Effectiveness* (New York: McGraw-Hill Book Company, 1966); E. A. Fleishman and D. R. Peters, "Interpersonal Values, Leadership Attitudes, and Managerial Success," *Personnel Psychology,* 15 (1962): 127–43; Norman George and Thomas J. Von der Embse, "Six Propositions for Managerial Leadership," *Business Horizons,* December, 1971, pp. 33–43.

[39]See George and Von der Embse, "Six Propositions"; also Norman George and Thomas J. Von der Embse, "Leadership Attitudes: Emerging Patterns," *Manage,* October, 1970, pp. 6–11.

[40]Tannenbaum and Schmidt, "How to Choose", pp. 95–101.

[41]Alex Bavelas, "Leadership: Man and Function," *Administrative Science Quarterly,* March, 1960, p. 495.

[42]Ernest J. Hall, Jane S. Mouton and Robert R. Blake, "Group Problem Solving Effectiveness under Conditions of Pooling vs. Interaction," *Journal of Social Psychology* 59 (1963): 147–57.

[43]Robert L. Kahn, "Role Conflict and Ambiguity," p. 649.

[44]*Ibid.,* p. 645.

[45]See Jack J. Holden, Jr. "Decision-Making by Consensus," *Business Horizons,* April, 1972, pp. 47–54.

[46]Tannenbaum and Schmidt, "How to Choose", pp. 95–101.

[47]Scott, *Organization Theory,* p. 73.

[48]Alex Bavelas, "Leadership: Man & Function," in S. G. Huneryager and I. L. Heckman, *Human Relations in Management* (Cincinnati: South-Western Publishing Co., 1967), p. 283.

[49]Scott, *Organization Theory,* p. 77.

[50]*Ibid.,* p. 198.

[51]Gibb, "Communication and Productivity," in Huneryager and Heckman, *Human Relations,* p. 525.

[52]*Ibid.,* p. 525.

CHANGE

Incident	*Page*
THE NEW COMPUTER AT FOURTH NATIONAL BANK	208
Gerald B. Martin	
Analysis 1	209
Analysis 2	211
JOB ENLARGEMENT	214
S. E. Williams	
Analysis 1	215
Analysis 2	216
THE OFFICE MANAGER	221
Larry M. Hudson	
Analysis 1	222
Analysis 2	224

THE NEW COMPUTER AT FOURTH NATIONAL BANK

Mr. Jones, 45 years of age, has been with Fourth National Bank since he graduated from high school. He was an ambitious and hard working trainee and went from the position of teller to assistant controller in 10 years. When the bank merged with another in 1966, he became vice-president of Bank Operations, primarily due to the efforts of a senior vice-president who had originally hired Mr. Jones. He had no formal education beyond high school except for some banking seminars and training courses.

Mr. Smith, about 55 years old, was made vice-president in charge of Data Processing Operations after the merger. He was given this position as a result of his background in computer work with one of the banks joined by the merger, and the recent completion of the courses necessary to gain his college degree.

With the approval of the president and controller, the bank is currently increasing its computer capabilities to handle the expanding data processing workload. The new computer system, selected by Mr. Smith and the controller, has the capability of assisting the tellers in the branch offices in their work but it would require that they change many of their methods of making entries and processing items (checks, etc.) that they handle every day. Mr. Jones has been against the purchase of the new system ever since the president decided (at the urging of Mr. Smith and the controller) to switch from the Bank's less sophisticated Apex computer system that Jones had favored and buy a U.B.M. package with the needed memory capacity and improved applications. Since the branch bank operations were under Mr. Jones, he felt he had the necessary authority to run this segment of the bank as he wanted. With Mr. Jones's very limited knowledge of the computer, Mr. Smith and various U.B.M. representatives found it impossible to explain the concepts or advantages of the new system to Mr. Jones and it wasn't long before he refused to listen to anything Mr. Smith had to say concerning the new system. Antagonism between the two developed to a point where Mr. Jones refused to cooperate and went ahead and ordered new teller equipment for the branches from the old supplier realizing full well that the equipment could not function effectively with the new system.

The situation was further complicated by the feelings of some of the bank operations and branch personnel who had worked under Mr. Jones for years and saw this conflict as an opportunity to show their loyalty for him. When the time came to test the new system in their area of responsibility, they gave as little cooperation as possible, were quick to criticize it to other employees and were very slow to learn the proper operation of it. This caused numerous errors, required more time from the computer staff and pushed the cost of conversion to the new system over the budgeted amount.

ANALYSIS 1: *The New Computer at Fourth National Bank*

Much has been recorded and observed about the introduction of EDP into various work organizations. There is much, too, that is now passé. The use of the computer is a fait accompli, especially in the banking industry. Therefore, one cannot approach this situation from the standpoint of computer vs. no computer. It is better to view the matter as a system change centering on improved rather than new technology.

There are several questions which must be raised in relation to the facts surrounding the incident. For purposes of this analysis, we will depart slightly from the format developed throughout this text and raise these questions in the body of the analysis.

CHANGE

An obvious point is that Jones perceives the new computer system as a threat to himself and probably to his position with the bank. People tend to have an adverse reaction to change when they see this change as a threat to their sense of importance and personal worth. It would be helpful to know how Mr. Jones was introduced to the changeover to the new computer system. In all likelihood, the root of the problem lies in Jones's exposure to the new system. Workers react most favorably to change when they are familiar with the organization's approach to change and if they can be made to want the change themselves. Indeed, as Cartwright suggests, the work group is best approached as both a target and an agent of change.[1] In this incident, Jones was on the periphery of the decision-making process —neither the agent of change nor the target as such, but rather something of an "involved" bystander. It appears that Jones's work group constituted the strongest opposition to the change. It would be necessary to find out more about the nature of their resistance—whether due to perceived threat to their job security or because of a reluctance to change their work relationships. Jones might be communicating his own apparent fears to the employees, thereby compounding the problem. Had he been involved in the actual planning of the new system, the transition could have been made with minimal resistance.

There is probably no experience more frustrating to a manager than an action in which he/she has virtually no mastery and yet is faced with the prospect of living with the consequences. Jones may be experiencing a combination of what Argyris refers to as the four most frequent threats; anxiety, conflict, frustration, and failure.[2] Jones does not understand the system, a factor which would compound any fears he might have about his lack of formal education. By condoning the cost overrun created by subordinates, he was in effect joining them for protection. By going ahead and ordering equipment that is not compatible with the new system, Jones is trying to destroy any chances of the new system succeeding.

The actions of the employees to support Jones exemplify small group behavior found under these conditions. Small groups exist because of a common goal or purpose and they will tend to resist changes that threaten their survival. However, because the incident mentions their loyalty to Jones, the group action suggests that Jones might also be looked upon as an informal as well as the formal leader. If informal leaders do in fact serve the function of articulating the needs of the group, then Jones is fulfilling that role to some extent, if only out of self-interest.

COMMUNICATION

The incident suggests that a communication problem also exists. The president and Mr. Smith should have anticipated the hostility that this change would likely arouse. Of course, it is not known how vociferously Jones relayed his own perceptions about the change to the U.B.M. system. It is possible that he may have given tacit support in his face-to-face meetings with the president and with Smith, for fear of appearing uncooperative. What is even more important than the message itself is the reduction of uncertainty that accompanies the communication. In this instance, however, Jones was apparently well aware of the impending change, but his own role in the process was not clearly spelled out.

For example, perhaps the new system could have been presented to Jones as an efficiency measure which would increase rather than threaten his stature in the bank. The use of what Beckhard calls an "organization confrontation" meeting could be helpful toward getting Jones involved in the change.[3] Beckhard indicates that this meeting is especially useful for getting the group mobilized rapidly in order to deal effectively with an organizational crisis.[4] One advantage of this type of meeting as applied to the bank situation would be that a number of key employees could be brought together with top management, apprised of the problems confronting them and asked to mutually help solve it.[5] Chances are the employees would arrive at a similar conclusion; i.e., the bank needs the new U.B.M. system. At least they would be sounded out on the matter, even if their conclusions failed to agree with those of top management. And as a communication network this type of meeting would likely result in greatest satisfaction for group members, consistent with the observation that the circular, round-table type of communication pattern, though more cumbersome and time-consuming, results in higher member satisfaction.[6]

There are other issues here, of course, such as authority and group behavior. These have been touched upon indirectly above, but one that looms especially important is the question of Jones's authority. Will it be undermined by the actions taken? Some would argue that a manager cannot be held accountable for resources over which he/she had no decision authority in selecting. Aside from the classical authority-responsibility equation, the behavioral implications are considerable. It has been suggested earlier that Jones is likely experiencing considerable frustration over this situation and that his sympathizing with the workers may be a convenient sanctuary for his fears. Having had little control over the present change, Jones is provided with a neat rationalization for any accountability problems that result. Again, a few hours of consultation by top management with Jones could have resulted in a quite different situation, and would have been time well spent.

ANALYSIS 2: *The New Computer at Fourth National Bank*

Two central issues are involved in this incident. They are the bank's reorganization and the introduction of a new computer system. Changes of such magnitude may easily disrupt the equilibrium of an organization, the relationship of the employees and the patterns of role and status. This analysis will be an attempt to explain the reactions of Mr. Jones, one of the prime executives, to the aforementioned changes.

According to Scott, "Change even under the most desirable circumstances, causes social and psychological dislocations which must be restored in new status positions."[7] Status passage, the basic social process of regularizing an individual's status, was absent in this incident. The suddenness of the merger precluded this normal adaptive process. Hence, conditions for further change were less than desirable.

Mr. Jones was vice-president of Bank Operations; the new merger created a new, and somewhat parallel, position of vice-president of Data Processing Operations. In a banking system, needing real-time information for its everyday operations, these functions of the two vice-presidents must be highly integrated, or, at a minimum, they require a high degree of interaction to successfully execute operations.

The situation at Fourth National before the computer change contained unsettled role conflicts, as well as status incongruencies. Under these conditions, attempts to regain positional equilibrium elicited role defenses. Mr. Jones may have perceived his lack of education as a deficiency, causing him to have a feeling of insecurity; and, as a result, he overcompensated with his hard work.[8] A factor which complicated Mr. Jones's readjustment was the introduction of the new computer. His possible insecurity due to the lack of education, the role and status disequilibriums due to the merger, and the uncertainty of technological change, may have caused Jones to develop dysfunctional pathological role defenses.[9]

Mr. Jones's lack of expertise in computer technology and the certain overlap in his functional area by the new complex computer system may have created in him a state of anxiety. He might have thought this new system would require different management techniques or a reorganizational alignment that he did not comprehend. He possibly foresaw the necessity to implement and train his employees for the new system, a function we infer he was not capable of performing. In this case, Mr. Smith would have to take up the slack, as he apparently did, and cross functional divisions and train Mr. Jones's employees. In this situation, Mr. Jones was losing to Mr. Smith one of his prime sources of power, the power of knowledge or "Expert Power" as defined by French and Raven.[10]

Another possible explanation of Mr. Jones's behavior was the fact that his first power act failed. He failed to prevent Mr. Smith from proposing and implementing the new U.B.M. system. The incident states that Jones was a man who was accustomed to "getting his own way."

Upon perceiving a newcomer, Mr. Smith, oppose him, Mr. Jones's second action might have been a substitute power act as defined by Goldhammer and Shils.[11] In this incident the substitute power act by Jones was to deliberately undermine the project so that the computer and its proponents would fail. We know that he ordered incompatible teller equipment. We might also comment that this action is a very risky one. Mr. Jones has started an overt power struggle, and according to Jennings, great personal risk is involved when power drive is not used subtly and silently.[12]

Thus, we have two possible explanations for Mr. Jones's behavior. He may, first of all, have perceived a threat and reacted to a certain degree. Or, secondly, seeing his opposition to new equipment fail, he may have reacted to sabotage the project.

ADDITIONAL INFORMATION DESIRED

The degree of Mr. Jones's reactions could be better predicted if we knew his leadership style. The more he relied on traditional authority, the higher up decision making would be pushed. Very likely then, Mr. Jones would be called upon to make decisions in areas where he was not competent. If Mr. Jones had delegated authority, he would have entrusted to a competent person the task of supplying the necessary expertise to the decision process concerning computers and not have feared losing influence and position. Thus, the more democratic a leader, the greater the possibility of mitigating the effects of change on his position.

It would also be helpful to know the organizational relationships prior to Jones's promotion and the merger. Prior to his promotion, a formal organization triad could have existed. If Jones was the protege of a senior vice-president, as indicated in the incident, together, they may have counter-balanced the formal power and authority of the minority member, Jones's boss.

JOB ENLARGEMENT

The manufacturing operations at Plant Y of the Crestline Corporation consist of fabricating and assembling a major consumer durable product. Traditionally the manufacturing systems have been designed and built around the typical high speed assembly line operation.

As general production superintendent of Plant Y, Mr. Brown, who has developed through the management ranks largely by following traditional management principles, must give final approval to all systems changes that will affect his operations.

A new design of one of the major components for the ultimate product has been completed by product engineering. In turn it has been released to manufacturing engineering for implementation into the assembly line system.

The manufacturing engineering group recently studied the available research relative to the advantages of the job enlargement principle versus the paced conveyor system—in terms of providing relief from monotony and boredom. Realizing that job dissatisfaction has been and continues to be an apparent problem, a system which includes job enlargement was developed to assemble the new component along with the traditional paced conveyor system. Each system was then presented to Mr. Brown for his approval with the recommendation from the manufacturing engineering group that he adopt the job enlargement systems design.

Mr. Brown, being aware of the perceived monotony and boredom of the assembly line, decided to accept the recommendation and adopt the job enlargement principle.

As the production date arrived the facilities were completed and a number of operators moved from the assembly conveyor to a new job. They, in turn, were told to completely assemble the component and stamp their work with a personalized identification stamp which had been provided.

Output and quality during the first week was below that which was anticipated and showed very little improvement during the next several weeks. In fact, the output was significantly below that of similar work at an adjacent paced conveyor operation.

Mr. Brown's boss is upset, to say the least, since efficiency is low and excessive overtime is necessary to meet schedules. Mr. Brown, realizing that he is responsible for production, is trying to determine what happened and what course of action to take at this point in time.

ANALYSIS 1: *Job Enlargement*

It is possible that we have a perception problem due to the fact that people see the same thing differently because of their past experiences.[13] Mr. Brown and the Manufacturing Engineering Group perceived that the workers on the assembly line were experiencing monotony and boredom due to the high degree of specialization which required the workers to do the same simple task over and over again. Maybe the workers' view of their work was not one of boredom and monotony and they were happy doing just what they were doing.

Possibly the ideas of Dubin and Strauss are applicable to the production workers. Dubin says that work in many instances is not the central life interest for its participants.[14] Strauss emphasizes that not all people seek self-actualization on the job.[15] In this incident it may be that the workers were relatively happy performing their simple specialized task and did not desire more stimulating or difficult responsibilities. It appears that Mr. Brown was basing his decision on the idea that work is the central issue in a person's life, and the work must therefore provide for satisfaction, independence and possibly some creativity. This concept of work being the central life issue is directly or at least indirectly defended by authors such as Argyris, McGregor, Maslow, and Herzberg when they imply that self-actualization is the true motivating force.[16]

It appears from the incident that Mr. Brown did nothing more than tell the production workers that so many of them would be working on the new job enlargement program. This approach ignored two important aspects of the communication process—understanding and feedback. The production workers did not know why the change was taking place. Also, they did not have a chance to express their opinions on the new job enlargement program. By having no communication and thus no feedback, Mr. Brown has only his perceptions and those of the Manufacturing Engineering group, and no real idea of how the production workers perceived their jobs.

RECOMMENDATIONS

First of all, we should look at what happened and then consider the appropriate action to take now.

What Happened. By incorrect perception and failure to use communication, Mr. Brown changed the production workers' job from one of specialization to one of job enlargement. The workers' output and quality decreased and Mr. Brown was responsible for finding out why. Mr. Brown should have realized that people's perceptions of the same thing are different. Mr. Brown should have talked to the production workers and tried to find out what their reaction would be to the proposed plan for job enlargement. Feedback from employees could have provided Mr. Brown with some insight to the employees' perception of the situation.[17]

Action Needed Now. By communication and feedback from the production employees, Mr. Brown will be able to find out how many of the workers are satisfied with their present job and how many would like the opportunity to change to the job enlargement program. Mr. Brown may be able to find enough workers interested in the job enlargement program to continue it and at the same time increase the output and quality up to acceptable levels. If Mr. Brown cannot find enough workers interested in the job enlargement program, he probably should adopt a long-range program based on the ideas and concepts expressed by Williams.[18]

ADDITIONAL INFORMATION DESIRED

1. What was the basis for determining that job dissatisfaction was a continuing apparent problem?
2. What was the basis for determining that the workers on the assembly line were bored and that they considered their jobs monotonous?
3. How much training was given the employees relative to the new operation?
4. What was the intent of the personalized identification stamp, as perceived by management?

ANALYSIS 2: *Job Enlargement*

Past history indicates that the paced assembly conveyor system has, as its major advantage, the ability to govern production rates and provide a predicted output with reasonable accuracy. Characteristics of this system are the high degrees of specialization and repetition required of the operators. As a result of this, the operators experience relatively high degrees of boredom and monotony, both alien to the values of many people in our complex industrialized society. These factors can affect job satisfaction, motivation and productivity.

Job enlargement (whereby an individual performs a greater number of tasks, or even completes a whole job) is one approach that has been used successfully to offset some of the disadvantages inherent in traditional assembly line systems. This approach has led to increases in productivity and quality in several situations, particularly where skilled employees are concerned. Improved job satisfaction and morale have resulted from these types of situations.[19]

However, it is important to realize that the results are not always as anticipated, as can readily be observed in this incident.[20] A more complete analysis of the incident would be made if the following were known:

(a) the union-management relationship and the viewpoint of the union toward job enlargement;

(b) the type of pay system used (piece rate, daywork, measured daywork, etc.);

(c) mutual perception of employee and management roles;

(d) the experience level of the manufacturing engineering group particularly as related to work design;

(e) Mr. Brown's real attitude toward job enlargement principles and his past relationship with the engineering groups;

(f) the needs, motives, and attitudes of the employees on the conveyor line;

(g) other programs that may have been tried relative to improving output and quality;

(h) the type and nature of communication channels between management and employee;

(i) the type of leadership pattern used by management and the methods used in handling their authority;

(j) the level of influence imposed upon the individual by the informal social organization or prime group.

ORGANIZATION CHANGE

Each of the above questions would, of course, have particular utility in solving the efficiency problem. The attitudes of Brown and the engineering group are especially important, because of their effect on worker acceptance of the change. In other words, the approach toward making the change (in this instance enlarging the jobs) may be more important than the changes themselves. It is evident that employees when confronted with an unknown, particularly as it is related to their own jobs, are likely to perceive the change as a threat to their security and to their existing state of need satisfaction. This threat may be either real or perceived, but as long as it exists, it will have a definite effect upon attitudes and motivation.

There is some controversy, though, over the amount of participation desirable in implementing change. Coch and French showed highly desirable results in programs involving workers in planning for change.[21] Yet, Herzberg maintains that, at least in job enrichment programs, participation is not essential and in fact could be dysfunctional.[22] The Herzberg rationale appears to be that workers will respond positively to efforts made toward intrinsically improving their jobs and that often this must be done unilaterally in order to efficiently implement the program. While this smacks of some "We know what's good for you" elitism, it is obvious that in certain instances, union opposition would thwart job enrichment efforts were the decision left to the workers. This opposition can, however, be diminished, as Myers suggests, through proper orientation and collaboration.[23] Therefore, it may be possible to launch such change programs in a directive fashion, but participation could add an important dimension in terms of resolving conflict and getting commitment to the new system.

Management at Crestline, not being fully aware of the structure of need satisfaction and conflict situations, did not give adequate consideration to the consequences. Objectives of the program were obviously not clearly explained to the employees and little attempt was made to clarify and/or reduce potential conflicts that existed between the goals of the workers and the goals of the job enlargement system. Management over-simplified the situation and assumed that its workers were experiencing boredom and a lack of self-esteem and creativity. This is not necessarily true, since many employees can satisfy these needs outside the shop in other activities such as home, church, and community relations.[24] Granted, this drive to satisfy these higher needs undoubtedly existed in many of the employees involved. But even in these cases, many probably still perceive the change as a threat to some of their lower-level needs such as security, group belongingness, and positive social interaction which were ostensibly satisfied in the paced-conveyor system.

Then, too, there is the gnawing question of job enlargement itself. In the 1950s it was thought of by some in salvationist terms. Yet, the test of time has relegated it into disfavor and since then, it has shared a fate similar to that of the old "human relations" movement. The problem with job enlargement is that it simply adds more activities rather than real responsibilities.

It does not especially encourage involvement of the sort which promotes self-esteem. As Sorcher points out, ". . . there is little difference between a dull four-step job and a dull two-step job," particularly when other forms of incentive are absent.[25]

This is not to question Brown's sincerity nor to impugn his managerial capabilities. He is obviously attempting to do what managers are responsible for—getting productive and efficient effort. Nor did he have the luxury of armchair quarterbacking for which we academicians are sometimes known. Job enlargement and pollyannish human relations have bitten the dust in the test of time. There is evidence that job enrichment and participative management could also succumb, heretical as that might seem.[26] The qualifying factor for survival would appear to be the extent of systematic development of these approaches, introducing and integrating them within the organization framework, adapting the structure itself to accommodate the change, and especially focussing them on issues rather than on change per se.[27]

In the Crestline incident, little planning was done toward assimilating and implementing the job enlargement program. In summary, it is believed that failures occurred in the following areas:

(a)   Not enough research was done to determine the needs that were being satisfied with the present system. Without this knowledge, it is not possible to know the amount of job satisfaction the employees are experiencing nor is it possible to determine what will motivate them to perform better.

(b)   There was a lack of concern for the employees' role as a member of the prime group that existed around the work stations on the conveyor system. The effects upon the social system and the interaction between the individual and the group were not anticipated as a result of the changing environment.

(c)   Communications between management and workers were not effective. Evidently management did not clearly present the purposes and objectives of the new program, or at least the employees did not perceive the program as management had intended. Management has not communicated to the employees in such a manner that they perceive management's role as trustworthy individuals full of understanding and consideration for their needs.

(d)   Participative management was not used in any aspect of the program, and management depended solely upon their own edict to develop and implement the system. The support of the group or informal organization was not realized in any phase of the program.

(e)   The selection process to determine the initial group to try out the new system was not effective. The process was rather random in nature and did not take into consideration the motives and levels of aspiration of the trainees. It is of utmost importance that the initial group be sold on the program since they will be the ones who will sell it to the remainder of the group. As stated before, failure in this area is largely due to the lack of research into the individual backgrounds of employees.

THE OFFICE MANAGER

During his first month at the bank, Mr. Kline appeared to be extremely happy with his new job. He seemed always to be in a good mood, and his cheerful personality helped him to win acceptance with ease. At the end of the first month the bank's president surprised all of his employees, except for three of his eight top officers, with the announcement of the bank's planned merger just hours before the news was to be released to the public. Everyone was surprised but Kline seemed more so than any other. Kline later explained that the merger was to be with the holding company for which he had previously worked. He expressed a strong dislike for their policy of making officers only of college graduates, which he was not. For a few weeks, Kline was noticeably less cheerful at work, and several co-workers began speculating as to the reason. Then his mood improved when he learned that a new position was being created specifically for him. He was to become the "office manager" with the overall responsibility of seeing that "things get done." He would be given a degree of latitude in defining his specific duties, but when a problem came up they would look to him for the solution.

During the next eight months Kline submitted several proposals for innovations in job descriptions and practices. While he was trying to defend one proposed change on the grounds of improving employee morale, the idea was vetoed by his superior, who said "The people under you aren't supposed to like you." Twice he was allowed to implement minor changes only to be chastised later for wasting his time on unimportant matters. None of his major proposals were accepted, and Kline became discouraged. After a few months passed, he was submitting fewer and less radical proposals. He was less cheerful than before, evidencing a degree of tension as if he were under some sort of strain. He appeared to avoid people, preferring to keep to himself much of the time. One day it was rumored that Kline had submitted his resignation. He left, and the bank did not replace

221

him after he was gone; the position of office manager was abolished.

ANALYSIS 1: *The Office Manager*

Within the framework of an incident of this type, it becomes difficult to separate the effects caused by misunderstood communication and those resulting from the corresponding incorrect perceptions. In order to determine the cause in this incident, it would be necessary to know whether it was a policy of the bank to not promote anyone but college graduates to the officer positions. Assuming that this man's education was not an automatic disqualifier, it appears that there was not sufficient feedback to eliminate this perception.

Using this overall feeling as a reference point, it can then be shown that perhaps part of this individual's feelings of frustration could be caused by this impression. As Leavitt reports, "People perceive what they think will help satisfy needs; ignore what is disturbing; and again perceive disturbances that persist and increase."[28]

The manager in this case probably perceives the initial assignment as a challenge and perhaps as an opportunity to show he could advance to officer level. His initial failures were probably then passed over, but repeated efforts to accomplish his ideas led to this ultimate frustration.

It does appear that the man left the organization because he felt he was not contributing. It would, therefore, be beneficial to determine if the job responsibilities were outlined in any more detail than those given in the incident. If not, there is a high probability of role ambiguity and perhaps role stress.[29]

The changes that occurred as a result of the merger cannot be labeled as the primary cause of the dissatisfaction and eventual departure of Kline. Yet, they are important as precipitating factors leading to the difficulties involved in obtaining support for Kline's proposals.

ORGANIZATIONAL CHANGE

Effects of a merger at the top level are often not visible at the operating level. Yet, where the merger involves changes in managerial philosophy, there are likely to be some repercussions throughout the organization.[30] The creation of the new position for Kline appears to be a positive step toward accommodating individual needs in the inevitable post-merger adjustments. But in this instance this action was an obvious two-edged sword. The role ambiguity mentioned earlier represents the seamier side of this change.

The creation of the role problem could be a direct result of uprooting Kline from his original position, even though he held that position only for a brief period. Coupled with the apparent lack of job definition, we have a situation where one could predict the type of response made by Kline; namely, trial-and-error behavior, leading to failure, frustration, apathy and eventual resignation. It is one thing to issue the charge to an individual to "get things done" but quite another to give the individual the type of support which encourages an action orientation. Lurking beneath this observation is a major question of motivation which we should briefly address at this point.

MOTIVATION

Reference has been made in other areas of this text to different concepts of motivation. Therefore, we will not go into the details of the various theories and concepts involved. Rather, the factors apparent in this incident will be underscored and evaluated. For example, the organization apparently is conscious of fulfilling hygiene factors. This is evident in the care given to providing job security for Kline and presumably for others in this situation.[31] But it is not clear that Kline is preoccupied with security needs at this point. He is certainly not fixated at this need level. What appear to be more important are those factors which would motivate Kline toward achievement—recognition, opportunity for advancement, results-orientation, support and encouragement for his proposals, feedback on his ideas, constructive criticism along with reasons why the proposals were not acceptable. The earlier encouragement and perceived freedom propelled Kline to seek out improvements in the organization. The continual reinforcement by way of ongoing communication with Kline would be necessary to maintain that level of behavior.

ADDITIONAL INFORMATION NEEDED

In analyzing this incident, it would be helpful to know under what conditions Kline left the holding company which merged with his present employer. It is possible that the situation described was a resurgence of a previous episode. Also, it would have been helpful if the changes proposed by Kline were explained in more detail. It is possible that they were *too* innovative. More detail of the conversations that took place between Kline and his superior might have provided more insight into the reasons for the incident.

ANALYSIS 2: *The Office Manager*

The overall approach to this incident will be in terms of March and Simon's analysis of decisions to participate.[32] Our analysis consists of three basic stages through which Kline proceeded one by one. We will explore each in turn and enumerate the factors leading to his transitions and the effects each stage had on his behavior.

STAGE 1

Kline probably made some calculations during his preemployment interviews concerning the reward structure offered by the bank and compared them to his calculations of the role structure expected of him. Since this evaluation is a subjective process, it is impossible for anyone but Kline himself to know the relative weights he attached to each specific reward and demand. We can infer from his decision to participate in the organization (to accept the job offer) that he considered the inducements to be greater than the demands.

In addition to this inference, we can explore some of the common features of preemployment interviews which influenced his evaluative process. An interview is an act of communication and, as such, is subject to the problem of communication breakdown. One of the causes of communication breakdown is filtering or conscious manipulation of information in favor of the sender.[33] Both the interviewer and Kline were very likely guilty of some conscious manipulation, leaving out some facts and emphasizing others more favorable to their respective positions. A second cause of communication breakdown is what Leavitt has called selective perception.[34] The job was probably perceived by Kline as promising precisely those rewards that his previous job lacked, especially if these rewards were critical to his needs. Each party in the interview perceived what the other was saying according to his own expectations, hopes and fears. A third cause of breakdown is social distance.[35] Since the two parties spoke from different frames of reference, it was difficult for the interviewer to make Kline understand what working for his organization would be like. To the extent that these barriers to communication were operating, Kline's evaluation of the rewards and demands of the job offer tended to be inaccurate. His decision to accept the job offer was, then, based on a somewhat inaccurate perception of the relative rewards and demands of the job. His perceptions were, however, subject to continual revision.

Once Kline was actually on the job he began experiencing first hand the new organization's reward and role structures. As he began to detect discrepancies between his intitial calculations and his experience, a precarious situation arose. Now facing apparent denials of his conviction, he had to choose either to accept the fact that he had been wrong or to delude himself into thinking the job was as expected. To accept his mistake would have meant subjecting himself to some degree of anxiety and tension. In terms of Festinger's theory of "dissonance reduction,"[36] Kline chose to delude himself into thinking favorably about the job until a point was reached when a critical and unequivocal denial occurred. In this incident the critical denial was the announced merger, for it meant Kline would be subject to the identical organizational policies he had sought to escape by leaving his previous job. From this point forward, Kline's perception of the relative rewards and expectations of the job took on a new balance.

Before investigating the new state of Kline's thinking we should take notice of the leadership style displayed by the bank's president. The president subscribes to the traditional or "top-down" theory of authority, which means that the source of authority is at the top and is delegated down.[37] The president does not feel that it is important for him to consult his subordinates before making decisions that will affect them. He merely makes the decision and announces it, which corresponds to what Tannenbaum and Schmidt call "Boss centered leadership" in which the leader uses all of his authority and leaves no freedom for the subordinates.[38] Since the decision to merge was viewed as critical by Kline, it was natural for him to resent being hired without being informed of the possible upcoming merger.

STAGE 2

Once the merger was announced, Kline's evaluation of the rewards and demands of his job entered the second phase, in which he considered them to be approximately equal. At this point he was neutral toward his job, and thus continued acquiring information concerning his alternatives.[39] Then the bank promoted him to office manager which gave him renewed hope that in spite of the merger he might be able to enjoy a successful career at the bank. His promotion and new duties may have been interpreted by Kline as an indication that his lack of a college degree would not hold him back professionally.

Kline's decision process can be described in terms of Barnard's concept of "zone of indifference."[40] Kline had been indifferent to nearly all demands and expectations with which the bank confronted him during his initial experience on the job. His zone of indifference was wide so he regarded nearly all demands on him as acceptable. But, as experience forced him to re-evaluate the relationship between the rewards and demands of his job, his zone of indifference tended to become more and more narrow. Some of the demands were regarded as acceptable, others were not. A major reason for his refusal to accept some of the demands resulted from his perception that the demands were incompatible with his personal goals.

Although at this stage Kline viewed his job as less than ideal, he nevertheless found it satisfactory. Kline's level of aspiration and search behavior was induced.[41] But his negative work experiences also caused him to adjust downward his level of aspiration so that the level of satisfaction he was able to derive from his job was acceptable to him, although it was not at a maximum.

It is apparent that Kline's newly created position as office manager was structured with conditions making conflict inevitable. First, he became a focal person between two groups or role senders, his superiors and his subordinates.[42] Second, he had no real authority or freedom to implement solutions without prior approval of his superior.

Another dimension to this incident is the relationship between the organization's norms for management and the personal norms exhibited by Kline. From the statement "The people under you aren't supposed to like you" we can infer that the normal practices of management were "structure" oriented rather than "supportive."[43] In spite of this, Kline displayed a strong interest in improving employee morale by submitting proposals to this end. Showing support for subordinates in order to improve morale was not a high priority concern of the bank. In effect, Kline did not embody the values of management and therefore was never accepted as a full member of this primary group. Initially he had earned for himself a "fringe status position" but over time he tended to become an isolate.[44] In this capacity he was deprived of the many psychological rewards which group membership provide. Finally he was no longer able to tolerate the tensions and pressures that resulted from his nonconformity, and he began submitting fewer radical proposals. Kline probably realized that sponsoring relatively minor changes would involve less personal risk.

STAGE 3

According to Presthus's transactional view of leadership, there is a reciprocal relationship between a subordinate and his superior.[45] If Kline had successfully negotiated what he considered necessary improvements in the subordinate-authority relationship with his superior, he might have remained with the bank. Instead, he believed after a time that his situation was not improving to an acceptable level. Eventually a point was reached at which Kline considered the demands of his job to be greater than the rewards. The bank had failed in both of Herzberg's categories, motivation and hygiene.[46] Kline was not properly motivated because his job was not designed to serve his basic needs, and he was also dissatisfied with the policies, practices, and working conditions.

ADDITIONAL INFORMATION DESIRED

It would be helpful to know why the bank elected not to fill the position after Kline resigned. If the position was created especially for Kline and then not filled after he resigned, we would be in a position to know more about the philosophy of top management and the organizational climate that prevailed.

It would be beneficial if we knew more about the attitudes, norms and values of the employees who were under Kline's supervision. With this information we would be able to more fully analyze the existence, if any, of role conflicts experienced by Kline.[47]

FOOTNOTES

[1]Dorwin Cartwright, "Achieving Change in People: Some Applications of Group Dynamics Theory," *Human Relations* no. 4 (1951), pp. 381–92; See also Lippitt's model of the change process, in Gordon Lippitt, *Organization Renewal* (New York: Appleton-Century-Crofts, 1969), esp. part 1, pp. 5–57.

[2]Chris Argyris, "Personality and Organization," in D. R. Hampton, Charles E. Summer and Ross A. Webber, *Organizational Behavior and the Practice of Management* (Glenview, Ill.: Scott, Foresman and Co., 1968), pp. 141–42.

[3]Richard Beckhard, *Organization Development, Strategies and Models* (Reading, Mass.: Addison-Wesley Publishing Co., 1969), p. 38.

[4]*Ibid.*

[5]Several possibilities for developing this participative arrangement are presented in Dan H. Fenn, Jr. and Daniel Yankelovich, "Responding to the Employee Voice," *Harvard Business Review,* May-June, 1972, pp. 83–91.

[6]Marvin E. Shaw, Gerard H. Rothschild and John F. Strickland, "Decision Processes in Communication Nets," in Donald E. Porter, Philip B. Applewhite, and Michael J. Misshauk, *Studies in Organizational Behavior and Management* (Scranton, Pa.: Intext Educational Publishers, 1971), pp. 489–504.

[7]William G. Scott and Terence R. Mitchell, *Organization Theory: A Structural and Behavioral Analysis* Revised Edition (Homewood, Ill.: Richard D. Irwin, Inc., and The Dorsey Press, 1972), p. 203.

[8]Chris Argyris, "Personality and Organization," in Hampton, Summer and Webber, *Organizational Behavior,* p. 144.

[9]For a comprehensive coverage of Bureaucratic Role Defenses, see Victor A. Thompson, *Modern Organization* (New York: Alfred A. Knopf, Inc., 1961).

[10]John R. P. French and Bertram Raven, "The Basis of Social Power," in Dorwin Cartwright and A. F. Zander, eds., *Group Dynamics* 2d ed. (Evanston, Ill.: Row, Peterson and Co., 1960), pp. 607–23.

[11]Herbert Goldhammer and Edward A. Shils, "Types of Power and Status," in Hampton, Summer, and Webber, *Organizational Behavior,* p. 481.

[12]Eugene E. Jennings, "The Anatomy of Leadership," in S. G. Huneryager and I.L. Heckman, *Human Relations in Management* 2d ed. (Cincinnati: South-Western Publishing Co., 1967), p. 254.

[13]Scott and Mitchell, *Organization Theory,* pp. 71–73.

[14]Robert A. Dubin, "Person and Organization," in William T. Greenwood, *Management and Organizational Behavior Theories* (Cincinnati: South-Western Publishing Co., 1965), p. 488.

[15]George Strauss, "The Personality vs. Organization Theory," in Leonard R. Sayles, *Individualism and Big Business* (New York: McGraw-Hill Book Co., 1963), pp. 67–80.

[16]*Ibid.*

[17]Mr. Brown could have precluded this problem had he been more knowledgeable of the importance of planning for and implementing change. He could have benefitted had he been familiar with a highly relevant and related article by Edgar G. Williams, "Changing Systems and Behavior," *Business Horizons,* August, 1969, pp. 53–58.

[18]*Ibid.*

[19]Note the discussion of job enlargement studies in Edwin B. Flippo, *Management: A Behavioral Approach* (Boston: Allyn and Bacon, 1970), pp. 252–54.

[20]And in other studies on job enlargement; see, for example, Ronald C. Bishop and James W. Hill, "Effects of Job Enlargement and Job Change on Contiguous but Nonmanipulated Jobs as a Function of Workers' Status," *Journal of Applied Psychology* 55, no. 3 (1971): 175–81.

[21]Lester Coch and J. R. P. French, Jr., "Overcoming Resistance to Change," *Human Relations* 1 (1948): 512–32.

[22]Frederick Herzberg, "One More Time: How Do You Motivate Employees?" *Harvard Business Review,* January-February, 1968, pp. 53–62.

[23]M. Scott Myers, "Overcoming Union Opposition to Job Enrichment," *Harvard Business Review,* May-June, 1971, pp. 37–49.

[24]The reader's attention is directed to the discussion of Dubin's central-life-interest concept in the "Motivation" section of this book.

[25]Melvin Sorcher,"Motivation, Participation and Myth," *Personnel Administration,* September-October, 1971, p. 21.

[26]See Thomas H. Fitzgerald, "Why Motivation Theory Doesn't Work," *Harvard Business Review,* July-August, 1971, pp. 37–44; also, Herzberg's "dissatisfiers" might become "satisfiers" under varying conditions, as shown in Raymond L. Hilgert, "Satisfaction and Dissatisfaction in a Plant Setting," *Personnel Administration,* July-August, 1971, pp. 21–27.

[27]Larry E. Greiner, "Red Flags in Organizational Development," *Business Horizons,* June, 1972, pp. 17–24.

[28]Harold J. Leavitt, *Managerial Psychology* 2d ed. (Chicago and London: The University of Chicago Press, 1964), p. 33.

[29]Role conflict and ambiguity tend to be lower when structure is provided as shown in John R. Rizzo, Robert J. House and Sidney Lirtzman, "Role Conflict and Ambiguity in Complex Organizations," *Administrative Science Quarterly* 15 (1970): pp. 150–63.

[30]An excellent treatment of the post-merger human problems is given in Charles M. Leighton and G. Robert Tod, "After the Acquisition: Continuing Challenge," *Harvard Business Review,* March-April, 1969, pp. 90–102.

[31]For review of the concepts in this discussion, see references to Herzberg and Maslow in the "Motivation" section and in the "Job Enlargement" incident in this section.

[32]James G. March and Herbert A. Simon, *Organizations* (New York: John Wiley and Sons, Inc., 1958), chaps. 3, 4.

[33]Scott and Mitchell, *Organization Theory,* pp. 159–60.

[34]Leavitt, *Managerial Psychology,* pp. 32–33.

[35]William G. Scott, *Organization Theory: A Behavioral Analysis for Management* (Homewood, Ill.: Richard D. Irwin, Inc., 1967), pp. 302–3.

[36]L. A. Festinger, *A Theory of Cognitive Dissonance* (New York: Harper and Row, Inc., 1957).

[37]Scott, *Organization Theory,* pp. 201–3.

[38]Robert Tannenbaum and Warren H. Schmidt, "How to Choose a Leadership Pattern," *Harvard Business Review,* March-April, 1958, pp. 95–101.

[39]March and Simon, *Organizations,* chaps. 3, 4.

[40]Chester I. Barnard, *Functions of the Executive* (Cambridge: Harvard University Press, 1938), pp. 168–69.

[41]Herbert A. Simon, "Theories of Decision-Making in Economics and Behavioral Science," *The American Economic Review,* June, 1959, p. 263.

[42]R. L. Kahn, "Role Conflict and Ambiguity in Organizations," *The Personnel Administrator,* March-April, 1964, pp. 8–13.

[43]E. A. Fleishman, "Leadership Climate, Human Relations Training, and Supervisory Behavior," cited in Edgar H. Schein, *Organization Psychology* (Englewood Cliffs, N. J.: Prentice-Hall, Inc., 1965), p. 43.

[44]Scott, *Organization Theory,* pp. 93–97.

[45]Robert V. Presthus, "Authority in Organizations," *Public Administration Review,* Spring, 1960, pp. 86–91.

[46]Frederick Herzberg, "The Motivation-Hygiene Concept and Problems of Management," *Personnel Administration,* January-February, 1964, pp. 3–7.

[47]Arthur N. Turner, "A Conceptual Scheme of Describing Work Group Behavior," in Paul R. Lawrence and John A. Seiler, *Organizational Behavior and Administration* (Homewood, Ill.: Richard D. Irwin, Inc., and The Dorsey Press, 1965), pp. 154–64.

ORGANIZATIONAL CLIMATE

Incident	Page
THE LETTER OF RESIGNATION	231
William F. Davis, Jr.	
Analysis 1	232
Analysis 2	234
THE PUB INCIDENT	237
John C. Powell	
Analysis 1	238
Analysis 2	240
THE MANAGEMENT TRAINING PROGRAM	245
James Bridenbaugh	
Analysis 1	245
Analysis 2	249

THE LETTER OF RESIGNATION

R. S. Howell was the manager of profit planning of a large multi-divisional corporation. He reported to the treasurer of the corporation. The function of his department was the consolidation and analysis of the profit plans submitted by various divisions of the company. Mr. Howell's staff consisted of an assistant manager, secretary, two female clerks and five financial analysts. Mr. Howell had held his current position for about five years and was considered very competent by his superiors. He had been with the company nearly fifteen years. The employees of the department were all under thirty years old. None of the financial analysts had been with the company more than four years and most were on their first job out of college.

Mr. Howell had become increasingly concerned with turnover among his financial analysts. Within the past three years, four of his analysts either asked for transfers to other departments or left the company. The situation reached a crisis when John Bounds, who had been with the company fifteen months, submitted a letter of resignation to Mr. Howell, with a copy to Howell's supervisor.

Bounds stated the following reasons for his resignation:

1. No analysts in Mr. Howell's department had ever been promoted to management positions in other departments. Analysts in the controller's division had been promoted on many occasions. "I don't feel there is any future for me in this division."

2. He felt that he had not been given adequate responsibility, nor was any other analyst in the department.

3. He did not feel there was a "professional" atmosphere in the department.

4. He did not feel he had been given proper recognition for his work.

5. Overall morale among the analysts was low.

Mr. Howell, when confronted by his superior with John's resignation, made the following remarks: "I don't understand it. I

231

have given John two substantial increases in only fifteen months. If that isn't recognition I don't know what is. I was very pleased with his work until the last few months. I can't create openings for promotions. All I can do is try to give my people as much exposure as possible. I'm about ready to give up. It seems no matter what you do, you can't satisfy these young people today."

ANALYSIS 1: *The Letter of Resignation*

It is assumed that the facts given by John Bounds on the reasons for his resignation are correct. There are several areas which bear closer scrutiny, among them motivation, perception, and communication, all of which add up to an assessment of the organizational climate.

The first area to be examined is motivation. What sort of motivation has Howell provided for in his analysis? It would appear that Howell is lacking in this area, especially when we consider that within the last three years, four analysts have left his department in addition to Bounds, who is in the process of resigning. The area of motivation relates to Howell's statement regarding salary increases. From the incident it would seem that Howell believes that money is the only motivator. Perhaps a reassessment of his (Howell's) understanding of Herzberg's ideas on motivation and hygiene, respectively, would shed some light on his personnel problems. He should realize that motivation is far more complex and consists of more than a pay raise. Sirota and Wolfson, in referring to Herzberg, state

> there are certain job content factors that, when present, 'satisfy' and 'motivate' employees. Conversely, he says, there are 'hygiene' factors that, when absent, dissatisfy employees but whose presence is not satisfying per se.[1]

> Thus, if a person is not paid well (pay is a hygiene factor), he will become dissatisfied, but to pay him well will have little effect on his satisfaction or motivation–he will simply *not* be dissatisfied.[2]

Perhaps the jobs themselves do not require college trained personnel; if they do, however, an evaluation of jobs along the lines of job enrichment might solve some of the problems. Sirota and Wolfson state

> Job enrichment may be defined as the redesign of a job to provide a worker with greater responsibility, more autonomy in carrying out that responsibility, closure (a complete job), and more timely feedback about his performance.[3]

This situation, then, relates directly with what Sorcher states, ". . . the manager should be aware that employees can become more involved in their work if the incentive is a highlighted sense of self-esteem."[4]

The next area for consideration is the one of perception. We must question how Bounds perceives his job situation and his environment and, conversely, how Howell perceives his employees. As stated by Scott, "Perception imparts to the brain through the senses what is 'seen' in the world outside the person."[5] But sensing is not perceiving. As Berelson and Steiner put it,

> sensory information does not correspond simply to the perception that it underlies. The fundamental reason for the difference between sensory data and perception is that sensory impulses do not act on an empty organism; they interact with certain predispositions and states already there . . .[6]

The process of perception does not stop there. Perception is selective; i.e., what is seen interacts with the personal state and therefore certain things that are "seen" are admitted and others omitted. It is apparent that both Bounds and Howell are experiencing selective perception in their situations.

It would appear that Bounds, judging from his statements in the incident ("he felt" and "he did not feel"), was perceiving aspects of his job environment selectively. As Leavitt states, "Most of us recognize that the world-as-we-see-it is not necessarily the same as the world-as-it-really-is."[7] On the other hand, the very same argument may be applied to Howell. He has the attitude of perceiving things the way they have always been. His statements that he doesn't understand the situation would lead us to assume that he is rather closed-minded to changes in personnel expectations.

Closely related to perception is the area of communication. It appears that there is ineffective communication between Howell and his analysts—Bounds in particular. Communication is a two-way process. Judging from Bound's statements, we would surmise that both upward and downward communication is limited.

Additional information is needed to make a thorough analysis of this incident. We would want to know the hiring policies of the firm. How are personnel selected for the jobs? Are college degrees really required for the successful performance or execution of all jobs?

It would also be helpful to know more about the climate of the corporation, especially in regard to the treatment of professionals. Are professionals treated differently from other white-collar workers or clerks as far as policies, supervision, independence of work, etc., are concerned? We should know more about Howell's leadership style.

Exactly what was the atmosphere for free exchange of information between supervisor and employee (Howell and Bounds)? Were channels of communication open and were there means to effect communications without filtering and distortion? Were there any barriers to communication, such as those mentioned by Stieglitz, i.e., individual differences, corporate climate, or mechanical barriers?[8] These are factors which must be considered, especially the one concerning corporate climate.

CONCLUSION

Based on our analysis of motivation, perception and communication, we can conclude that the organizational climate is not conducive to providing an environment for that professional growth and development of employees needed to enhance achievement of company goals.

ANALYSIS 2: *The Letter of Resignation*

Mr. R. S. Howell supervises five financial analysts, and fails to understand why four of these people, young and fresh from college, have become dissatisfied and left his organization within the past three years. One of them, Mr. John Bounds, provided some clue in his letter of resignation, but Howell did not discern the nature of the problem. One should not castigate Howell, though, without first examining his reasons. These constitute a part of the missing information in the incident and should be mentioned here before proceeding further. For example, how valid were Bounds's criticisms? Exit comments are among the most candid of all feedback, but that does not necessarily make them valid. In other words, they convey honest feelings, but these feelings might have little basis in fact. Surely, what one perceives is most important, but solving the problem involves the company's system of developing its financial analysts.

A system change based upon unsubstantiated criticisms could produce even greater criticisms after the changes are made. In addition, what were the job market conditions in this field at the time? Perhaps the mobility of financial analysts was quite high, in which case they might leave primarily for reasons of finding better opportunities, even though many positive qualities existed in the present situation. Assuming that workers attempt to maximize their inducement-contributions ratio,[9] the analysts could simply be searching for an even better deal.

CORPORATE CLIMATE

The above questions and speculations relate directly to the climate, both in the larger organization and in this department. It is possible that conditions are not favorable toward self-development in this company. One factor could be that of size, since the incident mentioned that it is a large corporation. Studies have shown that size is inversely related to satisfaction, especially at lower corporate levels.[10] In addition, there appears to be an almost universal deficit in satisfaction of self-actualization needs, as shown in the Ivancevich and Strawser study.[11] This would suggest that the more idealistic and self-fulfillment-oriented employee would also experience a larger gulf between perceived and desired need satisfactions under the conditions described in the incident.

Most of the personnel involved are young college graduates experiencing their first professional employment. They undoubtedly came to the company expecting to develop their skills and eventually move on to managerial positions. Instead, they have found an atmosphere lacking in challenge and opportunity. Apparently, this situation is widespread in business today, or is at least perceived to be by college students. Various observers have lamented, in recent years, the failure of business to attract highly-educated young people.[12] Although much of the commentary is more in the order of a general indictment of business than of a synocure for the young, there is undoubtedly a message of significance in the words of the critics. This incident typifies the kind of organization which has become virtually stereotyped in the literature—one which fails to actualize the potentialities of its employees. What is frequently overlooked, though, is the complexity of the problem.

Not everyone can or will advance to the rarified atmosphere at the top of the organization. Space there is severely limited. In a way, one can understand Howell's view that he cannot create promotions but can only give people exposure. The exposure, if it is present, would be an important factor in promotability, according to Jennings' research.[13] In that respect, Howell is apparently supporting the aspirations of the analysts. But there is another way of approaching the concept of advancement. It is the view that considers advancement a perceptual matter rather than an upward physical move. In other words, employees can advance within positions as well as among them. This type of advancement occurs in the form of personal growth through achievement and commitment. It is in this latter area where Howell has possibly misinterpreted the needs of the analysts. His approach of giving them large salary increases is well-intended, but it is largely hygienic. Were the salary increases construed as a form of recognition for high achievement, they could serve as a form of recognition. But this would require a systematic approach including such prefatory steps as developing expectations, delegating authority and eliminating performance barriers.[14]

LEADERSHIP

Mr. Howell appears to be bureaucratically-oriented in his managerial philosophy. Economic reward and security are evident, but personal growth and adaptation to change are deficient.[15] Stability is, of course, desirable in an organization, but so are flexibility and adaptability. Howell apparently has chosen the stability route, at the expense of considerable loss of talent. One expects stability-orientation in a large organization, but it is also possible, as Hellriegel and Slocum demonstrate from case studies, to achieve a dynamic balance between stability and adaptability.[16] In other words, policies and procedures can be established and high-risk choices avoided, but simultaneously management can be thinking and planning toward the future, especially the future of employees who demonstrate potential for achievement and/or promotion.

THE PUB* INCIDENT

Jason Howe was an affable bachelor who had gone to work at a
military installation as a male stenographer following his
discharge from the Armed Forces after World War II. Jason
eventually worked his way up into a buyer's position, which
required a bachelor's degree or equivalent business experience. It
was not known who decided that Jason possessed the equivalent
business experience, but by 1960 Jason was considered a
journeyman buyer in an office which procured relatively simple
and common materials. At that time Jason lost his job due to a
reduction in force; however, the Base Personnel Office found him
a job with equal pay in another procurement organization. This
was a drastic change for Jason, as the new office procured ground
support equipment for modern weapons; consequently, the
equipment was much more complex, the prices were much
higher, much more documentation was required to support a
contract award, and the contracts themselves were more complex.
Jason maintained his outward pleasantness, however, and
whatever insecurity he suffered was not apparent.

The new office consisted of an immediate supervisor, two
secretaries and about ten buyers. The latter twelve people were
unofficially divided into two groups, each of which was led by
one of the senior buyers. These two buyers were in effect working
supervisors and were not accorded official supervisory status.
Solution of most of the buyers' routine problems, as well as much
of their daily supervision, came from these two senior buyers;
however, the immediate supervisor was not inaccessible when he
was needed.

A new immediate supervisor was brought into the office about
six months after Jason's arrival. In the following several months
the senior buyer under whom Jason worked expressed skepticism
to the new supervisor about whether Jason was really capable of
working in the office, as he (the senior buyer) had to work so
hard with Jason to obtain his procurements. One Friday when
both Jason and his senior buyer were absent, the Division

*Pleasant but Unproductive Buyer

237

Commander (a general officer) called the Branch Chief (a colonel) to his office and told him that he (the general) had been called by an unsuccessful bidder who had written or called Jason Howe three times asking, without getting an answer, the basis for an award to one of his competitors. The general told the colonel to get an answer out that very afternoon, and to see what should be done with Howe. The colonel and the immediate supervisor, after an exhausting search of Jason's crammed desk, found the disgruntled bidder's letters and sped off a reply promptly, as no real problems were involved in the response. The next day, a Saturday, the immediate supervisor made a six-page handwitten inventory of all old and superfluous materials in Jason's desk.

On Jason's return to work the following Monday, the colonel and the immediate supervisor related last Friday's incident to him and asked if he had any excuses for it. Jason had none; he was then shown the six-page inventory made on Saturday, and was told that he would receive a reprimand and probably be removed from his job within ten days. He was also told that if he left the Division before then, the reprimand and removal action would be dropped. Before the ten days elapsed, Jason departed, having obtained another buying position with the same salary at another military installation within the commuting area.

ANALYSIS 1: *The Pub Incident*

According to Friedrich, one of the tests for the extent of bureaucratic development is the degree of qualification for office.[17] The military is an example of an organization that establishes specific qualifications for each position. However, these qualifications are not always objective standards. For example, how does one determine what constitutes business experience equivalent to four years of college? A determination of this sort is necessarily subjective and lends itself to a high degree of bias.

When any organization lists requirements for employment in its various positions, these requirements should be consistent with both the specific tasks of the job and the pay. This consistency implies that jobs with equal pay will be at least approximately equal in skill requirements.[18] When Jason was being considered for a position as buyer in the second procurement organization, his placement was based on the fact that he had previously worked in a position with a similar job description and similar requirements. However, Jason's first job as buyer actually required considerably less expertise than did his new job as buyer.

This incident points out the importance of scientific job selection,[19] or placing the man in a job which is consistent with his abilities. If the Base Personnel Office had had available to it more adequate information concerning Jason's abilities and the actual requirements of the job, it might have found him a job more similar to his previous one. A placement decision based on more accurate information could have prevented Jason from being assigned a job which was "over his head," so to speak. Assigning individuals to positions in which they can contribute to the overall performance of the organization is of great importance. An alert manager would recognize that Jason's incompetence was a symptom of a larger organizational problem— poor job placement. The manager should attempt to discover (1) how it was possible for a worker to be placed in a job in which he is unproductive, and (2) how the organization might have detected the lack of productivity sooner, so that the employee might be either retrained or reassigned. In reference to the former, the basic cause is the disparity between the skill requirements for jobs of equal description. This disparity is dysfunctional since it allowed the Base Personnel Office to assign Jason to a job for which he was unqualified.[20]

How can such a disparity in skill requirements for jobs of equal description come about? Caplow points out that "large organizations afford more chance for greater vesting of interests than small organizations."[21] For example, an executive might be motivated to increase the qualifications for positions below him so that he could appear relatively more important. This motive should be held in check by some organizational function which is responsible for ensuring that job requirements are consistent with the skills and abilities actually needed on the job.

Once Jason was assigned to his new position, measures could have been taken which would have detected the disparity between Jason's skills and those needed on the job. Some sort of appraisal of Jason's performance was needed. Performance appraisals would have provided not only information with which the supervisor could judge how well Jason was doing, but also information with which Jason could judge his own strengths and weaknesses. It is quite possible that evaluations would have motivated Jason to improve his performance.[22] We get the impression that not even minimal performance appraisals are common practice in Jason's office unless they are unilateral, secretive and subjective.

The apparent lack of performance appraisals is an indication of a general lack of effective supervision. The responsibility for getting the work done was vested in the two "working supervisors," but they had no authority to oversee in an official capacity. Their supervisor was not "too accessible," creating a lack of upward communication. We are tempted to infer from this incident that the office supervisor does not function as a manager, except to the extent of locating and firing incompetents when he perceives a risk of personal blame. It appears that the supervisor's search of Jason's desk was partly to find the bidder's answer and partly to find evidence to use against Jason.

The supervisor, if he were a good leader or manager, would know why Jason had failed to give the bidder an answer; if not, he would attempt to discover the reason. For only if he understands the reason for Jason's failure can he take actions to insure that Jason will do better next time. By firing Jason he loses an employee who may have possessed untapped potential, and he signals to the other employees what may happen to them if they fail to please him. The result of the latter could increase tensions and fear, which could in turn cause the other employees to conceal their shortcomings rather than seek the assistance of their supervisor (or others) in developing their abilities to do their jobs.

We are also tempted to infer that the organizational climate as evidenced by the leadership (or lack thereof) is a major causal factor leading to Jason's dismissal. There is evidence (large backlog of work in Jason's desk) to indicate that objectives are not clearly established, nor are there policies or procedures for measuring accomplishments. Additionally, the disciplinary action (immediate dismissal with no consideration of alternatives) would indicate that discipline is used as punishment rather than as a means of improving required behavior. Progressive discipline such as that advocated by Odiorne[23] would seem to be a basic philosophy that, if adopted, would benefit this organization.

ADDITIONAL INFORMATION NEEDED

It is unclear why Jason failed to provide the bidder with the information he requested. Did Jason know the answer to the bidder's question but withhold it either because he thought it to be confidential, or in order to conceal his own incompetence in handling the contract? Or did he not know the answer and, in an effort to hide his ignorance, intentionally block the communication? Or was Jason so disorganized that he had not yet attempted to respond to the bidder's inquiry? Or did Jason not recognize the whole matter to be important or to require his attention?

ANALYSIS 2: *The Pub Incident*

Quo vadis? Another employee who has advanced to his level of incompetence? In a more serious vein, perhaps it is more complex than that. One is intrigued, though, by what has been dubbed "the organizational stupidity factor,"[24] so named because of the purported effects of exponentially advancing technology combined with the operation of the Peter Principle.[25] The result is, in short, an increasing gap between the expertise required for task performance and the actual capability of the incumbent.[26] Presumably, the concept is intended to apply to governmental organizations, but it is conceivable that all bureaucratic organizations are similarly afflicted to some degree.

There are several issues in this incident, among which are motivation, leadership, communication, and role behavior. The facts given suggest, though, a large area is covered, including such various factors as leadership, attitudes, work systems, tasks and policies, all playing significant roles in the sizing up of the situation. Therefore, it is preferable to begin on the topic of climate while at the same time recognizing the specific aspects of that dimension.

ORGANIZATION CLIMATE

Jason Howe will probably be identified by some as the typical civil servant. That is, of course, an unfair label, but it has been popularized to the point that the image of the governmental employee has suffered considerably. If there is indeed an inexorable process at work which encourages and even rewards incompetency, the cause resides more in the organizational climate than with the individual. For example, in our incident Jason Howe was simply transferred after bungling the job. The result is that some other division must now wrestle with his obvious limitations. Furthermore, having been transferred at the same salary could produce a morale problem of major proportions among those who feel they "earned" their respective grades and salaries through meritorious service. From a macro-perspective, this practice can only, in the long run, drive competent personnel from the organization.

The organization might be left with what Barnes calls "socials"—employees who are not work-oriented and are not concerned with advancement or achievement. "Socials" are described in contrast with "Organizationals" and "Professionals," particularly in the context of engineering groups. The latter two—organizationals and professionals—are more work-oriented, the organizationals toward internal advancement and the professionals toward achievement in their disciplines.[27] Evidently, all three types are needed for balance in organizations, but in the present situation, the climate appears to attract the "socials" more than it does the other types.

It would be instructive at this point to trace the genesis of the current problem with Jason. The initial blunder occurred when the Base Personnel Office assessed Jason's capability for undertaking the more complex procurement work. Backtracking even further, the evaluation of the new job was probably erroneous. It was equated with the simpler job that Jason had previously held. In order to fully understand the implications, the reader must also be acquainted with the federal civil service system, which differs conceptually from that of private industry promotion systems. There are two bases for qualification at a particular level of salary and classification. One resides with the employee and is his/her qualification level. The other lies in the position, which has a particular classification. An employee can move to a higher classification only upon qualification by examination, tenure, etc. Were the new position in this incident classified at a higher level than Jason's old position, he would have had to formally qualify or be "detailed" to the job for a probationary period. The other option would be to reclassify the job in order to match it with the person's qualification level.

The position evaluation, then, was a more serious error than the transfer of Jason, because it enabled him to move without requalifying, which he probably could not have done. This factor, coupled with the apparent inflexibility of the promotion-demotion-discharge system in the bureaucratic structure, breeds dissatisfaction among those who are of greatest potential value to the organization. Turning to the research in the area of satisfaction, there is much that is inconsistent and even contradictory. Satisfaction has been shown to relate indifferent directions with factors such as productivity and leadership style. The satisfaction paradigm itself is a veritable jungle of interpretation. Yet, a few basic relationships appear consistently throughout the studies; namely, that perceived satisfaction is associated positively with job performance, supportiveness of management and opportunity for higher level need fulfillment.[28] In the context of this incident, the supportive conditions are not present, neither are the inducements for higher level need satisfaction. This is not to say that employees could not self-actualize on the job. One would think that an important position such as procurement, working with suppliers directly and assuming responsibility for allocating taxpayers' money in the interest of national defense, could indeed produce intrinsic satisfactions. But, apparently, the service orientation required for this attitudinal posture was not sufficiently recognized nor continually encouraged.

RELATED ISSUES

This incident can be useful for illustrating another area discussed in other incidents in this text.[29] The application of OD has been discussed earlier. There is no intent here to give disproportional attention to this behavioral area, but it deserves comment simply because it is a frequently discussed and somewhat controversial one. Moreover, public and semi-public organizations appear to have been in the forefront as far as its use is concerned, for various reasons such as public funding, interagency cooperation, cumbersomeness of structure and certainly the minority group problem. One can readily see the need for application of some of the fundamental OD concepts such as team development, cooperation, revitalization of structure and systems. At least these areas constitute the major focus of some OD consultants.[30] Undoubtedly, an effective OD program, one which takes a system perspective, can change the attitudes and relationships to the extent that the "Jason Howes" in organizations are assigned work consistent with their capabilities. Such a program could also lead to upgrading the skills of personnel such as Howe in order to make them promotable.

There is also a note of skepticism, sounded by Greiner and reiterated by this analyst; i.e., the relative inattention given in many OD efforts toward task objectives.[31] In Howe's situation, it may be possible, for example, to make him more aware of the need for interaction with those in his internal role-set. But his most important role responsibility is to his external clients —primarily the national interests, but also the suppliers. He has already demonstrated social capability; perhaps greater emphasis on task competency would prevent him from in effect withdrawing from his responsibilities by procrastinating on handling bidders' inquiries. In all fairness to OD programs, there is usually some content emphasis in the training and development process, but some of it, judging from exercises observed by this analyst, is too artificial to allow prediction of transfer of learning to real work situations.[32] Continuing briefly on this topic, there is another shortcoming which, ironically, some OD consultants (e.g., Eddy)[33] attribute to "canned" or packaged programs; namely, the inflexibility of design for which packaged, or preferably, "predesigned," programs have received a bad press in the literature. Yet, there is no assurance that so-called unstructured programs are flexible in design. Predesigned programs spell out the structure explicitly, while in less structured programs, the model is often implicit and resides in the sometimes rigid assumptions and objectives of the facilitator or conference leader. Moreover, as Bennis has stated in regard to the industrial humanism movement, which underlies the OD philosophy, there is a distinctly human bias in the direction of democratization of the organization.[34] This could very well be appropriate, but might not be, either, in view of this incident and the findings regarding contingency theory discussed in the Leadership section of this text.

One should be aware, too, of the senior buyers' role in the supervision and development of Howe. Since each was responsible for the work of six buyers, it would appear that they could check periodically, especially on new buyers. A question arises regarding their training and preparation for the supervisory role. Apparently, these buyers perceived themselves as specialists rather than as supervisors. There would undoubtedly be training exercises available to these senior buyers which could strengthen their understanding of their leadership role. This would be especially true of governmental installations, which often require a certain number of training days per year for managerial personnel. For example, an effective supervisory program would help to equip the buyers with leadership skills and styles needed in handling situations such as this. The findings reviewed in the Leadership section of this text suggest a situational style—more specifically, in this instance, a directive approach which conveys to Jason specific instructions and monitors his performance very closely. The Branch Chief and the regular supervisor did in fact move quickly, but only after the situation became unredeemable.

ADDITIONAL INFORMATION NEEDED

There is, of course, much that is not known about the incident that would be helpful toward accurately sizing it up and eventually developing a solution. For example, what was Howe's background? Might he have qualified for some other position at a comparable level? Also, could the new position be handled by other buyers until such time as a competent individual could be located to take over the position? If the installation were linked up to the computerized personnel placement system in the civil service, certainly this avenue could have been pursued. Such a system has existed since the early 1960s—a former classmate of this analyst assisted in developing this nationwide system. Finally, in departing somewhat from our format in the text, we can provide additional information that the student/reader would find of considerable interest. Because of its unusual nature, we will disclose this information. Jason lasted one year at the other military installation before he was again discharged. He returned to the organization cited in our incident and assumed the duties of a male stenographer, but attempted, unsuccessfully, to again attain a buying position. A few years later, an accident took his life. Quo vadis? Jason, in the happy hunting ground of civil servants, with no triplicates, classifications, transfers, routings, priorities, seniorities, and no File 13s.

THE MANAGEMENT TRAINING PROGRAM

Five years ago, top management of a large manufacturing corporation decided to add a number of college graduates to the organization in first line supervisory positions. Fifteen such candidates were hired and assigned to various departments ranging from metal stamping to assembly line operations. The purpose of such a program was to insure the company a supply of well-trained and experienced personnel to assume greater responsibility in middle and upper management positions. These college graduates were each responsible, as foremen, for supervising approximately thirty hourly rated employees who were represented by a strong international union. These foremen reported to a general foreman, who reported to the superintendent who in turn reported to the plant manager.

The fifteen foremen were paid on a salaried basis and their salaries were above scale for persons with comparable qualifications. Four years of "training" had passed when the plant manager requested the personnel department to send up the folders of the fifteen foremen so that he could review their progress. He was shocked to find that only two of the original fifteen remained, and from their performance records it was clear that they would never be suitable for higher positions. He immediately asked the personnel department for reasons why they could not retain the sorely-needed lost talent.

ANALYSIS 1: *The Management Training Program*

Before examining the issues, there are several items of additional information that would be helpful toward developing a solution. First, what type of training program was involved? From the facts of the incident, the training was primarily on-the-job, but were there discussions and seminar sessions as well? If the positions existed originally, what had happened to the previous foremen? This information would assist in determining whether or not the trainees were subjected to an environment of embittered employees who had a degree of loyalty for the displaced workers, or if they were confronted with the situation of trying to fill a new position that the hourly-rated workers felt should have been filled by a qualified member of their group.

How was the training program developed and what instructions were given concerning its implementation? Who was to monitor the training program and how often was management to be informed of its progress? This kind of information would give an indication as to who should be held accountable for training as well as provide an insight into the reasons for the trainees' departures.

Did management explain the reason for having the trainees, their relationship to upper management, hostilities likely to be encountered, and the policy of management regarding communication? This type of information would allow one to decide whether or not the trainees were prepared for the realities of the job.

The issues here are difficult to identify, simply because the reasons for the apparent failure of the program could lie in several different areas. Communications and leadership are ostensibly relevant. Also, motivation and perception could be important. The pervasiveness of the turnover problem, however, suggests that the atmosphere is not conducive to developing and keeping good foremen. Thus, the climate in this plant appears to be a major causal factor. This climate consists of management attitudes, policies, structures, philosophy, day-to-day relationships as well as worker morale, among other factors.

CLIMATE

It seems unusual that the plant manager would ask the personnel department why the company was unable to keep this young talent. Since the two remaining trainees had poor ratings, it seems logical that the plant manager would have suspected that a similar type of record could be responsible for the departure by the other trainees. In addition, one would think that the person most familiar with the reasons for the departure would be the immediate supervisor and not the personnel department. This suggests that another barrier may be the organizational structure itself. Who has the responsibility for the training function? Was the training policy ever clearly stated? The functional responsibilities in the organization may not have been adequately delineated. If the authority and responsibility for the training program were vested in the personnel department, the trainees' supervisor may have been apathetic toward the arrangement. If, on the other hand, the supervisor was completely responsible for the training program, he might have become more involved and attempted to be constructive insofar as operating problems were concerned.

It is virtually axiomatic today that trainees' superiors participate in a meaningful way in the training process.[35] Apparently, top management did not monitor the training program on any ongoing basis. This can be inferred from the four-year lapse between inception of the training and the subsequent evaluation. It is desirable, of course, to evaluate training on a long-term basis. Too often training effectiveness is measured within a few short months after the experience, if at all! But in this incident, there was little evidence of constant surveillance, or at least of an annual check on the process by management.

As indicated earlier, the actual content of the training program is not known. If it involves strictly on-the-job training (OJT), there are several weaknesses that are associated with this approach. Perhaps the benefit of immediate productiveness is desirable to the company, but it can be dysfunctional over the long run. Among the disadvantages of OJT, which could be highly relevant to this situation, is that little skill development and breadth can be expected as a result of OJT, in contrast to other types of training programs.[36] Although the structure of monetary rewards would appear to be favorable, the conditions for intrinsic motivation may be absent; i.e., opportunity for advancement, interesting work, sense of achievement and recognition. The emphasis by top management might be too egalitarian in the sense that meritorious performance is not recognized accordingly. This is evidenced by the fact that the remaining two foremen were rated as having low promise. As Sidney Wilson suggests, timeliness is a highly important element in rewarding managerial performance. The reward can take many forms, but the emphasis should be on job performance rather than verbal performance.[37]

There is another question which involves the leadership climate especially. This is the matter of delegation of authority to the foreman trainees. In other words, were they permitted or encouraged to make decisions and take specific positions on views that confront them? Viewed in another way, there was an obvious absence of commitment by the foremen. This commitment, in turn, develops out of ego involvement in one's work. As Rhine and Poloworick found, in a study on attitude change, one of the most important factors in producing both attitude change and commitment is that of taking a stand on specific issues.[38] Perhaps the foremen were sheltered in this regard, preventing them from becoming involved in the problems of the work units.

A final observation regarding climate concerns the union situation. The presence of a strong union is an important constraint on any foreman.[39] The new foreman just out of college might experience considerable disappointment and frustration upon learning the severe limitations on his/her discretion.

OTHER SALIENT ISSUES

The general foreman, superintendent, personnel department and the trainees may have all been unclear as to their roles in the training program. Conflict may have arisen from the relationship of the trainees' supervisor to the hourly rated personnel and to management, or the relationship between the trainees and management. Robert L. Kahn, in references cited elsewhere in this text, suggests different role conflicts that can exist in an organization. The inter-role type of conflict has application in this setting. In this case, the role pressures associated with membership in one organization are in conflict with pressures which stem from membership in other groups. The general foreman or superintendent may be impeding communication because of his inter-role conflict. He knows he is closer now to membership in the management group, but remains loyal to the group of hourly-rated workers. The hourly-rated group may be exerting pressure informally on the general foreman or superintendent who in turn has elected to remain in good standing with the informal group at the expense of the trainees. Again, this pressure may be stemming from perceptual differences that are affecting the hourly-rated employees. The latter may perceive the trainees as outsiders who have taken over positions that should have been filled by members of their group. Also, the higher salaries may be perceived negatively insofar as incentives are concerned.

Role ambiguity would appear to be one of the main reasons why the trainees departed and this condition persisted due to the lack of communication. Since the training continued for four years with ostensibly very little communication with upper management, the trainees probably felt that they were grossly neglected. Kahn determined that ambiguity is caused, among other factors, by the way in which one's supervisor evaluates one's work, opportunities for advancement, and scope of responsibility.[40] He also cites certain consequences of ambiguity conditions. These include low job satisfaction, low self-confidence, a high sense of futility and considerable tension.[41] Any of the first three factors would definitely contribute to the decision of the trainees to leave the firm.

COMMUNICATION

The assumption is made that the departed personnel were upset or frustrated at the events or situation at work, because it seems unlikely that such a large number would leave had they felt otherwise. Regardless of the reason(s) it would appear that their concerns were not adequately addressed by the plant manager. This observation is based upon the plant manager's complete surprise when he found out that the foremen had left, plus the fact that he was not aware of trainee endeavors over the relatively long training period. Assuming that the new foremen were unable to solicit management attention, it is useful to examine the communication area and its relationship to the functioning of an organization.

The goal of communication is and should be complete understanding. This requires a continual process of listening and responding—of consultation between the employee and supervisor. There are various impediments to communication which are spelled out in virtually every basic text on the subject. The implication here is that regardless of position, members of this organization were no doubt placing different interpretations on the events surrounding the existing situation. This may have been the result of individual or group interests, but nevertheless the communication barriers need to be removed. In this incident, communication can be facilitated by setting forth an explicit policy. Lack of such a policy may be interpreted by a supervisor as a lack of interest by management in communicating. The result in this incident is that the general foreman or superintendent may have elected to communicate sparingly with the plant manager because of the ambiguity or lack of company policy regarding the training of new supervisors.

ANALYSIS 2: *The Management Training Program*

While there are several areas of behavioral science relating to this incident which could be discussed, this analysis will concentrate primarily on perception, communication, motivation, and managerial development; all have a direct impact on the prevailing organizational climate.

PERCEPTION

It is quite obvious that the new foremen and the plant management did not share the same concepts regarding the role of the foremen in the organization. If this had been so it is quite likely that some of the capable foremen would have still been employed by the firm when they were needed. Management perceived this program to be a long-term training program, while the foremen obviously did not. Such a disparity is not unpredictable, because of differences between sensory data and perception. Even though the sensory data may be the same it interacts with predispositions.[42] Since new foremen trainees in all probability do not have the same predispositions as top management, the perceptions of the same sensory data will be different. The attitudes of the foremen and top management are products of their backgrounds and serve to screen their sensory perceptions, so that they see that which they think will satisfy their needs. Each group therefore arrived at a unique set of conclusions concerning this situation. This uniqueness is a fundamental problem. In order for management to predict employee reaction to a given set of sensory data, it must first have a clear understanding of employee perceptions.[43] In this incident it appears that management made no attempt to analyze the perceptions of the foremen. If they had, they could possibly have avoided the consequences.

The foremen, after a prolonged period of limited interaction with top management, probably perceived their role in the organization as merely foremen whose job it was to manage the various production departments. This role resulted in conflict with their personal goals which were to advance themselves through the company's ranks into more responsible positions. There are also several aspects of role ambiguity which may have significance in this incident: uncertainty about supervisory evaluation criteria, opportunities for advancement, scope of responsibility, and the expectations of others regarding performance.[44] Each of these were probably sources of concern for the new foremen, concern which eventually led to levels of job satisfaction and feelings of futility which were inconsistent with their perceptions of a satisfactory work environment.

COMMUNICATIONS

A prominent factor in this incident is the apparent lack of communication between the new foremen and the higher levels of management. Had the foremen been impressed from the start with the fact that the company considered these foreman positions as merely a training ground and "jumping off place" for more responsible positions within the firm, the foremen as a group may have been more highly motivated to perform well in their positions. The role ambiguity could conceivably have been eliminated by the establishment of channels of communication between the foremen and their supervisors. Communication channels are essential for congruent reciprocal communication, mutually accurate understanding of the work situation, psychological adjustment for everyone concerned, and mutual satisfaction in the relationship.[45] Without these channels the foremen found themselves incapable of resolving the ambiguities between their actual role and their desired role.

It is difficult for any organization to function effectively without a systematic communication program. When problems arise in the communication system they are usually traceable not to the communication media but to filtering and perception of the communication by the personnel concerned.[46] Thus it is important that effective communication channels be established to correct such situations.

MOTIVATION

Without the proper communication channels to reduce the misconceptions of the foremen's role it was impossible to motivate them in the performance of their work. There are several discussions of human motivation which might be appropriate but perhaps the most appropriate is Maslow's.[47] In this incident three of the five basic needs, physiological, safety, and love, were probably satisfied. There is some question as to whether the esteem need was satisfied since the lack of communication did not allow the foremen to assess their position adequately. Thus, there may have been doubts in their own minds as to the level of esteem that others held for them. Surely, the foremen perceived a lack of opportunity for self-actualization. With no visible means of achieving their personal goals for advancement within the manufacturing company, the foremen sought to find means of doing so in other companies.

MANAGERIAL DEVELOPMENT

The fact that the manager waited for four years to check the records of a group selected for training indicates that the firm had no real formal training program. It has become increasingly common in industry to have formal executive development programs for employees. Such programs should provide the means for obtaining the information which the executive must have, both technical and managerial, about the prospective executives.

If the program does not have the support of higher levels of management (primarily in the form of increasing acceptance of the developing manager's opinions) the program will fail to accomplish its goals. The lack of program support was evident in this incident. By the time contact was again established the foremen had reached the point of frustration and had sought work elsewhere.

The types of development programs are varied. On-the-job-training, understudy plans, short- and long-term formal education, and position rotation are just a few. The least effective, at least as employed in this incident, is on-the-job-training. Some positions require so much technical detail that there is no time for development. On-the-job-training is often costly and time consuming as related to effectiveness. Finally, it is often inefficient, more of a hit-or-miss program than a formal program.[48]

The position of foreman was a poor choice for the application of an unsupervised training program. The position is an in-between level, not worker but not quite management.[49] It requires experience and training in dealing with two different types of people. In this incident, personnel direct from college were expected to effectively deal with two types of personnel immediately. Without experience, or someone they could turn to for guidance, the feeling of being "forgotten men" was probably exaggerated. The foremen could not determine their role within this company and therefore probably perceived it necessary to relocate in a firm in which they could.

ADDITIONAL INFORMATION NEEDED

Why did it take four years for the plant manager to learn that only two of the fifteen foremen remained with the company? What was the extent of personnel turnover among other employees? Did the personnel department know the extent of turnover and the reasons for it prior to the time that the plant manager requested the information? Answers to these questions would provide us with a more comprehensive insight as regards the organizational climate within this company.

CONCLUSIONS

Although there is nothing that the firm can now do to regain the four lost years of "training," they can take measures to assure that an incident like this will not occur again. The only way to accomplish this is to establish an organizational climate with attitudes and practices conducive to formal training programs. This will obviously require revamping of the personnel office which, itself, is the best exhibit for the need of formal training. Until they themselves realize the benefits obtainable from formal training they cannot institute such a program in other departments of the company.

FOOTNOTES

[1]David Sirota and Alan D. Wolfson, "Job Enrichment: What Are the Obstacles?" *Personnel,* May-June, 1972, p. 15.

[2]*Ibid.*

[3] *Ibid.*, p. 8.

[4] Melvin Sorcher, "Motivation, Participation and Myth," *Personnel Administration,* September-October, 1971, p. 21.

[5] William G. Scott, *Organization Theory: A Behavioral Analysis for Management* (Homewood, Ill.: Richard D. Irwin, Inc., 1967), p. 67.

[6] Bernard Berelson and Gary A. Steiner, *Human Behavior: An Inventory of Scientific Findings,* cited in Scott, *Organization Theory,* p. 67.

[7] Harold J. Leavitt, *Managerial Psychology* 2d ed. (Chicago and London: The University of Chicago Press, 1964), p. 28.

[8] Harold Stieglitz, "Barriers to Communication," in S. G. Huneryager and I. L. Heckman, *Human Relations in Management* (Cincinnati: South-Western Publishing Co., 1967), pp. 563–71.

[9] See James G. March and Herbert A. Simon, *Organizations* (New York: John Wiley and Sons, Inc., 1958), chap. 3.

[10] John M. Ivancevich and Robert H. Strawser, "A Comparative Analysis of the Job Satisfaction of Industrial Managers and Certified Public Accountants," *Academy of Management Journal,* June, 1969, pp. 193–203.

[11] *Ibid.*, pp. 199–203.

[12] See James L. Sheard, "College Student Preferences for Types of Work Organizations," *Personnel Journal,* April, 1970, pp. 299–304.

[13] Eugene Emerson Jennings, *The Mobile Manager* (New York: McGraw-Hill Book Co., 1967), chaps. 1, 4.

[14] See Robert C. Miljus, "Effective Leadership and the Motivation of Human Resources," *Personnel Journal,* January, 1970, pp. 36–40.

[15] Roger Harrison, "Understanding Your Organization's Character," *Harvard Business Review,* May-June, 1972, pp. 119–28, especially p. 127.

[16] Don Hellriegel and John W. Slocum, Jr., "Integrating Systems Concepts and Organizational Strategy," *Business Horizons,* April, 1972, pp. 71–78.

[17] Carl Friedrich, "Constitutional Government and Politics," cited in Scott, *Organization Theory,* p. 250.

[18] Wilfred Brown, "A Critique of Some Current Ideas About Organization," in Huneryager and Heckman, *Human Relations,* pp. 492–93.

[19] Scott, *Organization Theory,* p. 273.

[20] Brown, "A Critique," pp. 492–93.

[21] Theodore Caplow, "Organization Size," cited in Scott, *Organization Theory,* p. 251.

[22] Douglas McGregor, "Human Side of Enterprise," cited in Scott, *Organization Theory,* p. 270.

[23] George S. Odiorne, "Discipline by Objectives," *Management of Personnel Quarterly,* Summer, 1971, pp. 13–20.

[24] Clarence A. McComber and Nan B. Jenkins, "The Organizational Stupidity Factor," *Government Executive,* January, 1972, pp. 52–54.

[25] Laurence J. Peter and Raymond Hull, *The Peter Principle* (New York: William Morrow and Company, 1969).

[26] McComber and Jenkins, "Organizational Stupidity," p. 53.

[27] Louis B. Barnes, "Organizational Systems and Engineering Groups: A Comparative Study of Two Technical Groups in Industry," in P.R. Lawrence and J.A. Seiler et al., *Organizational Behavior and Administration* (Homewood, Ill.: Richard D. Irwin, Inc., 1965), pp. 199–201. Miller discusses the Barnes model in terms of teamwork. See Thomas E. Miller, "Building

Teamwork in Organizations," *Personnel Administration,* September-October, 1971, pp. 38–45.

[28]For a synthesis of the major satisfaction and leadership studies, see Karlene Roberts, Raymond E. Miles and L. Vaughn Blankenship, "Organizational Leadership, Satisfaction and Productivity: A Comparative Analysis," *Academy of Management Journal,* December, 1968, pp. 401–14.

[29]See the The Adams School incident in the "Communications" section of the text.

[30]S. R. Ganesh, "Choosing an OD Consultant," *Business Horizons,* October, 1971, pp. 49–55.

[31]Larry E. Greiner, "Red Flags in Organization Development," *Business Horizons,* June, 1972, pp. 17–24.

[32]Some exercises are intended only as skill-developers with no intent to simulate reality. The analyst is referring here to those which attempt to imply a reality base, but do not approach the complexities of organizational life.

[33]William B. Eddy, "From Training to Organization Change," *Personnel Administration,* January-February, 1971, pp. 41–42.

[34]Warren G. Bennis, *Changing Organizations* (New York: McGraw-Hill Book Co., 1966), chap. 8.

[35]See Robert J. House, *Management Development: Design, Evaluation and Implementation* (Ann Arbor: Bureau of Industrial Relations, The University of Michigan, 1967), chap. 4; also Gordon Lippitt, *Organization Renewal* (New York: Appleton-Century-Crofts, 1969), chaps. 13, 14.

[36]See Paul Pigors and Charles A. Myers, *Personnel Administration* (New York: McGraw-Hill Book Co., 1965), pp. 377–93.

[37]Sidney R. Wilson, "The Incentive Approach to Executive Development," *Business Horizons,* April, 1970, pp. 15–24, esp. pp. 19–21.

[38]Ramon J. Rhine and William A. J. Poloworick," Attitude Change, Commitment and Ego-Involvement," *Journal of Personality and Social Psychology* 19, no. 2 (1971): 247–50.

[39]See Fritz Roethlisberger, "The Foreman: Master and Victim of Double Talk," in Lawrence and Seiler et al., *Organizational Behavior,* pp. 434–38.

[40]Robert L. Kahn, "Role Conflict and Ambiguity in Organizations," in Huneryager and Heckman, *Human Relations,* p. 645.

[41]*Ibid.,* p. 650.

[42]Bernard Berelson and Gary A. Steiner, *Human Behavior: An Inventory of Scientific Findings* (New York: Harcourt, Brace and World, Inc., 1964), pp. 98–101.

[43]Leavitt, *Managerial Psychology,* p. 35.

[44]Kahn, "Role Conflict," p. 649.

[45]Carl R. Rogers, "A Tentative Formulation of a General Law of Interpersonal Relationships," in Lawrence and Seiler et al., *Organizational Behavior,* p. 313.

[46]Michael J. Jucius, *Personnel Management* (Homewood, Ill.: Richard D. Irwin, Inc., 1971), pp. 304–19.

[47]A. H. Maslow, "A Theory of Human Motivation: The Basic Needs," in D. R. Hampton, C. E. Summer, and R. A. Webber, *Organizational Behavior and the Practice of Management* (Glenview, Ill.: Scott, Foresman and Co., 1968), pp. 27–40.

[48]Jucius, *Personnel Management,* pp. 264–81.

[49]L. A. Dale, "The Foreman as Manager," *Personnel,* July-August, 1971, pp. 61–64.

Incidents
Without Analyses

INDEX TO PART III INCIDENTS

Incident   *Page*

LONG HAIR   260
    David Haskins

THE NEW CLERK-TYPIST   261
    Thomas R. Robinson

THE EAGLETON AFFAIR   263
    Thomas J. Von der Embse

AMALGAMATED METALS, INC.   265
    James Ward

WHITE IMPLEMENT COMPANY   267
    Stephen L. Christian

WHAT HAPPENS TO SALLY?   269
    Scott M. Probst

THE DOUBLE-BAG AFFAIR   270
    Thomas Schneider

THE SHORT SKIRTS   271
    Roger R. Werling

THE RESEARCH GROUP   272
    C. L. Bellanca

THE MOCK COMPANY   274
    Jon M. Heslop

THE COMPUTER SYSTEM   276
    William E. Huxhold

STUDENT CONFLICT 277
Michael A. Babick

SECRETARIAL CONFLICT 278
J. W. Householder

ACE PAPER COMPANY 279
Paul M. Comolli

TECHNICAL SYSTEMS DIVISION 281
Jerry W. Woodruff

SUMMER HOURS 283
Charles Closz

THE FOREIGN ACQUISITION 285
W. Schuberth

THE TECHNICIAN-SALESMEN 286
A. A. Gurtner

SHIFT CHANGE 288
David W. Boerger

SCIENTIFIC INVESTIGATION 290
Rudy C. Beavin

THE PRINTING SERVICE 292
Frank Hall

HIDE-AND-SEEK AUTHORITY 293
Nancy C. King

THE CONTROLLER'S SUCCESSOR 295
Thomas B. Picciano

WILL THE REAL LEADER
PLEASE RISE? 296
William E. Quinn, Jr.

THE BOARD OF EDUCATION 297
Dennis Thayer

TECHNOLOGICAL INNOVATION 298
John V. Murray

THE OFFICE REPLACEMENT 300
Charles E. Kamke

THE EXPERIENCED FOREMAN 302
Dennis Brockman

THE PERPLEXED FOREMAN 303
Anonymous

THE ENGINEERING CHANGE 304
Paul A. Schroeder

LONG HAIR

Exco is a very large, decentralized company with a generally conservative view toward employees. Groups of employees with similar jobs, training and education (generally college level) are scattered throughout the country. Supervisors are usually grouped together and are many miles removed from their subordinates. Communication is done basically by mail, although the telephone is used for important matters, and face-to-face communication limited to one meeting every two to four weeks. Subordinates are engaged primarily in public contact; therefore, neat appearance is essential.

Six months ago a division-wide conference was held, including field personnel, their supervisors and some home office top management. Supervisor Williams had noticed a gradual trend of longer hair and long sideburns among his seven subordinates. About two weeks before the conference he distributed copies of a written home office policy regarding appearance. The tone of the policy was conservative, stipulating such items as no sideburns, no untrimmed moustaches and no beards. Mr. Williams made a point of calling certain individuals regarding this policy, particularly with respect to long hair and sideburns. All members of this group subsequently complied with Mr. William's direction.

The trend of this group since the conference has been to have long, but neat, sideburns, and otherwise neat appearance. Recently, however, Mr. Glass has let his hair grow quite long, his sideburns grow longer and is wearing a moustache for the first time. He has also taken on a very "Mod" appearance in his dress. Mr. Williams is aware of Mr. Glass's appearance and on a recent field trip during an informal gathering of the group there was much banter about the appearance of Mr. Glass. Mr. Glass is a fair performer and fits in well with the group except for his appearance. Mr. Williams is afraid of what top management will say about Mr. Glass's appearance and believes he must do something soon.

THE NEW CLERK-TYPIST

Earlier this year, Mr. Henry Jackson, senior partner in the law firm of Johnson and Watson, deliberated on the performance of his office staff. The firm at that time employed two married women in their early twenties: Sandra, his secretary and Gloria, a bookkeeper-receptionist. Gloria had been with the firm for three years. Sandra has worked there about two months, but has had about seven years' experience in secretarial work. Mr. Jackson concluded that it would be necessary to hire an additional clerk-typist to support an expanding practice. Gloria was asked to seek out and hire a student from a local business school to work part-time, as the projected expansion would probably not be realized for several months. Mr. Jackson also implied that the person selected for employment would be considered for a permanent position upon graduation. Gloria obtained a referral from the Upton-Mulvaney Business College and arranged an interview.

Nora, the interviewee, was nineteen years old, single, living with her parents and had no previous experience. Her expected graduation date was within the next five months. She apparently satisfied all the requirements for employment and was therefore hired. No other applicants were sought for interview. Gloria introduced Nora to Mr. Jackson and he explained that she was to help Sandra with her work. Specifically, she was to do all filing and various typing assignments passed on to her by Sandra.

The next afternoon when Nora reported for work, Sandra explained to her the firm's filing and other office procedures. Sandra sensed that Nora resented this instruction, but let it pass without incident. Throughout the following workdays, Nora frequently conversed about her relationship with a certain young man she was dating. Gloria and Sandra tried to be courteous listeners but were really not interested because it interfered with their work. Nora's work performance had been satisfactory, despite the tendency to converse.

About a month later, Sandra observed that Nora was behind in her filing. When this was brought to her attention, Nora indicated that the filing would be done as soon as she finished typing a business letter. Several hours passed and the filing was no better. Sandra noticed Nora writing a personal letter. She reflected a moment and began contemplating what action, if any, should be taken when Mr. Jackson returned to the office.

THE EAGLETON AFFAIR

At the 1972 Democratic National Convention, U.S. Senator
George McGovern became the Democratic candidate for
President. Senator McGovern's support was considerable and he
was elected on the first ballot. The Vice-Presidential nomination
was little different insofar as the Convention's vote was
concerned. But, by Senator McGovern's own admission, the
Vice-Presidential running-mate, Senator Thomas Eagleton, was
not Mr. McGovern's first choice. In fact, he was rather far down
a list headed by Senator Edward Kennedy. Nonetheless, the
Convention readily endorsed Senator McGovern's choice for a
running-mate and elected Senator Eagleton with little opposition.

Shortly after the Convention, Senator Eagleton disclosed to
Senator McGovern that he had undergone psychiatric treatment
earlier in life. This disclosure rapidly became public knowledge
and questions began to arise over Mr. Eagleton's status on the
ticket. Senator McGovern remained steadfast in his selection,
stating that he was "1000 percent" behind Mr. Eagleton. During
this time, columnist Jack Anderson reported that he had
information from reliable sources that Senator Eagleton had
several DWI and reckless driving violations on record in his
home state of Missouri. This revelation by Jack Anderson
compounded the pressures on Senator McGovern to "dump" Mr.
Eagleton.

Senator Eagleton, meanwhile, maintained his position that he
was highly qualified for the office of Vice-President, that the
charges of Mr. Anderson were false and that he was
psychologically sound and had the physicians' documentation to
support it. He stated that he had no intention of resigning as a
candidate. He also claimed that his own mail was running
overwhelmingly in favor of his candidacy.

A couple of weeks after the initial accusations against Senator
Eagleton, Mr. McGovern decided to replace Mr. Eagleton on the
ticket. Senator McGovern cited party and national unity as a
major reason and suggested that this decision should in no way
disparage Mr. Eagleton's integrity or qualifications. The

Democratic Central Committee accepted the recommendation (indeed, there was some indication that Committee members forced it!) to replace Mr. Eagleton and the latter resigned at a nationally-televised conference. A couple of days before the announced resignation, columnist Anderson issued a full retraction of his earlier allegations regarding Mr. Eagleton's traffic record.

Senator McGovern, searching for a new running-mate, selected R. Sargent Shriver, again after having exhausted a list of other possible candidates, all of whom refused the invitation for various stated reasons. A subsequent Gallup Poll showed the new McGovern-Shriver ticket running even further behind the Republican ticket of President Nixon and Vice-President Agnew than had the McGovern-Eagleton ticket.

AMALGAMATED METALS, INC.

The engineers in the Metallurgical Department of Amalgamated Metals, Inc., formed an informal group to discuss with management the working conditions and fringe benefits of salaried, nonsupervisory employees. This group was formed partially to stop an attempt at unionization of these employees, of whom the engineers were the majority. Most of the engineers were antiunion, but were very dissatisfied with their working conditions, and agreed that some attempt should be made to talk to top management. They were especially upset with the way the unionized engineers' aides were rapidly closing the wage and fringe benefit gap that had existed between engineers and aides, a move that began shortly after the aides became unionized. It appeared to many of the group that the president, who had held office for over thirty-five years, was ignoring their problems and that the personnel department, headed by the president's brother-in-law, was so busy placating the different unions in the company that they did not want to bother with the engineers' complaints. The personnel department was perceived as ineffectual by most engineers.

A committee was formed to present a list of items for management's consideration, including such things as salary levels, performance reviews, fringe benefits and recognition of the committee as an advisory agency to management in matters pertaining to engineers. The list was given to the department vice-president, Mr. Collins, who forwarded it to the personnel department, as he said most items dealt with company-wide policy. After about six weeks and much prodding by the committee chairman, Mr. Atkins, an answer was given by Mr. Collins. He stated that the company was already doing many of the things requested and had been doing them for a long time. Salary levels were being examined. Most of the other items that emerged were too complicated to go into in detail, but the company was looking out for the engineers' best interests. The group committee would be used as an advisor, but Mr. Collins didn't really see that it was needed, as matters were being taken care of by the personnel department. More detailed answers would follow after further study.

About four weeks later, the company granted raises to most of the engineers, including Mr. Atkins, stating that this action would bring salaries to standard for engineers. No mention was made of the committee's work at this time, and no other results were apparent. Most older engineers were satisfied with the raises, but most of the younger ones were not. An informal poll conducted by Mr. Atkins of all salaried, nonsupervisory employees indicated that any unionization movement would fail by about two to one vote, with older engineers being the decisive factor against unionization.

WHITE IMPLEMENT COMPANY

On April 1, 1967, Mr. John Holloway retired as the controller of the White Implement Company and was succeeded by Mr. Richard Flynn. Mr. Holloway had been with the company for 47 years and had been controller for the last 22 years. Mr. Flynn was new to the company. He was a 36-year-old graduate of a large midwestern university, had a graduate degree in finance and was a Certified Public Accountant. Mr. Fred Holiday, the financial vice-president of White, had great faith in Mr. Flynn and felt that he would continue to run the accounting department in the same efficient manner that Mr. Holloway had.

Mr. Flynn had spent February and March working with Mr. Holloway and by April had become well versed in White's accounting system and the reports it was to generate. However, to give Mr. Flynn a chance to "get his feet on the ground," Mr. Holiday had decided that no major changes should be attempted in the accounting methods, procedures, or routines for at least the next six months.

After only three months, it became apparent to Mr. Holiday that all was not well in the accounting department. The monthly operating statements were unusually slow in coming out, monthly closings were taking almost twice as long as they previously had, and two of the accounting personnel had quit. Both of these employees had been with the company for over 15 years and Mr. Holiday viewed their departure as a great loss.

Troubled by this unexpected turn of events and unable to get any ideas from a meeting with Mr. Flynn, Mr. Holiday began to consult with the accounting staff concerning what had gone wrong in what had previously been one of the best departments in the company.

Mr. Holiday first talked to Mrs. Pearl Ridler, the general ledger bookkeeper and a 24-year employee in the accounting department. Mrs. Ridler stated "We never know what we are doing these days. Mr. Flynn gives us a job assignment but he never tells us what to do on it. When I ask him a question, he ends up by asking me four questions to every one that I ask him.

When Mr. Holloway was here, you got a straight-forward and fast answer to your questions; he knew his job."

Mr. Holiday next talked to Mr. Winters, the accounts payable bookkeeper. Mr. Winters's complaint was, "All Mr. Flynn wants to do is talk. I need my problems solved, not a lot of talk." Mr. Frank Thomas, the cost accountant, commented, "Mr. Flynn is continually asking me questions about my job. He is always asking my opinion on things. I sometimes wonder who is really running the accounting department."

WHAT HAPPENS TO SALLY?

Sally had been promoted from the steno pool in March as an executive secretary to Mr. Roberts. He informed her of her new duties and responsibilities and stated that although she would still report to Mr. Scott, supervisor of the pool, she could expect to be kept occupied full-time by Mr. Roberts.

Sally had eagerly and satisfactorily accepted her new position, but her peers and other managers had not accepted the change with any degree of satisfaction. Sally began to drift away from the steno pool group and formed friends among other personal secretaries. The managers began to complain about Sally being too busy to do their work, and voiced their dissatisfaction at no longer having available the fastest typist in the department. Mr. Scott told the managers of the change in Sally's assignment and the need for them to understand the demands Mr. Roberts made upon her schedule. However, Mr. Scott noted that this explanation did not fully satisfy the managers and that frequent arguments still occurred at Sally's desk.

In June, Mr. Roberts was taken ill and was to be out for the remainder of the year. His supervisor, Mr. Paul, vice-president of the division, assumed temporary leadership. One of the first problems brought to his attention by the managers was the steno pool/Sally situation. Mr. Paul had his secretary deliver a memo to Sally and the stenos stating that until Mr. Roberts's return, everyone was of equal status and would report to Mr. Scott.

Sally became increasingly indignant over the situation, constantly refusing work for the reason that she was still doing catch-up work from Mr. Roberts. Mr. Scott talked to Sally about the situation on three different occasions, indicating the temporary nature of the directive, and the need for her cooperation. However, Sally became more difficult, coming into work late and leaving early, taking long lunch hours and leaving the department without telling anyone where she was going.

During a week of heavy typing to meet deadlines, Sally came in one morning an hour late. After working for one-half hour she left and did not return for forty-five minutes. Her absence caused a delay in the work and as she returned to the department, Mr. Scott contemplated what course of action to take.

THE DOUBLE-BAG AFFAIR

While James West attended college and worked part-time at
Allied Markets as a cashier, the company initiated some
cost-cutting measures; one of them was to use one bag (single
bag) instead of two (double bag) when sacking a customer's
order. The only time that double bags were permitted was when
the cutomer requested them. Some of the employees were
informed by the manager, Mr. Kane, about the new policy of not
using double bags and others were informed by word of mouth
from other employees.

The no-double-bag policy was the idea of the district
supervisor, Mr. House. Mr. House had just recently been
promoted to supervisor. He was formerly a store manager and
since he became supervisor, he started many new policies which
were supposed to increase efficiency and cut costs at the various
stores in his district. Most of these ideas had not been too
successful.

One day while James West was operating the cash register, he
had to bag most of the orders himself (cutting the number of
"baggers" was another of Mr. House's economy moves). Jim had
placed just one gallon of milk in a bag, and when the customer
attempted to pick it up, the bottom of the sack split. From this
episode, Jim decided it would be much better for the customers if
he put the gallon cartons of milk in a double bag. This would
avoid having any customers come back in the store angry because
their bag had torn and the milk had been spilled.

Mr. House came in for one of his routine visits that afternoon
and shortly thereafter Mr. Kane came up to Jim telling him that
Mr. House had noticed he was double-bagging for many of the
customers. Kane proceeded to remind Jim that he was to use just
one bag instead of two and warned him that if this continued in
the future, he could be subject to a reprimand.

THE SHORT SKIRTS

It was the first day of school, with its customary first principal-teacher meeting of the year. One major issue seemed to dominate the discussion. The principal had noticed girls' skirts had gotten rather "mini" in length. The conclusion was finally reached that any teacher, man or woman, who observed any girl with a skirt that looked too short should send her to the principal who would administer disciplinary action.

During the intervening months a few girls were sent to the office because of short skirts. However, these girls' comments were usually the same, "Other girls wear skirts this length, why can't I?" Of course, to emphasize their comments, they always cited a few examples of other girls who wore skirts the same length as theirs.

The principal immediately called an emergency meeting of all high school teachers. "I have seen many short skirts around this school lately, why don't you teachers follow through and send these girls to the office?" A quick response came from the men teachers with such comments as: "What do you call a short skirt, anyway?"; "If we start looking at the girls that closely, they will accuse us of eye-balling them."; "I kind of like short skirts on girls." Thereupon, the women came in with comments as: "A short skirt is anything that is two inches above the knees."; "You men can tell what a short skirt is." Promptly, the men teachers replied, "What should we do, carry a tape measure around with us and measure each and every skirt that we think is too short?"

The conclusion was that it was indeed difficult to tell if a girl's dress was too short. In fact, it was brought out that some girls could walk a certain way so that a short skirt was not even detected. Indeed, some skirts look shorter than others on different girls.

The principal was at his wits' end over what should be done about the short skirts. By this time the emergency meeting was at a standstill and all rational discussion had been abandoned.

THE RESEARCH GROUP

Dr. Smith was a research manager for a subsidiary of a leading chemical company. The subsidiary was formed to work specifically on government research and development contracts in the chemicals and materials fields. The function of research manager in the organization entailed responsibility for clearly defined areas of research. The responsibility included the development of new business in these areas, and managing current programs, both technically and financially. In the current programs, the research manager reported to the contracting agency to ensure effective and efficient performance.

Dr. Smith, in the short length of time he had been with the company, had developed a reputation among his subordinates as a very demanding, inflexible individual who would not tolerate mistakes. In addition, those who were not subordinates but were considered sub-peers felt he was extremely inconsiderate in his dealings with sub-peer groups. For example, in working with service and maintenance groups, they believed that Dr. Smith used his position to unfair advantage by requesting service at the expense of other groups whose requests were submitted earlier and were probably as important and as urgent as his.

One of the programs for which Dr. Smith was responsible was subcontracted from a large aerospace firm. The technical performance of the program was supervised by Mr. Jones who, as a group leader, reported to Dr. Smith. The employees under Mr. Jones consisted of two professionals and three nonprofessionals.

Mr. Jones was frequently criticized by Dr. Smith for his performance, not only from the technical standpoint but also on the way he handled his subordinates. Dr. Smith believed that Mr. Jones was too easy on his people, and by being a "nice guy" to his subordinates was failing to get the utmost work from them. Dr. Smith also criticized the performance of the professionals and nonprofessionals. A frequent criticism was that an insufficient quantity of work was performed and that the quality of work could be improved. Criticisms were often directed to individuals without Mr. Jones's knowledge.

272

Morale in the group was considered low, with frequent complaining to Mr. Jones about Dr. Smith's methods in handling his subordinates. The progress of the program was considered to be unsatisfactory by the contracting aerospace firm.

THE MOCK COMPANY

A group of four engineers was formed to organize and advise a high school civics class in the operation of a mock manufacturing company. The company would be entirely composed of the students and would actually produce and sell low-priced items, such as candles and notebooks. Officers in the company were to be paid monthly salaries, salesmen were to receive commissions, and all other class members were to be paid hourly wages for production efforts.

The engineers (advisers) arranged to meet with the class instructor one morning for a two-hour period in order to get the program started—to discuss the basic concepts of the mock company and what would be expected of the students. On the day of this initial meeting, the instructor arrived late and was forced to leave due to "prior commitments," after only forty-five minutes. The advisers expressed the opinion that although the instructor seemed enthusiastic about the endeavor, he was not willing to devote much of his time to coordinating the activities. They went on to say that they believed the instructor possessed only the most basic ideas concerning the mock company.

Before the initial meeting the advisers had hoped to spend at least two hours a week with the students for the purpose of manufacturing the product and keeping the company finances in order. During the meeting, the advisers were told that the civics class met regularly, five days a week, from 12:00 noon to 12:55 P.M. The students ate lunch from 11:30 A.M. until class time. The advisers were informed that they would only be allowed to take over the class for one 55-minute period each week. Feeling that this would be an insufficient amount of time, the advisers developed a plan to conduct the class from 11:30 A.M. to 12:55 P.M. with the students eating in two groups at different times during this period. The instructor expressed support for this plan.

The first meeting between advisers and class went smoothly. Officers were elected, product lines were determined, and capitalization procedures were discussed. After the class, the advisers asked the instructor to have the six officers come to class

274

at 11:30 the next week. The remaining fourteen members of the class were to eat at 11:30 and come to class at 12:00. The officers were to go to lunch at 12:30. When the advisers came to class the next week, they discovered that through a misunderstanding the whole class had been instructed to come in at 11:30. However, only eleven students and one officer were there, and as a result, the second meeting was a complete failure. Also, it became evident during the second meeting that the instructor had given the students several bits of false information at other regular class periods concerning the mock company.

THE COMPUTER SYSTEM

Mr. Meng is the branch chief within a large division of a computer-oriented organization. He has thirty employees, consisting of computer analysts, clerks, and systems engineers. There are three supervisors reporting to him, one for each group of job titles. The systems engineering group is unique to the branch. The engineers all have less than two years experience, are 24 to 28 years old, and are on their first job since graduating from college. The two other groups consist of much older, more experienced personnel.

Mr. Brown, 30 years old, is the supervisor for the systems engineers. He holds an advanced degree, is very close with each engineer, both personally and professionally, and is very permissive with them as long as their projects produce results. He often allows them to initiate their own projects. Mr. Meng, 15 years older, has a bachelor's degree, communicates very little with the engineers, and has a history of project failures in the company. He is unresponsive to projects initiated by the engineers and repeatedly conveys these feelings to Mr. Brown, who usually supports the projects.

Within the last five months, two engineers have quit and morale within the group is low. Pete, one young engineer, has initiated his own project of a rather technical nature. The results could mean important improvements to the design of a large-scale computer system and the project has aroused the interest of some managers outside of Mr. Meng's branch. However, Mr. Meng will not support the results of Pete's project because ". . . nobody asked us to do a study in this area; I don't feel that we should be responsible." In spite of Mr. Meng's resistance, Mr. Brown told Pete to complete the project and report it as an unofficial study to the affected branch. Nothing resulted from the report and soon Pete quit to find another job.

STUDENT CONFLICT

For the past two years the student council at a large midwestern state university has not had strong leadership. This year, enterprising leaders are attempting to control the student council. One is Mr. Rosenberg, the president. The second is Mr. Goldstein, the chairman of the social affairs committee. The number of members on the council is limited, and often all the members must work together to promote and create a successful event.

Early in October, Mr. Rosenberg called a special council meeting. Mr. Goldstein and a few of his friends did not attend, since they were not notified. At this meeting, Mr. Rosenberg introduced the idea of creating a Coffee House requiring the efforts of most of the members for the next twenty weeks. Mr. Rosenberg explained the benefits to be derived from the Coffee House, but did not elaborate on the problems that would have to be faced by the members. They decided to endorse this program at this meeting.

At the regular meeting two days later, Mr. Goldstein introduced the idea for a series of major social events, in the course of which top entertainers would be brought to the campus every month. As Mr. Goldstein began to explain his program, Mr. Rosenberg interrupted and said, "Never mind! The council has already decided to vote for my program." Mr. Goldstein insisted on explaining his program to the council. Grudgingly, Mr. Rosenberg gave his permission. After a limited explanation, Mr. Rosenberg called for a vote on which program to accept. The council voted for Mr. Goldstein's program.

SECRETARIAL CONFLICT

Miss Dane, a Negro secretary, began working in a predominately white engineering office. She reported directly to Mr. Hart and performed the typical secretarial duties for his group of some twenty engineers, designers, and technicians. Her experience prior to this job was minimal; however, her attitude was very good. Miss Dane adapted rapidly to her new work environment.

One of the secretary's major duties was to answer the telephone for the department. She would then page the person being called via a loud speaker system. However, a problem existed when Miss Dane had to leave her desk. No specific person was assigned the responsibility for answering the telephone. Consequently, the telephone would ring as many as twenty times without being answered when Miss Dane was absent.

Mr. Hart reminded Miss Dane of her obligation to answer the telephone, whereupon she made it a habit to spend more time away from her desk. She started missing work more frequently, made less effort to arrive at work on time, and spent extended periods of time in the ladies' room. This situation continued for several weeks, whereupon a crisis developed.

Mr. Scott, Mr. Hart's boss, attempted to call Hart on a given afternoon, and no one answered the telephone. In fact, Mr. Scott tried unsuccessfully several times in a one-hour period. At this point a very perturbed Mr. Scott and Mr. Hart held a meeting with Miss Dane. She was told that her rebellious tactics had been carried far enough. She became quite indignant and said, "You wouldn't be doing this to me if I had been a white secretary." Mr. Hart must now take corrective action toward solving this conflict.

ACE PAPER COMPANY

The Ace Paper Company, in the Miami Valley of southwestern Ohio, is a principal manufacturer and supplier of quality printing and writing paper. Since the mill's daily production is rather small, great emphasis is placed on producing quality paper and on achieving customer satisfaction. This intensely customer-oriented policy has been very successful for Ace, and it has become a respected, integral part of the Printing Papers Division of the parent corporation.

Largely responsible for Ace's profitable and enviable status in the market is John Dewey, resident manager of the plant. He is highly touted by corporate executives for his demonstrated ability in moving out of his previous assignment within the corporate ranks in order to assume managerial responsibilities of Ace when it was acquired in 1965.

Mr. Dewey spends considerable time at the plant and encourages his subordinates to do the same. In order to keep abreast of the previous day's activities and performance, he initiated daily production meetings in which production problems, customer specifications and maintenance projects could be discussed each morning with his supervisory subordinates. It was at one of these "morning meetings" recently that a particular problem regarding the failure of production personnel to comply with customer instructions received much attention.

"I happened to be walking by the wrapping crew a while ago," observed Mr. Dewey, "when I noticed that they weren't numbering the rolls in sequence on that Regal order. There are three order numbers on that manufacturing order, and every time we change an order number we're supposed to number those rolls beginning with 1, 2, 3, etc., on the wrapper. What's wrong with those guys? Didn't somebody tell them about how to number those rolls for Regal? We got a charge-back from them on the last order a month ago for not keeping roll numbers separate on different order numbers. And now, roll-wrapping is making the same mistake again."

Mr. Mace, production manager of the Ace plant, responded: "John, I wasn't aware of this situation. When I came in this morning, the foreman told me that we were having trouble meeting 'specs' on the paper machine, and, frankly, I just wasn't thinking about wrapping instructions. I guess Carl (the foreman) thought the roll-wrapping crew could handle it this time, because he didn't say anything to me about it."

"The damage has been done now," observed Mr. Dewey. "We'll have to unwrap the rolls made so far and renumber them." Turning to his quality control supervisor, Dewey said: "Bob, have your technicians work over to stay with each roll-wrapping shift to make sure each crew doesn't mess things up again. For the present, maybe Al can spare one of his engineers to unwrap and renumber the rolls that are marked wrong. I want the shift foremen to stay on the machine and make sure we maintain test specifications. They just won't have time to fool with this problem."

TECHNICAL SYSTEMS DIVISION

A year had gone by since Colonel Landa had been promoted from chief of the Stellar Division to chief of the Largest Directorate of the Solar Systems Command. The Stellar Division was one of the six divisions now under his supervision. The product of the division was analysis of technical systems which were most often presented in the form of written reports. The majority of the employees in Stellar Division were engineers and scientists. Colonel Landa was a democratic sort of leader and had worked hard at improving the morale of his people. While division chief, Colonel Landa had observed some improvement in the division.

When Colonel Landa was promoted, Colonel Smith was selected as his replacement. It didn't take Colonel Smith long to let everyone know that he knew more about this organization than anyone else because he had used its products at his previous job. He let it be known that he would shape up this division and would do it "with an iron hand."

Colonel Smith immediately began to involve himself personally in many of the projects, an approach which no previous division chief had used. Not much time had passed before the employees began to realize that Smith lacked sufficient technical knowledge to add anything to the technical content of the work. Colonel Smith also realized his lack of technical knowledge, yet was determined to have some personal involvement in the projects, so he began to take a more than active part in determining the grammatical content and appearance of the reports. Because of this, he became known as a "nitpicker" and was the subject of much criticism from his employees. He was not only slowing up his division's work, but was duplicating that of the quality control division.

The morale of his division was low, the technical quality of the work was substandard, and problems that should have been handled by the division chief were being neglected. Colonel Landa was concerned because of the complaints he had received about the quality of work being put out by this division. Many of the military personnel were asking for transfers and three of the best civilian engineers had quit.

After a director's meeting the organization's commander called Colonel Landa aside and told him that he had been informed that higher government officials were seriously considering that the Stellar Division be dissolved because of its partial duplication of work with other agencies and because of the poor quality of its product.

SUMMER HOURS

Tipton College is a small private midwestern coeducational liberal arts school. For most of its history, it has operated on a conventional semester program with no classes during the summer months. Although efforts had been made to bring conferences to the campus and thereby achieve more productive use of the idle facilities during the summer, this had never been too successful.

All administrative activities slowed down during the summer and it had been a custom to close the offices at 4:00 P.M. rather than the normal hour of 5:00 P.M. The revised hours usually started on the Monday after graduation, which came around the middle of June, and extended through Labor Day. Approximately fifty clerks, typists, stenographers, and bookkeepers were affected by the change. Each year, late in May or early in June, they were notified about summer hours in a memo from the director of nonacademic personnel.

Earlier during the current school year, the Board of Trustees had approved a plan to switch Tipton College to the academic quarter plan and enroll freshmen students in both summer and fall quarters. It was believed that this would ensure more effective use of the facilities, thereby easing the ever present financial strain and also fulfilling an obligation to help provide college education for the rapidly expanding group of young people seeking college entrance.

Plans for the switchover had been going smoothly and Mr. Canfield, business manager and vice-president for financial planning, called a staff meeting during May to review the overall situation. During the course of the meeting, Mr. Alfred, the assistant treasurer, indicated that with a regular complement of students on campus during the summer, his staff was going to have difficulty getting its work done during regular hours and still get in vacations. He was assuming, he stated, that shortened summer hours were a thing of the past.

At that, the director of public relations said that he had assumed that the reduced summer hours would still be in effect and he knew from speaking to members of his staff that they were making their plans accordingly. Others indicated that they didn't know how their staffs felt, but that shortened summer hours had been a normal situation for many years. The director of nonacademic personnel immediately replied that no memo had gone out because he had not yet discussed the matter with Mr. Canfield, and so the employees should not be making any assumptions.

THE FOREIGN ACQUISITION

Martin Schmidt & Company, a Chicago based firm, acquired a previously well-known producer of farm machinery in Germany, Hanz Zimmer AG, and renamed it Schmidt-Zimmer AG.

The executives of Schmidt-Zimmer started a complete reorganization program and brought in U.S. managers from the home office. About one month after the new U.S. managers had taken over, they determined that the plant employees were in their opinion mostly "alcoholics." The employees were drinking wine during breaks beginning with breakfast. The drinking created a matter of concern among the U.S. managers and the workers were ordered to stop it. Workers and Works Council rejected the order; as a result, management fired the Works Council and the leaders of the disobedient workers.

The Labor Force went out on a strike endorsed by their union. A German court reinstated the Works Council, and after a strike of about four months and various court actions, the U.S. management team was recalled and replaced by an all-German management team. The employment of the "alcoholics" was continued and the restriction on alcohol was discontinued.

THE TECHNICIAN-SALESMEN

The Cox Manufacturing Company had developed a number of new products which were considerably more sophisticated than those they were currently selling. In order to present this new equipment to the top management of each customer, the Company reasoned that the structure of the sales force for these new products would need to be different from the existing force; it called for salesmen who had more formal education and sales skill.

The new sales force was aggressively recruited and chosen for its abilities and motivational aspirations. It was then decided to pay these salesmen a straight salary since the company hoped to establish a consultant-type image in its field. A new salary class was established which would give the salesmen a very generous salary with wage progressions based upon performance. Other than this difference in salary, all attempts to distinguish between salesmen would be minimized.

A broad sales policy was established which basically stated that the company would attempt to discourage sales when the salesmen thought it was not in the customer's best interest to buy. There was also a set of sales techniques defined which were to be applied on every contact with the customer.

The managers for these groups were chosen from those managing the existing sales force. They were given their markets and the sales objectives and left to devise their market strategy.

Each salesman was to have complete responsibility for the satisfactory installation of the system once it was sold. This responsibility required him to act as a project manager by coordinating the activities of engineering, installation and training. Each department, however, was rather rigidly structured with its sets of operating procedures. This required the salesman to continually seek help from his manager to accomplish his tasks.

The responsibilities were discussed with the salesmen at the time of interviewing and hiring. There was no formal process providing for an evaluation interview with each salesman to appraise his results. However, it was made clear through the lines of organization and reinforced in sales training meetings that selling skills were most important.

After the operation had been in existence for a time, top management was disappointed with the results of the operation, including a decline in sales and unsatisfactory installations of most of the jobs. To correct the situation, top management transferred the existing managers and replaced them with salesmen who were most skilled at getting their jobs installed correctly. It was top management's feeling that these leading salesmen would be better equipped to control the technical areas with the other salesmen and, more importantly, they had demonstrated their skills in accomplishing results through others.

Management was shocked to witness the turnover in the sales force which occurred shortly after the moves were effected and sought to find reasons for this behavior.

SHIFT CHANGE

There are eight employees in the Reliability Test Laboratory. The laboratory performs a quality control function by testing random samples of daily production for physical characteristics. Until January of this year, the employees had worked from 6:30 A.M. to 3:00 P.M. each day. Don Kuntz, a Reliability Engineer, was in charge of the major product line tested in the lab and held the secondary responsibility of managing the lab. As a result, the lab employees were relatively unsupervised.

In mid-December when it became evident to top management that Kuntz was overworked in this dual capacity, David Barnes was advised that he would become foreman of the lab effective January 1. Barnes had previously worked in an office adjoining the lab as a nonsupervisory member of the Reliability Engineering Department.

When Harry Boyles, supervisor of Reliability Engineering, advised Barnes of his new assignment he also cautioned him that employees were not working between 6:30 A.M. and 8:00 A.M. Don Kuntz had worked from 8:00 A.M. until 4:45 P.M. in order to handle his engineering responsibilities, and as a result, the lab had been unsupervised early in the shift. To combat this, Boyles had decided to change the hours for all lab employees to 8:00 A.M. through 4:30 P.M. effective January 1. Boyle also informed Barnes that the lab employees had already been informed of the change.

On January 1, when Barnes was introduced as the foreman of the lab, reporting directly to Kuntz, the change in working hours became effective. The change in working hours met with drastic reaction. The men had worked the same shift (as in all the production areas) for an average of twenty-three years each, and immediately began requesting consultation with their union representatives in order to fight the shift change. They were told that such action was legitimate, according to the labor agreement. Next, the group began a work slowdown in protest. After approximately two weeks, Charles Turner approached Kuntz with the comment, "we know that the shift was changed because we weren't working before 8:00 A.M. If you will return the shift to the original time, we will promise to begin work promptly each morning." Kuntz told him that management was pleased with the new arrangement and had no changes in mind.

One of the policies of the company was that safety glasses were to be worn at all times in the lab area; however, Kuntz had been quite lax in enforcement of this rule and Barnes had been told by Boyles to remedy the situation. He relayed this message to the group and everyone wore their glasses the first day until about 4:00 P.M. The group had gathered around a table to the rear of the lab, and Barnes noticed the absence of the glasses as he approached the table. He reminded the group to wear the glasses and they all responded except for Turner who replied, "Why doesn't Kuntz wear his safety glasses over there in his office;" Barnes replied that it was necessary to wear the glasses only around the moving machinery in the lab. Turner responded, "I won't wear my glasses unless Kuntz does." With this, several other employees removed their glasses. Barnes then told Turner, "You are suspended for the balance of this shift and one day, with no pay."

The next day there were five employees absent from work.

SCIENTIFIC INVESTIGATION

Dr. Peter Pulaski desired to utilize students who were nearing completion of their master's degree program with various universities, to assist with investigation of problems related to the instrument lab. It was anticipated that concurrent with their assistance in these investigations, sufficient creativity together with comprehensive analyses would be elicited to enable them to use these lab experiences for their theses.

One such student was Mr. Charles Doevich, from the electrical engineering department of a local university. Mr. Doevich's thesis advisor, Dr. Stanley Durland, had arranged with Dr. Pulaski for Doevich to participate in the investigation of the operation of Avalanche Photon Detectors as a function of ambient temperature. There was a keen interest in elevated temperature operation; e.g., 70 to 100 degrees Centigrade. Prior to Mr. Doevich's employment, Dr. Robert Brown of the instrument lab, at Dr. Pulaski's direction, assembled specific electronic and thermal conditioning apparatus intended for use during the planned evaluation of Avalanche detector operation.

Mr. Doevich collected a series of data upon which he performed analyses prior to preparing a rough draft of the experimental and analytical sections of his thesis. Dr. Durland and Dr. Pulaski then reviewed the rough draft. Following telephone consultation between the two advisors, Mr. Doevich was called to Dr. Pulaski's office for discussion. The principal point for discussion was Mr. Doevich's failure to fulfill either the university's or lab's expectations and/or requirements in the report of his findings.

Dr. Durland held that Mr. Doevich's work lacked sufficient theoretical intensity to support the reported data while Dr. Pulaski was of the opinion that insufficient weight had been placed on developing and showing empirical evidence. Both his thesis advisor and his supervisor, however, were in agreement that several potentially significant parameters had been inadequately treated by Doevich, experimentally and analytically. Concerning this latter point, Mr. Doevich's response was that the equipment provided for his investigations would not allow full treatment of the parameters. He further observed that the necessary elements for these studies were available in the overall laboratory complex.

Following his consultation with Mr. Doevich, Dr. Pulaski again phoned Dr. Durland to discuss the status of the investigation being conducted. The two discussed various possibilities for continuing support of Mr. Doevich's investigations in order to fulfill his thesis requirements as well as to provide a completed experimental report for the lab. This discussion was necessary because the current contract supporting Mr. Doevich's investigations would expire in less than two weeks and its extension was improbable unless it were demonstrated that continuation would produce relevant results. To be able to continue support, a decision within a week would be necessary in order to meet administrative requirements.

THE PRINTING SERVICE

In a large government printing plant, the manager, Mr. Zimmer, retired after more than thirty years of service. His assistant of fifteen years, Mr. Olds, moved up to manage the plant. The number three man, Mr. Hanley, formerly head of the highly-innovated electronic printing section, became deputy plant manager.

Prior to taking his new position, Mr. Hanley had often discussed occurrences in the various sections with the systems automation specialist, a staff consultant from headquarters. Hanley was critical of the lack of delegation of authority, of the slow action from his superiors in filling jobs and generally of the stagnation which he felt had crept over all operations.

After a few weeks as deputy manager, Hanley talked again to the systems specialist. "You know, I've been working to change things around here. I've instituted weekly meetings with the section heads, to exchange information, hear their complaints and arrive at new procedures. There has been some success, but they are still letting most of my instructions go into one ear and out of the other. I really don't know what to do. One, in particular, goes his merry way. Actually, he could have retired several years ago, but is staying on in order to maximize his retirement. He's not yet at the mandatory retirement age. A couple of others will soon be due for retirement. I suppose that will solve most of my problems."

HIDE-AND-SEEK AUTHORITY

If there was one thing Dan March didn't need today it was a complaint from the staff. The printers had finally delivered the galley sheets ten weeks behind schedule and he was itching to look at them. The Provost's words from yesterday's meeting of department chairmen still echoed in his ears—"no more money. We're all going to have to trim expenses." Dan wondered, too, if Professor Perkman was giving the candidate for the opening in his department a too-honest tour of the medium-sized community in which S.L.A. University (*S*mall *L*iberal *A*rts *U*niversity) was located. But he neatly swallowed his sigh as Professor Stone's spare frame towered in the doorway.

"Do you have a minute to spare, Dan? This is important."

"Sure, however, I meet my class in twenty minutes; we'll have to be brief," he replied.

"What in the world are you thinking about?" Stone began. "That young man you introduced to us at lunch is all wrong, even though he seems OK personally. His field is Modern British Literature and you know very well we have two men already. Last term only three students signed up for that Eliot seminar that was offered; how can you hire a third man?"

Dan nodded his head in response. Bob Stone continued, "We'll all be out of a job soon, the way kids are flocking to the political science department and their automatic A's and B's. Something's got to be done and soon. Either don't replace the people who resign and thus spread the work around, or do something about attracting more students our way. I'm going to talk to the other tenured faculty in the department and maybe we'll get together. We'll want to know what your thinking is on these issues."

"Now, wait, Bob," Dan countered. "I've got facts and figures to show that our department enrollment has begun to rise. And as for not hiring for replacements—if we allow a cut in staff now, it will be years before we can get them back. The money situation is not getting any better."

"I don't agree," Stone persisted, "and I'm not alone. I'll get back to you after I've seen some of the others." He turned and headed down the hall to his office.

This time the sigh did escape his lips as Dan March gathered his lecture notes and tried to focus on Moby Dick and his Captain Ahab, if only for an hour.

THE CONTROLLER'S SUCCESSOR

Ralph Hart, the controller of King Division of a large industrial firm, was transferred to the Spear Division in another city across the country. Many of the personnel in the accounting and data processing departments of the King Division felt relief and had a "good riddance" attitude because they considered Hart to be a "two-timing," "behind your back" politician.

The assistant controller of King Division, Carl Pritchard, felt he had proven himself in his five years with the firm and thought he should get the vacant position. Most of the employees in the accounting and data processing departments also thought Pritchard was the only man for the job.

Even though he was a "hard driver," the employees under Pritchard respected him and enjoyed working with him because he was fair and empathic. Pritchard fought for his men when "raise time" came around and always placed them first.

Since Pritchard, a CPA, was the controller of a smaller firm before joining King Division, he believed he had the necessary qualifications, experience, and intelligence for the job.

Before leaving to take over the controllership of Spear Division, Ralph Hart had a long talk with Harry Valance, the General Manager of King Division and his good friend, about who should replace him as controller. Hart recommended Larry Evers, also a CPA and sales manager of King Division, for the position.

Valance, knowing how valuable Pritchard was, let it leak out that Evers would probably be the next controller. When the employees heard that Evers was being considered above Pritchard, many came to Pritchard and expressed their displeasure; some even threatening to quit if Pritchard did not get the post. Pritchard, also dismayed, went to Valance and asked to be considered for the job.

About a month later, Larry Evers was named controller of King Division and Carl Pritchard was given a raise in salary.

WILL THE REAL LEADER PLEASE RISE?

Prior to Mr. Connelly becoming chief of the specifications division of Willy-Nill, Inc., Mr. Morrow, a long-time employee of the firm, had been serving as acting chief for a period of eighteen months. Although Mr. Morrow was a veteran in the field, a good manager and was well-liked by his subordinates, he was not made permanent chief of the division because he lacked a certain requirement for the position. Mr. Connelly joined the firm in July, 1969, having been with various firms in the industry for approximately twenty years. Upon his arrival, he was informed by Mr. Grabowski, the Procurement Director, and Mr. Connelly's immediate supervisor, that he would be taking over as chief of the specifications division, with Mr. Morrow reverting back to his permanent job as branch chief, under Connelly.

The firm had adopted a rigid set of methods and procedures which were closely adhered to by the employees. Mr. Connelly, having been new to the firm and having served in various other firms in the industry, was quick to recognize certain faults in the management structure of the Procurement Division, as well as the procedures for accomplishing the tasks for which it was organized. A rather blunt and straightforward man, Connelly took these matters up with Mr. Grabowski, long-time member of the firm's management. Mr. Grabowski listened to Connelly but took no action on his suggestions. On other occasions, Mr. Connelly argued with Mr. Grabowski concerning policies and procedures of the director and the division.

As the months passed, Mr. Grabowski began circumventing Connelly in relaying information and policies to the specifications division. In personnel and operational matters, Grabowski often went directly to Morrow without informing Connelly. He often held Connelly responsible for these same matters. In December of 1969, Connelly was removed from his position as manager and supervisor of twenty people, and was given the job of office manager, indirectly responsible for three people. He was replaced by Mr. Ward, a man inexperienced in that particular field, but who had been serving as chief of another division.

Mr. Grabowski called Mr. Ward and Mr. Morrow into his office for orientation into the operations of the division.

THE BOARD OF EDUCATION

The West Carlton Board of Education and the West Carlton
Education Association (W.C.E.A.) have been locked in long and
hard negotiations for the past five months. The bargaining
climate between the two teams has not been ideal. Early in the
bargaining period members of the W.C.E.A. threatened a walkout
but a last minute reconciliation averted a possible strike.
However, tension has remained at the critical level. In fact, just
last week two members of the four-man W.C.E.A. negotiating
team attempted to resign but were persuaded to remain with a
vote of confidence. Both negotiating teams have become weary
and, in particular, the school board president has become
completely negative toward the idea of negotation. In spite of
these conditions, the negotiating teams were able to produce a
viable twenty-five-page contract which covers all certified
personnel of the West Carlton City School District. All major
portions of the contract have been agreed upon by both
negotiating teams. However, the Board president will not accept
the contract if the following sentence is included:

> Acceptance of this agreement precludes further negotiations of any issues
> until the time specified for resumption of formal negotiations as provided
> herein above, except, when mutually agreed upon by both parties.

The W.C.E.A. desires to retain the basic idea expressed in the
sentence. The W.C.E.A. negotiating team decided to meet with
all of the association members and evaluate alternative courses of
action.

TECHNOLOGICAL INNOVATION

The International Typographical Union (ITU) had been reluctant to cooperate with shop modernization measures at the High City Herald and Journal. In 1968, the company was eight to ten years behind comparable newspapers in printing technology. Early in contract negotiations that year, the union agreed in principle to the desired technological change. A high level company official said, "The only way we could get them to go along was to sell them on the training of their people. They are unable to do the jobs in the automated shops."

The company hired a specialist, Bill Dodson, who had recently gone through the same type of changeover at an out-of-state newspaper. Dodson was charged with the responsibility for the innovation project. In preparation for the coming change, all foremen in the shop were sent to Dodson's former plant to become familiar with the operation. Two of the new typesetting systems were installed and on-line training was begun for operators.

Meanwhile, negotiations with the ITU deteriorated because of economic issues and some work rule changes associated with the new technology. Some members of the local began work slowdowns. The printers made jokes about the poor quality of work on the new equipment and attempted to blame the machinery for missed deadlines. A typical comment: "One good linotype and a good operator will turn out more readable type than all that high-priced junk." When the contract expired in August, both parties agreed to a day-to-day extension.

Negotiations continued at dead center until late September when the company terminated the agreement and in effect told the printers, "As long as you come in and do the job, you'll get paid." Three days later, two employees with considerable seniority were fired for deliberately slowing down production. The ITU immediately walked out.

Mr. Dodson proposed that, in view of the union's past intransigence, the company should take advantage of the empty shop and remove all of the main production linotypes and install the new equipment throughout the shop. The printers, when they came back to work, would therefore have to produce on the new equipment or be in violation of the contract.

THE OFFICE REPLACEMENT

After one of his employees in the Cost Department left to take a position with another firm, Mr. Hailstone, general supervisor of the Cost Department for just over one year, started interviewing prospective employees to fill the vacancy. Although the current functions of the Cost Department were routine and monotonous, Hailstone was of the opinion that the company should seek a college graduate with a major in accounting. None of the existing employees in the Cost Department had an education beyond high school and all were in the 45–60 age range. Hailstone wanted to evaluate the functions of his section by developing an automated cost system utilizing the company's data processing center. At present, very little of the cost data involves data processing.

To attract candidates for the vacancy, Hailstone termed the vacant position as that of a "cost analyst." Several candidates were interviewed and one was selected. He was Joe Whitcomb, a recent graduate of a local university with a major in accounting. He was immediately placed on one of the department's most routine jobs. It was explained to him that he would first have to learn the current functions of the section before undertaking the assignment for which he has been hired; to help incorporate the cost section into the data processing flow.

After two months on the job, Joe started complaining about the routine character of the work and intimated to his co-workers that anyone who would continue on a job like this must have little or no initiative. After making his feelings known to Mr. Hailstone by saying that he was not hired for such work, he was given an assignment to automate the material cost portion of the cost system. Joe was to coordinate his effort through another supervisor in the cost section, Mr. Fields, and the data processing section. From the very beginning, Mr. Fields showed hostility toward Joe. Fields felt it unnecessary to hire a college graduate and told Mr. Hailstone that a woman could fill the vacant position just as well. His sentiments were, "We have been operating the cost section like this for 35 years—why change?" Mr. Hailstone's position was that the new program of automation could not be undertaken without hiring a person with the necessary drive and potential which were to be found in a man with a higher education.

At first, Joe showed a great deal of interest in his new assignment. He stopped complaining and became a very hard-working employee. His relationship with Mr. Fields was strained, but progress was being made on the materials program. At this point, the controller announced that, due to the continued loss of profits, new developments were to be curtailed. With his work on the materials program now severely cut, Mr. Fields put Joe back on his old routine job and he was told that as soon as things looked better, the materials program would open up once again. Almost immediately, Joe started complaining about the work he was doing. He wasted his own time and that of other employees in the section. He criticized his fellow workers and management on many occasions. Despite an initial warning concerning his behavior, Joe's attitude toward his job did not change.

THE EXPERIENCED FOREMAN

Bob Martin, the new foreman in Department 7 at the Meng Manufacturing Company, a producer of various types of automotive parts, was introduced to his new duties on Monday evening. He was to be in charge of an assembly group on the second shift. Since he was a former assembly line worker himself, he approached this assignment with confidence and energy.

Most of the first night was spent circulating among employees, getting to know them and letting them meet him. During the course of these brief interviews, he often asked questions such as: "Is that all you do, pack boxes?", or "Isn't there a better way to do that job?" At one point he picked up a box of parts and put it on the line to help a man who had gotten behind.

At the end of the shift he left feeling that he had made an excellent start at his new job.

When he arrived at work on the second day, he was dumbfounded to learn that no less than ten grievances had been filed against him by his employees. He could not understand what happened.

THE PERPLEXED FOREMAN

During their monthly poker game, six of the first line supervisors of the shipping and receiving department of the new Sturdy truck assembly plant were discussing the results of the past few weeks.

Dave Smith, the newest foreman in the department, began to talk about the problems he was encountering with his employees. "My people can't seem to work steadily and get all the stock unloaded from the trucks that come into my docks. I have to get on the backs of those forklift drivers all the time to get back to the dock after they have delivered stock, especially that clique of young guys from Northridge. Those lifts are critical to my operation. And to top it all off, the boss is giving some of my people orders and work assignments and not telling me about it until I tell them to do something. I'm their immediate boss. They should do what I tell them without question. After all, I know what the company's goals are. Now the boss says I had better have all the backlogged trucks unloaded and off of demurrage charges by Monday or else. What should I do, fellows?"

Several of the foremen offered suggestions that seemed practical, but none seemed to apply to Dave's own problems. They all agreed that they faced the same general problems at one time or another.

"Just concentrate on the problem that is of primary importance at the time and things will work out all right," was a friend's comment.

"It seems that I'm always having a confrontation with the union steward," Smith continued. "He tells me the contract says one thing, but I can never get in touch with the labor relations department to find out for sure. They are always 'tied up in negotiations' or 'out of the office.' Maybe I should just go back to my old job in the production office. Those were five happy years! At least then the pressure will be off."

THE ENGINEERING CHANGE

The Inverse Corporation is a diversified manufacturer of component assemblies for a variety of industries. A major Inverse product line consists of passenger seat constructions for the trucking industry. Federal safety standards (FMVSS) effective in August, 1972, required several major engineering changes to be incorporated into currently produced assemblies by that date. A meeting was called in June of 1971 to discuss the effects of these changes.

The Meeting

Manufacturing and Production Control agreed that the changes would not cause their areas any major problems. Process and Project engineering concluded that the changes were compatible with present manufacturing facilities and would pose no appreciable obstacles. Top management assessed the changes and concluded that they would primarily affect tooling.

The tool division, represented by its chief engineer, W. Track, and his two assistant superintendents, were divided in their opinions of the situation. Track, recently obtained from outside the corporation to head the tool division, believed the changes were compatible with present tooling and could be accomplished for the start of production in August of 1972. His two assistants, however, disagreed and predicted a November completion date as being more realistic. They based their opinions on past tooling practices and procedures.

Sales reiterated that a November date was impossible. L. Stanley, sales chief, pointed out that competitors, who have the same type of tooling as Inverse, have committed themselves to the August 1972 date and Inverse should be able to do the same. The meeting adjourned with Inverse committed to the August 1972 completion schedule. All were in favor of the decision except the two assistant tool superintendents, H. Jones and A. Smith. The following conversation between Jones and Smith occurred directly after the meeting.

304

Smith: "That young hot shot said he could do it but we're the ones who are actually going to do the work!"

Jones: "Did you hear him knuckle under to sales?"

Smith: "No one paid any attention to our arguments or suggestions. They acted as if we didn't know what we are talking about. We've been doing most of the work around here for the past twenty years and look who they listen to, a young outsider!"

Jones: "He thinks he's going to change the way we do things around here. Come August 1972 we'll see who is right, him or us, and believe you me it's going to be us."

After leaving the meeting Track knew he had a problem and pondered his possible solutions.